CAMBRIDGE CLASSICAL STUDIES

*General Editors*

J. A. CROOK, E. J. KENNEY, A. M. SNODGRASS

SCEPTICISM OR PLATONISM?

The Philosophy of the Fourth Academy

# SCEPTICISM OR PLATONISM?
## The philosophy of the Fourth Academy

### HAROLD TARRANT
*University of Sydney*

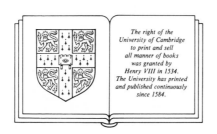

The right of the
University of Cambridge
to print and sell
all manner of books
was granted by
Henry VIII in 1534.
The University has printed
and published continuously
since 1584.

# CAMBRIDGE UNIVERSITY PRESS
### CAMBRIDGE
### LONDON   NEW YORK   NEW ROCHELLE
### MELBOURNE   SYDNEY

Published by the Press Syndicate of the University of Cambridge
The Pitt Building, Trumpington Street, Cambridge CB2 1RP
32 East 57th Street, New York, NY 10022, USA
10 Stamford Road, Oakleigh, Melbourne 3166, Australia

First published 1985

Printed in Great Britain at
the University Press, Cambridge

Library of Congress catalogue card number: 84–21346

*British Library Cataloguing in Publication Data*
Tarrant, Harold
Scepticism or Platonism?: the philosophy
of the Fourth Academy. – (Cambridge classical
studies)
1. Philosophy, Ancient
I. Title    II. Series
180'.938    B171
ISBN 0 521 30191 2

# CONTENTS

# PREFACE

This book is essentially an accident. It arose out of increasing dissatisfaction with the terms in which Academic and Platonic philosophy of the period from *c.* 100 B.C. to *c.* A.D. 150 had been understood. It is strange that little effort has been made before to understand the developments in epistemology during this period, particularly when authors have persisted in seeing a return to 'dogmatic' Platonism during it. Admittedly our evidence for the period is not good, but we do have rather more than might be supposed from the current state of the history books. One might tentatively suggest that some evidence has gone unnoticed because it accords poorly with the traditional view of the period.

Thus I have been forced to espouse an essentially new view of the period and to try to develop it here. It would be unkind, in the circumstances, to expect this volume to be packed with references to the supporting views of several generations of scholars. Most of the work which has stimulated me has come from the last decade, though there has still been literature from the previous century that has benefited me greatly. I have not seen fit to drum up artificial references to works which have not been helpful to me purely for the sake of 'scholarship'. Such a policy would disguise the fact that this book stems from a reading of the ancient literature with assistance from the modern: not vice versa.

I hope that the book will be read critically and that its conclusions will not be taken for granted. It is designed to be nearer to the first word than to the last on the subject.

I should like to express my gratitude to all those who have helped to make this book possible. Among institutions, the University of Sydney deserves thanks for allowing me leave at a key time in order that I should complete it, as do the Faculty of Classics and St John's College, Cambridge which provided facilities and privileges at that time. The Faculty of Classics, and in particular the editors of the Cambridge Classical Studies series, must also be thanked for enabling publication of the work; and I am grateful to Cambridge University Press for their early interest in, and final execution of, this project.

I have greatly benefited from the comments of Professor John Dillon and Dr David Sedley, and from discussions with scholars too numerous to mention here. I have received practical support from my mother, Mrs S. Tarrant, and encouragement from many quarters: especially from the ever-living spirit of Plato, Pyrrho, and Diodorus, and from my wife, who has exhibited great patience during the painful period of Platonic psychical procreation. My thanks to them all.

H.T.

*Sydney, 1984*

# NON-STANDARD ABBREVIATIONS

I have endeavoured to use abbreviations which are either standard or at least readily intelligible to all groups of readers for whom the book was intended. However, some works are referred to so frequently that they have warranted my own very short abbreviations. John Glucker's *Antiochus and the late Academy* has become *Ant.*, and John Dillon's *The Middle Platonists* has become *MP*. Less obscure abbreviations of books are established in my bibliography. From chapter 4 the anonymous *Theaetetus*-commentator has become A, and his commentary *K*. I frequently abbreviate Aenesidemus to Aenes. For easy reference, anon. *Prol.* refers to the anonymous *Prolegomena to Plato's Philosophy*, found, like the Didascalicus attributed to Alcinous (but here referred to as *Didasc.* without making assumptions about authorship), in C. Fr. Hermann's *Appendix Platonica* (Teubner Plato, vol. 6).

# INTRODUCTION

## i The people

It is my hope in publishing this study that I may be able to shed important new light on the nature of the Academic 'scepticism' and Platonism which are known to have influenced two major classical authors, Cicero and Plutarch. The importance of my findings will, I trust, be evident to those familiar with the philosophical writings of these great men of letters, and consequently I have not attempted to spell out in detail the ways in which they have been influenced by the Fourth Academic position, nor to assess the extent of that influence. One could, indeed, devote a separate book to such influences upon either of these thinkers. Moreover it is a sounder policy to attempt to examine our evidence for Fourth Academic thought independently of the question of Fourth Academic influence, for otherwise one's view of the latter may seriously imperil the objectivity of one's treatment of the former.

For this reason I have not afforded the usual dominant position to Cicero's writings as a source for Fourth Academic epistemology. One cannot avoid drawing upon him as a very significant source, but he should be used with caution where his attitudes do not agree with those attributed to the Academy of the period in other writings; except perhaps where he can provide those shades of colour which enable us to reconstruct a coherent and convincing picture of the Fourth Academic position. The fact that he wrote in Latin is an additional obstacle to any attempt to recreate characteristic Fourth Academic doctrine, since it is clear that terminology had become a crucial issue in the rivalry between the Stoa and the various Academic factions. Finally there are excruciating problems as to when Cicero is following a Fourth

1

Academic source; for his *Academica* is no two-sided debate between the positions of the 'sceptic' Philo of Larissa, leader of the Fourth Academy, and Antiochus of Ascalon, his apostate pupil; the orthodox, or 'Third Academic', position is also given prominence, and Cicero is by no means committed to the 'Fourth'.

The Third Academy, or that so labelled by Sextus Empiricus,[1] was that of Carneades, Head of the Academy for some decades until 129 B.C., and his pupil Clitomachus, who later held the chair until *c.* 110 B.C. During this time it would seem to me that the description 'sceptic' could have been used of the Academy without its being misleading, though I must emphasize that the nature of Carneadean thought was much disputed in the following century, and that, according to some accounts, the master was not *psychologically* sceptical, but *intellectually* so. On the death of Clitomachus, the Academy passed into the hands of his pupil Philo of Larissa; Charmadas, a former pupil of Carneades himself, is closely associated with Philo, and he too taught at Athens at the time; though philosophical rhetoric may have been his chief interest. As time progressed the Academy became more positive in its teachings under Philo, and hence it earned the reputation of being a separate Academy, or 'Fourth Academy', in its opponents' eyes.

Philo is known best for his 'Roman Books', written after the Mithridatic War had made the political climate in Athens too dangerous for philosophers to remain (88 B.C.), and before the text came to the attention of Antiochus of Ascalon at Alexandria in 87/6 B.C. These books are known to have argued that there was in fact only one Academy (Cic. *Ac.* 1.13), with a continuous tradition from Plato (or even from Socrates) down to his own day. The authority of the ancients was highly regarded at a time when the Romans busily tried to acquaint themselves with the literary and philosophical output of pre-Hellenistic Greece, and it was all but mandatory to claim some such authority for whatever position one favoured. The Academy felt such a need more than most schools, since there was something less than respectable in

Roman eyes about any discipline which espoused the cause of ignorance (cf. Cic. *ND* 1.6). Hence a more positive, more Platonic image was sought. As a propaganda exercise, the Roman Books were a failure, for the impression of unity which they set out to convey was built, at best, upon half-truths; as an attempt to reconcile Academic traditions with common sense, they may have had more success. They are, as I shall argue in chapter 3, the origin of a new Academic orthodoxy, an orthodoxy sufficiently different from earlier Academic thought to justify our use of the term 'Fourth Academy', however much continuity in diversity there had been.

By the 'Fourth Academics' I mean primarily Philo and Charmadas, with the possible addition of Metrodorus of Stratonicea, who foreshadowed their position in significant respects; secondarily I mean those who were inclined to follow the One-Academy thesis, and who acknowledged an allegiance to Plato as well as to Arcesilaus and Carneades, 'fallibilists' rather than 'sceptics', who emphasized the difficulties of knowing (in a general sense) but still sought to know. The Academy had always been, and still was as it tottered then on the brink of extinction,[2] an institution which encouraged free thinking, so one should not expect the 'Fourth Academics' to agree on the details of a well-thought-out system of belief; but there are, I would maintain, significant similarities in the philosophical approach of Plutarch, Cicero, and the anonymous *Commentary on the Theaetetus* which may be traced back to Philo of Larissa. Other names will appear in the pages which follow. I also inquire into the Academic position of Antiochus of Ascalon prior to his open break with Philo, for his development is not fully explicable without due weight being attached to his long and productive period spent under the guidance of Philo (Cic. *Ac.* 2.69).

My view that there was continued Academic activity of a Fourth Academic character between the death of Philo of Larissa and the time of Plutarch will be seen as rather unorthodox, and yet I believe that the evidence is quite conclusive.[3] Less easily proven is my view that Antiochus of

Ascalon had little influence among philosophers describing themselves as 'Academics' or 'Platonics' after the death of his brother Aristus, but this is not essential to my case. It must be noted that I do not postulate the survival of any continuous Academic school during this period, or even of any continuous oral tradition, certainly not a highly developed one. I should suppose that Alexandria became the principal seat of Academic activities (though Rhodes too may have played an important role), and that Eudorus of Alexandria, active in the third quarter of the first century B.C., was a key figure in the development of Academic Platonism.

Eudorus is, and will probably remain, a mystery figure, and though I now argue for his having been of Fourth Academic persuasions, I do not claim to be able to settle the issue finally. Owing to the tendency of scholars to see a gulf between 'sceptics' (among whom Philo of Larissa still features) and eclectic-dogmatists (including anybody who expresses, or appears to express, positive views which owe something to more than one school), Eudorus has had to be seen in eclectic-dogmatist terms, and this has led to his being associated with Antiochus or Antiochus' brother Aristus, i.e. with the Fifth Academy rather than the Fourth. But, as will emerge shortly, one cannot see this period in its true perspective if one persists with the sceptic—dogmatist dichotomy; moreover, eclecticism is not a Fifth Academic ideal, and is not compatible with the Fifth Academic belief in the concept of a single sage who has reached the full truth with unerring certainty. If any ideal of eclecticism had existed in any Academy, then it must have been the Fourth, as we see from Cicero at *Ac.* 2.7–9. Here the Academic is permitted a free, if cautious, choice between the various views available to him, without being pressured into accepting the complete system of some philosopher who is judged to be the sage.

Yet at present Eudorus cannot even be regarded as an eclectic with any certainty. For the most part we possess only reports of *his* reports of the views of other philosophers, and great caution needs to be exercised before the views in question may be attributed directly to him. His division of

4

moral philosophy shows us the quite unsurprising fact that he used many Stoic terms, and gives us some insight into his interests; it does not report his doctrine. His criticism of Aristotle's *Categories* tells us little. It seems likely that he differed from Antiochus on the question of the moral goal,[4] one of the two central issues of philosophy in Antiochus' eyes (Cic. *Ac.* 2.29), and we have nothing to show his position on Antiochus' other central issue, the criterion of knowledge. The only criterion we see him applying is the joint Platonic-Academic criterion of 'the likely', upon whose correct application Plutarch challenges him (*Mor.* 1013b); this will not suffice to brand him a Fourth Academic, but the terms in which Plutarch engages him suggests that he used the same standards as Plutarch does.[5] Other evidence suggests that the term 'Academic' would have been applied most readily to non-dogmatic philosophers in the age of Eudorus and for the following century.[6]

It is to Eudorus that one must look if one hopes to discern the origins of later Platonism, assuming that Arius Didymus (?) is continuing to follow him in his exposition of moral 'problems' in Stobaeus, *Ecl.* 2.45.11ff (Wachsmuth), where there is evidence of a new depth of Platonic scholarship and where the Middle Platonic moral goal first appears. To him may be traced the prevalent Middle Platonist metaphysic, based on God, Ideas, Soul/Mathematicals, Immanent Form, and Matter.[7] To him we may attribute Platonic elements in Philo of Alexandria.[8]

But Platonism required a suitable epistemological background from which it might emerge. Antiochus' championing of sense-perception was in conflict with the essence of Platonic philosophy: with the call away from this imperfect and unstable world of the senses towards what may be grasped by the mind in isolation. Platonism certainly needed something other than scepticism on which to build, but it needed no infallible elements of knowledge, and no certainty which followed upon these elements mechanically. What it did require was a mind totally liberated for inquiry; since knowledge, it was believed, was natural, and since the mind, in its natural state, became quickly attuned to the truth which it had once known, the chief requirements were freedom from alien doctrine induced by the senses and the faith to believe in those propositions to which unencumbered reasoning would lead us.

Thus Platonism emerged firmly wedded to the doctrine of the flux, relativity, and insubstantiality of the physical world; it emerged with doctrine, not dogma; it spoke in such a way as to trigger off an inner response, without laying down inflexible rules for either belief or conduct. As confidence increased over the years it was to lose some of this non-dogmatic character, but in Plutarch at least it is still present.

Thus there is an argument that the revived Platonism grew out of the 'Fourth Academic' approach to philosophy, cautious, critical of the senses, yet constructive. My study can neither prove nor disprove such a thesis, though it can, I hope, make it appear credible.

## ii The issue

The critical issue for determining the nature of any Academic influence on subsequent thought, Platonist or otherwise, is whether that thought accepted any Academic position on the criterion of knowledge, and if so which Academic position. Does it follow the Third, Fourth, or Fifth Academy? This must be determined with reference to the question of 'apprehension': what, if anything, did a thinker believe that we could 'apprehend' (Lat. *comprehendere*, Gk. καταλαμβάνειν), and in what sense? Sextus Empiricus uses their answers to this question to distinguish between New Academics, Pyrrhonists, and dogmatists at *PH* 1.3–4, where he apparently takes the position of Carneades and Clitomachus as characteristically 'Academic'; and it is again with reference to this question that he distinguishes between Pyrrhonists, Third Academics, and Fourth Academics (*PH* 1.226, 235).

It had been the 'Second Academy' of Arcesilaus which had first introduced the theme of 'non-apprehensibility' (ἀκαταληψία) into the academic repertoire, and adequate sources agree that he did so as a response to the Stoic position.[9] The terminology of 'apprehension' had been introduced to philosophy by the Stoa, and thus any early attack on 'apprehension' was inevitably an attack on the technicalities of the Stoic system, not on the possibility of cognition and knowledge: though it could have constituted part of such an attack.

'Apprehension' was for the Stoics an act of 'assent to an apprehensive presentation' (*SVF* 2.70, 90–1); this presentation was a mental impression arising from an 'existent' and registered in accordance with that 'existent' in such a way that it could not have arisen from a 'non-existent' (S.E. *Math.* 7.248 = *SVF* 1.59). Space precludes any detailed discussion of the 'apprehensive presentation' here, but it is perhaps easier to understand 'existent' as a condition of the material world or underlying truth than as a 'thing'. Thus an apprehensive presentation will appear such that it could only have arisen from an actual condition of matter or underlying truth; its very appearance will signify to us not only that it arises from an existent object, but also that the underlying condition of matter will be truly such as it indicates it to be. Thus it is true, and of such a kind that it could not be false (*SVF* 2.90 = S.E. *Math.* 7.152); that at least is how Arcesilaus understood it (*ibid.* and Cic. *Ac.* 2.77).

Arcesilaus' intention had been to show that no such 'apprehensive presentation' as the Stoics proposed could exist. The non-existence of such presentations would entail the impossibility of apprehension, so long as this was defined with reference to such a presentation (S.E. *Math.* 7.155). If the act of apprehension were impossible, all things would come to be non-apprehensible. This combined package of theses became known as the doctrine of non-apprehensibility. From the doctrine it followed that the Stoic sage, who assented to nothing non-apprehensible, would assent to nothing: he would 'suspend judgment' (ἐπέχειν).

While Arcesilaus' attack was directed against Stoic epistemology, and against the doctrine of apprehension in particular, it must be noted that Cicero represents him as *agreeing* with the Stoic definition of an apprehensive presentation (*Ac.* 2.77: 'consensit'). His agreement clearly did not indicate a belief that the term itself had been rightly defined, for the term was new in such a sense. His approval of the definition must have been given, if at all, as an approval of the requirements of a criterion of certain knowledge: if the apprehensible presentation were to serve as such a criterion, then it had to be such as the Stoics defined it to be. In that case to deny the existence of apprehensible presentations was to deny the existence of any criterion of certain knowledge. And thus the attack on the Stoa was bound to lead to clashes with other dogmatic schools concerning the possibility of knowledge, with the Academy attempting to demonstrate that no non-Stoic epistemology was sufficient to justify certainty.

It was in fact Carneades who was said to have extended the Academic attack so as to challenge *all* previous thinkers, not the Stoics alone.[10] Carneadean theory is presented as demanding something akin[11] to the Stoic criterion if certain knowledge is to be possible, though one is entitled to suspect pro-Stoic bias in the account, as Antiochus is named as a source (S.E. *Math.* 7.160–5). And thus, when Carneades did not admit the existence of anything akin to the Stoic criterion, the doctrine of non-apprehensibility acquired a more general significance, and was linked to the view that no school had yet discovered any criterion of certain knowledge.

Carneades and Clitomachus are singled out by Sextus as prominent Academics who treat things as *positively* non-apprehensible in a way which the Pyrrhonist would avoid (*PH* 1.3), and it is their school which Sextus has in mind when he claims at *PH* 1.226 that Academics confidently affirm (διαβεβαιοῦνται) that things are non-apprehensible. Carneades' confidence may be disputed, for Cicero makes it plain that he had not claimed to 'apprehend' that all things are non-apprehensible; but then he *could not* have made so contradictory a claim. The same passage (*Ac.* 2.28–9) also suggests that he had allowed the non-apprehensibility doctrine to acquire the status of a *dogma* or 'decree' of the

Academy, and so become one of the guiding principles of Academic philosophy.

Guiding principles, however, need not be based on intellectual certainty. They need to be workable, and able to command our general confidence. They are fundamental for the regulation of life. But for the regulation of life Carneades followed criteria which did not imply certainty: we should follow the persuasive (πιθανός, but Lat. *probabilis*) presentation; preferably when received in conjunction with other presentations which do not weaken one's confidence; preferably again when such attendant presentations have all been subjected to critical examination. The exact status of such presentations was the subject of much subsequent confusion. Galen (*Plac.* 9.778) actually held that the third kind had the same power as the Stoic apprehensive presentation; this cannot be quite correct, since it certainly did not have the power to produce infallible knowledge, though it might easily have been thought to have the same power for the regulation of man's life. Antiochus of Ascalon, on the other hand, was moved to claim that they had no power at all (Cic. *Ac.* 2.35—6). It seems probable that the Fourth Academy had tried to make more use of the three species of persuasive presentations than the Third would have done, and, to judge from *Ac.* 2.35, they had employed them as an excuse for making assertions, thus tending to give them a role in epistemology rather than in moral choice; though it must be noted that, to an extent, the process of making judgments of the likely truth or falsity of a given proposition is part of the conduct of our lives.

Fourth Academic innovation, however, was not most prominent here. Use was made of 'perspicuous' or seemingly self-evident presentations,[12] which nevertheless fell short of being actually self-evident.[13] Such presentations finally became the justification for Philo of Larissa's willingness to apply the term 'apprehend' in a non-Stoic sense, thus restricting the doctrine of non-apprehensibility to the denial of all apprehension *as defined by the Stoics.*[14] We learn from Cicero of a Peripatetic definition of apprehension (*Ac.* 2.112)

9

which would not render apprehension impossible according to Philo's theory.[15] There is, of course, no hint that Philo considered the Peripatetic definition to be a *correct* one (though by now, of course, the term would frequently have been used by non-philosophic persons in a non-technical cognitive sense), and no possibility that he would have acknowledged 'Peripatetic apprehension' to be a 'criterion of knowledge'. But admission of the word was bound to suggest the possibility of a more secure *grasp* of certain facts than Carneades was thought to have allowed for. It also seemed to herald a slackening of the Academy's attack on non-Stoic epistemologies.[16]

So long as the Carneadean attack upon all previous philosophies had been maintained, there was little room for the development of any commitment to Plato's views within the Academy. Cicero, speaking *in propria persona* at *Ac.* 2.142, speaks of Plato's position that judgment of the truth belonged to the mind and to reason rather than to the senses and to opinion, and yet Carneades had argued against reason or anything else being a criterion of truth (S.E. *Math.* 7.159). Philo's One-Academy thesis demanded that there should be no substantial gulf between Academic theory in his own day and Plato's theory. How could he move towards accepting Plato's theory (as the Academy represented it) without surrendering to the Stoics? The question is crucial to any assessment of the influence of Fourth Academic epistemology on subsequent Platonism.

But let us first consider whether Platonism could be better served by giving in to the Stoics on epistemology. The traditional anti-Academic jibe that critics of the senses 'throw out the light',[17] might equally well have been employed by the Stoics as a criticism of Plato himself. Rehabilitation of sense-perception would render all Plato's talk about the uncertainties of the sensible world redundant; it would no longer be opinable, as at *Ac.* 1.42, but, in many respects, truly knowable. Empirical formation of concepts from repeated sensation[18] would either demystify or else supplant the Platonic Ideas. It is not merely Platonic epistemology

which would be threatened by a move towards Stoic epistemology, but also Platonic ontology; and without an appropriate
ontology there would be no adequate context for Platonic
psychology; once the psychology has gone, the ethics and
politics are left without a foundation, and Platonism has
disappeared. It is not then surprising that Antiochus of
Ascalon, who in his *Sosus* took the step of approving the
Stoic apprehensive presentation and of defending sense-
perception, has had no visible influence on Middle Platonic
epistemology. *No apprehensive presentation is found there,
and no comparable faith in our senses as source of infallible
truths.*

Philo maintained the attack on sense-perception to a
degree, continuing to claim that no single presentation could
be of such a kind that it could not be false. But he allowed
that many seemed evident, and appeared to be confirmed by
similarly clear presentations received either by others or by
ourselves at different times.[19] The senses on the whole produced a coherent picture of the world, impeded only by
presentations received under abnormal conditions. It was
only the occasional fortuitous impression which both seemed
evident and yet was false. This was enough to remove complete certainty from the world of sensible particulars, even
for the man who judges only by seemingly evident presentations.[20] The doctrine of flux, which seemed to receive
adequate support from our senses, meant that our impressions
of sensible particulars could receive only limited support
from the presentations of others, who would necessarily be
viewing either at a different time or from a different angle.
There will be few, if any, witnesses to the fact that object $x$
seemed evidently $F$ at time $t$. I may try to examine all other
presentations which I receive between time $t - 3$ and $t + 3$,
and conclude that there is a persuasive case for $x$ having been
$F$ at time $t$, but there is always the chance that I was suffering
from hallucinations from time $t - 3$ until $t + 3$; I may even
have imagined that a few others were agreeing with me.

The difficulties experienced when trying to establish that
all objects belonging to the same species as $x$ always have the

property $F$, or rather *regularly* have that property, are less severe, provided that the proposition is (a) true and (b) attested by evident presentations among many witnesses. When natural regularities are the subject of inquiry, a multitude of witnesses of whom each has received many evident presentations can guard against the occasional fortuitous presentation, whether it has been caused by ill-health, drunkenness, or a trick of the light. Thus, when our studies concern the universal rather than the particular, the inadequacies of certain presentations arising from the senses present no obstacles to our knowledge.

Again, when the individual attempts to arrive at a universal concept, he will, according to the usual account, gather together a number of evident presentations of a similar kind.[21] Unique features of seemingly evident impressions will not be employed in the construction of the universal concept, and hence there will be an adequate safeguard against the fortuitous presentation which is false while appearing evident. This will not constitute a complete defence of Plato's attempt to see knowledge within the world of universal Ideas, chiefly because Plato would not accept the empirical account of concept-formation as a full explanation of our knowledge of the Ideas. But it is a defence sufficient to justify dichotomy between more knowable universals and less knowable particulars.

It is therefore not surprising that at the time of the Fourth Academy reference began to be made to the intelligible evident as well as to the sensible evident.[22] It may be that the intelligible evident was thought of as deriving from a number of evident sense-presentations,[23] but since this evident character has usually[24] been treated as a particular characteristic of good *sense*-presentations, we must assume that there was some positive new move towards the recognition of evident Ideas: a move most easily explicable within the context of an attempt to revive Platonism. The Platonist might be forced into a difficult position when asked whether or not these ideas were grasped by a presentation of a kind such that it could not be misrepresenting them, but it might have been possible to deny that they were grasped by a presentation at all.

Here I claim only that the Fourth Academy produced new epistemological ideas which appear to provide a more suitable epistemological framework for a revival of Platonism. This in itself did not constitute a revival of Platonism. Philo and his school have thus no claim to the title 'Fathers of Middle Platonism', and even their epistemology continued to have a more Hellenistic than Platonic character. The true beginning of Middle Platonism came with the combination of certain Fourth Academic epistemological attitudes with an in-depth interpretation of Plato inspired by Posidonius, and, through him, by the Old Academy. That combination was already in evidence by the time of Plutarch, and was *perhaps* achieved by Eudorus of Alexandria. But that is another story.[25]

At present we must be content to note that the Middle Platonists (a) do not in any extant text assume the existence of apprehensive presentations such as the Stoics demand;[26] but (b) do not seriously challenge the possibility of knowledge in some general sense. In this much they adopt a Fourth Academic position.

### iii The thesis

It will seem strange to many readers that the Academic 'scepticism' of Carneades could in time lead to a revival of Platonism. It therefore appears necessary, at the outset of this work, to show that such a development was *philosophically* plausible before tackling the historical evidence.

At first sight it would seem that any talk of a 'Carneadean–Platonist epistemology' would be absurd, and the phrase itself an oxymoron. It would be particularly scorned by those whose tinted spectacles see Plato as a dogmatic philosopher, Carneades as a sceptic, and the Platonic philosophy as supremely vulnerable to a sceptic's attack. Such persons would no doubt see less contradiction in the expression 'Antiochean–Platonist epistemology', for Antiochus was a dogmatist, Plato may be seen as such, and the Platonic philosophy may be seen as being in special need of a dogmatic defence. But an Antiochean–Platonist epistemology would also be a Stoic–Platonist epistemology, for in nothing did Antiochus come closer to his beloved Zeno[27] than in his theory of knowledge. And the Stoic and Platonist epistemologies were almost as different as any two epistemologies could be. Antiochus himself cannot hide the differences,[28] and he accepted the Zenonian 'corrections' of Plato's position. Even supposing that Carneades' school had been committed to the proposition 'There is no path to knowledge, either from sensation or from *a priori* knowledge', he would differ only in one respect from the Platonist, who holds that there is an a priori path to knowledge but no sensation-based empirical path. The Stoic differs from the Platonist on both counts.

What Carneades was committed to, however, was always far from plain. The two most obvious epistemological propositions to which we might hope to gain his assent are these:[29]

(A1)   No cognitive act (presentation) can present true data to the mind in such a way that they could not be false.

(B1)   One should follow a believable presentation $p$, received at time $t$, if it is not rendered suspect after thorough investigation of closely related presentations $p_1, p_2, p_3, \ldots p_n$ received between times $t - n_1$ and $t + n_2$.

The latter formula suits the evaluation of presentations concerning those sensible particulars which are observed for a limited period of time, and Sextus offers examples concerning such particulars.[30] The closely related presentations $p_1$ etc. will be received during the period of observation of the sensible particular concerned. The examination of $p_1$ etc. will assure us:

(a)   that the object under investigation *consistently* appears such as $p$ represents it to be;

(b)   that the conditions of light etc. under which the particular is observed *consistently* appear reliable;

(c)    that nothing is observed *inconsistent* with $p$;

(d)    that I, the observer, experienced *consistent* and *consistently believable* presentations such as would suggest the health of my faculties of judgment at the time of observation.

From this it will appear that the key to Carneadean decision-making is consistency. A believable presentation may be rendered more attractive by the observation that it is consistent with other relevant believable presentations, or at least with the vast majority of them.

But while it is rational to follow a believable presentation, received at 3.15 p.m., that this bird is black, if it is not rendered suspect after thorough investigation of related presentations received between 3.10 and 3.25 p.m., the situation is more complicated if the presentation claims that this bird is a raven; the temporal factor is only applicable to our judgment of this bird, not to our concept of a raven. If, however, upon viewing this bird, we receive a convincing presentation that all ravens are black, the temporal factor is largely inapplicable, and should be dropped from B1 to read as follows:

(B2)    One should follow a believable presentation $p$ when, on investigation of all other presentations relevant to $p$, $p$ is found to be consistent with them.

Strictly speaking, consistency with other presentations is not a confirmation that $p$ is true, but rather the elimination of objections to believing $p$. The Greek for 'consistency', however, is also the Greek for 'agreement';[31] thus it frequently means far more than the mere absence of disagreement. Accordingly the Fourth Academy tended to see the absence of contrary testimony as some kind of limited confirmation in its own right. The school which had so far made most use of lack of contrary testimony and of confirmatory testimony was that of Epicurus; Epicureans sought to distinguish between true and false opinions with reference to the confirmatory or contrary testimony of evident sensations.

(C)    One should follow[32] a belief $b$, when, on investigation, it is found to have confirmatory testimony and/or[33] not-contrary testimony from evident sensations.

Such sensation was vital to the Epicureans as being the only ultimate source of confirmation, and indeed there is not much point in seeking confirmation from anything which is not evident; for this in turn would require confirmation. For this reason the concept of the evident attracted the attention of the Academy, probably via the ex-Epicurean Academic Metrodorus,[34] who was first to promote the constructive view of Carneades' thought.[35] When the Academics adopt principle B2, therefore, the notion of confirmation through consistency is closely linked with the notion of the evident,[36] as in C.

The theory is as follows:

(D1)   If $Fx$ is evident, then $Fx$ will be consistently agreed upon in all normal presentations which purport to judge the $F$-ness of $x$.[37]

A Carneadean would resist the converse:[38]

(D2)   If $Fx$ is consistently agreed upon in all normal presentations which purport to judge the $F$-ness of $x$, then $Fx$ is evident.

But he might nevertheless adopt the following principle as a guide on which to base his conduct:

(D3)   If $Fx$ consistently *seems evident* in all the many presentations which purport to judge the $F$-ness of $x$, then $Fx$ is evident.

The Academic was obliged to consider carefully the terminology employed. Like the English 'obvious' or 'evident', the Greek ἐναργής and the Latin *perspicuus* or *evidens* appeared to imply the truth of any proposition which they were used to describe. As a result there must have been an early tendency for the school of Carneades to resist the concept of the evident, but Clitomachus qualifies their attack on it in a passage used by Cicero at *Ac.* 2.99. In effect he rejects the notion of any presentation which is *observably* true, but allows that there may be ones which are observably clear and persuasive, while being non-observably true; 'evident' *rather than* 'self-evident'. The rejection of the former sense, which follows necessarily from Carneadean principle A1, may be phrased as follows:

(A2)    There are no evident presentations, where 'evident' means observably true.

Hence if evident presentations were not to constitute a null-class, but were to retain something of the normal significance of the Greek term ἐναργής, they might have been defined by an Academic as follows:

(E)    Evident presentations are those which both seem evident and are true.[39]

Thus they would possess the highest level of persuasiveness conjoined with truth. But that which seems evident cannot, of itself, be relied upon as true.

Inevitably the issue of how we distinguish between presentations which seem evident only and those which are also true was now brought to the fore; and, if this was impossible, the Academics at least sought for a way of distinguishing true and evident *propositions* from those which merely seemed evident to certain individuals at certain times. For the only resource which the Academics had open to them was a further appeal to the principle of consistent agreement. They needed a theory similar to D3; Carneades, they believed, had shown the way by the introduction of the consistency-factor as in B2, while D1 had already established a link between consistent agreement and the evident. But was the jump to D3 too difficult for a follower of the Carneadean tradition to make?

Let us return to D1: if $Fx$ is evident, then $Fx$ will be consistently agreed upon in all normal presentations which purport to judge the $F$-ness of $x$. Suppose $Fx$ is not in fact evident; what other conditions could have produced the consistent agreement that $Fx$? The ancients might perhaps have assumed almost universally that the number of stars was even, but could they ever have assumed, almost universally, that the even-ness of the number of stars was evident? What conditions, then, other than the evident $F$-ness of $x$, might have caused consistent agreement *that Fx is evident*? Surely men could never come to a chance agreement that the earth is evidently cylindrical or that the moon is evidently green cheese. And while I grant that all men of a given period might agree that theological doctrine $T$ is evidently true if compelled by their creed to do so, it is not, ultimately, what proceeds from their lips which matters, but the presentations which are presented to their minds: can *these* consistently affirm that $T$ is evident? Can any proposition consistently present itself to men's minds *as being evident* and yet be false? Perhaps, but there is little hope for science or for philosophy if this is in fact the case. We have to operate upon the assumption that such things do not happen; we never *know* this, but we can have no *practical* doubt. Thus the followers of Carneades, correctly or incorrectly, took him to admit that it was only the occasional presentation which displayed believable clarity in spite of being false.[40] One supposes therefore that a Carneadean would regard as extremely rare those false presentations which displayed the highest degree of persuasive clarity. Was it conceivable that mankind should *consistently* receive a long string of occasional fortuitous presentations? Can consistency be the work of pure chance, devoid of any rational foundation? A constructive philosopher must resist such an idea as strongly as he would resist the notion that all ravens are pink.

If it was plausible to claim that Carneades would have resisted all talk of consistently repeated freak presentations, then it was plausible to claim Carneadean approval of D3 as a principle for guiding men's judgments: if $Fx$ consistently seemed evident in a multitude of clear presentations, then $Fx$ was indeed evident. And being evident it was also, according to definition E, true.

At this point the Academics had arrived at a method of judging the truth or falsity of various types of propositions. It may not have been infallible, but it was sufficiently reliable for one to be able to employ it with confidence; and it still seemed compatible with the principles of practical judgment left by Carneades. The Academics had managed to find a method of judging certain issues which would make allowances for the occasional false but clear presentations produced by abnormal conditions: sickness, madness, vivid dreams, drunkenness, tricks of the light, or other freak circumstances. The Academics had long concentrated on such presentations as these when attacking their dogmatist opponents.[41] The requirement that there should be consistent agreement covering a multitude of presentations would guard against abnormalities; the requirement that this agreement should extend to the evident nature of a given proposition guarded also against man's attempts to judge matters in which our faculties are not sufficiently accurate to be trusted.[42]

We have already noted that this method of judgment can seldom be applied to sensible particulars.[43] It applies most obviously to what is either universally or generally or frequently the case. It can establish that all ravens are black, that most ravens are noisy, or that a sub-set of corvines are ravens. It cannot establish that raven $r$ which I now catch sight of is black, unless perhaps via some universal law that if $r$ is a raven, then $r$ is black. The system thus encouraged one to look for universal rather than particular evident propositions. At the time concepts were thought to arise from repeated sensation,[44] and thus propositions implied by such concepts would have similar origins. Evident sensations could ensure that any concept formed out of them would be likewise evident,[45] and thus propositions implied by the concepts would be of the same character. And though one might be led astray by the occasional false presentation which seemed evident, one does not use such presentations (in so far as they differ from true ones) when forming concepts. One may be fooled by the evening light into supposing that this gull is pink, but in the absence of any other presentations of pink gulls one does not use this presentation (or not in respect of its colour) for the formation of universal concepts. It is regularities which lead to concept-formation, and thus irregularities are weeded out. The dangers that beset our attempts to know particulars are no longer there in the case of universals. Men's concepts, particularly where they agree about them and agree that they imply a number of evident propositions, are reliable.

Once the Academics had accepted the existence of concepts

which were evident to the intellect, and had made the natural identification of these with the Stoic 'common' or 'natural notions' according to the links perceived between agreement and the evident (D1),[46] the door to Platonism was open wide. For it was accepted that men had these 'natural notions' concerning things of which there was no sense-perception, or at least no seemingly evident sense-perception. We had natural notions of God, natural notions of the virtues;[47] and from those natural notions we were thought to be capable of extracting evident propositions.[48] How could evident propositions arise from evident concepts, without those concepts having been implanted within the mind by evident sensations? The philosopher who accepted this kind of evident concept was bound to look towards some a priori knowledge as a possible explanation.

Any Academic of the time of Philo of Larissa would have been wary of giving a single explanation of such concepts, but if he accepted D3 then he would have been bound to regard any concept which was agreed to be evident as true. Analysis of such concepts would yield true propositions. Truth would belong to the intelligible world in a way which was alien to the sensible world; new foundations for Platonism would have been established.

If such theory has passed well beyond what Carneades would agree to (as I believe it has), then I believe that he would have objected principally to the last stage: to the admission of concepts which were generally agreed to be evident, but which had no basis in evident sensation. I doubt whether Carneades was prepared to give serious consideration to any origin of knowledge other than sensation, for it is sensation which he had in mind when he claimed that any criterion of knowledge would have to be linked with evident cognitive experience (S.E. *Math.* 7.160–1). Originally the term 'evident' had been applied to clear *sensation*; the notion of something evident to the intellect *and divorced from sensation* may never have occurred to him.[49]

Naturally Carneades would also have countered the application of D3 as a criterion of knowledge, but there is no evidence that any Fourth Academic ever tried to give such a principle that role. It was at best a guide. And if knowledge itself were admitted, then it was not out of a readiness to accept the existence of 'a mental state unable to be changed by reasoning',[50] but rather the result of a general desire to find some meaning for all those terms which men agreed to be meaningful. If men agreed that they had an evident notion of knowledge and of apprehension, then D3 demanded that there should be realities corresponding to those notions.[51]

Finally one may suspect that Carneades would have seen D3 as slightly inadequate. His own principle B2 referred to 'all other presentations relevant to $p$', while D3 reduces this to all presentations purporting to judge the issue. He might have been more inclined to accept it as a guide to conduct when revised as follows:

(D4)   If $Fx$ consistently seems evident in all the many presentations which purport to judge the $F$-ness of $x$, and if this impression is consistent with all other relevant presentations, then $Fx$ is evident.

# CHAPTER 1

# SCEPTICISM IN THE LATE ACADEMY?

We all know what we now mean by a sceptic. The Greeks and Romans of the late second century A.D. meant something slightly different by it, but knew what they meant. For Sextus Empiricus it was one who had grave doubts about the possibility of ascertaining anything or even estimating probabilities.[1] The near-legendary founder of the sceptic movement, Pyrrho of Elis, was thought to have perfected the practice of judging purely by the impression of the moment, freed from any preconceived ideas.[2] Precursors of scepticism had supposedly pointed to the difficulties of arriving at any certain knowledge, but they had fallen short of Pyrrho's example.[3] After a period when the study of uncertainty had been left to the Academy, the sceptic discipline had been revived in Alexandria during the first century B.C. by Aenesidemus,[4] and had survived more or less continuously until Sextus' day.[5]

We do not have to go much further back in time before a note of ambiguity is detected in the term. Aulus Gellius, following Favorinus,[6] explains that the term 'sceptic' is used of both Pyrrhonian and Academic philosophers (*NA* 11.5.6), even though he had previously (11.5.1) thought of it as a Greek *cognomen* for Pyrrhonians. While Favorinus saw only slight differences between Pyrrhonians and Academics, and seemed to see himself as an Academic with the authority to speak on Pyrrhonian subjects,[7] we do not receive the impression at *NA* 11.5.6 that it was his own idea that the terms 'sceptic', 'ephectic', and 'aporetic' should be applied equally to Academics; the Latin *dicuntur* suggests that those descriptions were regularly used of Academics, probably in the considerable body of literature which had already arisen concerning the difference between the two schools, and which had been mentioned at 11.5.6.[8]

A possible solution to the problem which appears in Gellius, and one which fits other evidence, would be to regard 'sceptic' as a *name* for the Pyrrhonians only, but as an appropriate *description* of the Academics as well. We do in fact hear that the Pyrrhonist-Empiric Theodosius rejected 'Pyrrhonian' as a name for the discipline because of doubts about Pyrrho's own attitudes, apparently preferring 'sceptic' as the correct name.[9] Such reservations may have been behind the tendency, discernible earlier in Philo (*QG* 3.33, if the Armenian translation is to be trusted), to use such terms as 'sceptic' and 'ephectic' as *names* for Pyrrhonian philosophers only, without eclipsing earlier, less technical usage.

Of the four terms which came to serve as names for Pyrrhonians ('sceptic', 'zetetic', 'ephectic', 'aporetic': D.L. 9.69–70), the first two derive from verbs meaning 'examine' or 'seek'. This origin was openly acknowledged, but an element of perpetuity had been introduced into terms which had not *per se* implied perpetuity: the words derived, they said, from examination *without finding* and from *constant searching for the truth*.[10]

In Philodemus and Philo of Alexandria we meet the adjective 'sceptic' in what must have been the original sense, 'given to inquiring',[11] a sense in which it could not possibly refer to any special group of philosophers. Philo, in extant Greek, only once refers to 'the sceptics' as if expecting the reader to identify a special group (*Congr.* 52). Not only do these people not see God (as only Israel does), they do not even see the heavens, which are the summit of the sensible world (as do the Chaldaeans and other astronomers); they see only inferior things (or an inferior thing) of this world. Failure to study the heavens sets them apart from most philosophers, but we learn at 53 that they are not interested in ethics either: not at least with any view to practical benefit. They are in fact interested only in matters of word and argument, though it would be a mistake to say that Philo associated them with logic: what he means is that they are incapable of dealing with a subject at a deeper level than that of mere word-quibbling and destructive paradox. They are associated

23

with sophistry.[12] One can imagine that many opponents of the Pyrrhonians would have viewed them thus, and I see no difficulty in identifying these 'sceptics' with the group who later bear that name,[13] even though the term may not, as yet, be well established in that sense.

On one other occasion Philo's extant Greek seems to use 'sceptic' in a similar sense (*Fug.* 209). The association with argumentative 'sophists' is again apparent (as in the Armenian of *QG* 3.33), and, as these people oppose all others, forcing them to defend 'their own dogmata, the conceptions of their minds', Philo appears to have Pyrrhonians in mind. On this occasion, however, he refers to their 'excessively sceptical intent' and portrays it as a disguise which they adopt, as if true 'scepticism' or moderate 'scepticism' were a genuine and commendable search *for the truth*. They claim to use 'scepticism', but is not the 'scepticism' which Philo recognizes elsewhere as a commendable quality.[14]

The clearest proof that 'sceptic' in Philo does not always refer to those whom we should describe as sceptics is found in the *De Ebrietate*. In this work the word is found twice in its natural significance.[15] One of these cases occurs in a section which has long been recognized as a retailing of the Aenesideman modes of suspension.[16] Here if anywhere one would expect to find 'sceptic' as the name of the Pyrrhonist school: if Aenesidemus had so used the term. Instead we find at 202 that the *scepsis* of all the *sceptics* had been directed towards the discovery of the truth, even though it had not finally achieved that goal.

We cannot be sure that Aenesidemus would have tolerated the use of the term found at *Ebr.* 202, because we do not know whether Philo is following Aenesidemus direct, freely adapting the original, or following a previous Academic adaptation.[17] The final possibility seems to me to be likeliest. But we do know that Aenesidemus referred to his own followers and predecessors as 'Pyrrhonians' when comparing them with Academics,[18] so that 'sceptic' had not yet been an official title. A passage of Diogenes Laertius suggests that Aenesidemus may have used the term *scepseis* for Pyrrhonian 'inquiries', for we meet the phrase αἱ ἐν ταῖς σκέψεσιν ἀντιθέσεις at 9.78, where Aenesidemus is apparently the source.[19] The counter-balancing of impressions and of arguments is of great importance to Aenesideman Pyrrhonism,[20] and this passage may indicate an early link between Pyrrhonist *scepseis* and the method of achieving suspension of judgment by the antithetic comparison of impressions and arguments. Sextus Empiricus, in the non-original prologue to his *Pyrrhonians* (1.8), describes *scepsis* as 'an antithetic power juxtaposing phenomena and intellectual considerations in whatsoever manner'.[21] It is natural to assume that because *scepsis* (*qua* 'inquiry') always led the Pyrrhonist to counter-balancing arguments, the word came to be applied to the practice of balancing arguments itself. Subsequently the adjective 'sceptic' would have developed a special usage, referring to those who employ the antithetic method as a road to suspension of judgment; so that the new sense of the word found in Philo (*Congr.* 52, *Fug.* 209, *QG* 3.33) is such as to imply devotion to non-constructive argument.

This account can adequately explain the newer use of the term in Philo of Alexandria, but how do we explain the more complimentary and apparently older sense in other parts of his work, and particularly at *Ebr.* 202? Here we must introduce material from Cicero's *Academica.* This work clearly presents inquiry as a virtue recognized by the Academy. They had claimed that Plato had anticipated the later Academics by inquiring (*quaerere*) into everything, advancing arguments on both sides and refraining from dogmatic assertion (1.46). The connexion between inquiry and counter-balanced arguments is much weaker than in Pyrrhonism; there is no suggestion that the arguments will always balance, just that one should examine both sides of the question. Similarly at 2.60 we find the Academics insisting that a pupil should use his reasoning powers rather than accept one side of the argument only from a dogmatic teacher. And in the important passage on the character of the New Academy at 2.7—9 we encounter the ideal of inquiring linked again with deep suspicion of all who submit to the authority of a single teacher without some consideration of all points of view. Words used for inquiring are *conquirere* (2.7) and *exquirere* (2.7, 9); the goal of inquiry is either the truth or the closest approximation to it (2.7), not suspension of judgment.

The Academic ideal of searching *for oneself* for truth or for something close to it is surely behind the more complimentary uses of the word 'sceptic' in Philo, and particularly the use at *Ebr.* 202, where all the *scepseis* of the 'sceptic' have so far failed to reach the truth which is their goal. This failure was unimportant: the Academic view expressed by Cicero, and recorded for us by Augustine *c. Acad.* 1.3.7, held that he who searched for the truth was blessed, whether or not he was able to attain it. The existence of such a sense explains why Philo can refer, apparently, to Pyrrhonists as excessively sceptical at *Fug.* 209, for their *scepsis* was indeed just an extreme form of a *scepsis* whose value was acknowledged. The *scepsis* of moderate Academics was the impartial examination of all sides of a question; Pyrrhonist *scepsis* contrived to conclude as well as begin with that same impartiality. The *scepsis* of moderate Academics was a necessary step towards approaching the truth; Pyrrhonist *scepsis* was given such prominence that perpetual inquiry was demanded, discovery being excluded.

The evidence of Cicero shows us quite clearly that the Academy as he had known it in his youth saw itself as a group of 'examiners'. What it does not show is what word the Academy used for their search and for their own inclination to search. Gellius suggests that the Academics could be described as both 'zetetic' and 'sceptic', just like the Pyrrhonists, and the verbs from which these terms derive (σκέπτεσθαι, ζητεῖν) could both be translated by the verbs which Cicero used: *quaerere* and its compounds. Of the (Greek) verbs the former is probably best suited to indicating a *critical* examination, and the latter for indicating a positive *search*. Plato could be seen as a powerful advocate of both practices, to judge from the number of times that σκεπτέον or ζητητέον occur in his works. Of the nouns, ζήτησις would convey the impression that the end was discovery, while σκέψις need not do so. Once again Plato had used both terms frequently.

It is when we come to consider the adjectives 'sceptic' and 'zetetic' that we are able to present more conclusive material. An important characteristic of the Academy in the first century B.C. is its desire to establish Socratic and Platonic precedents for its attitudes and activities.[22] The term 'zetetic' had been used by Plato in a sense which indicated his approval of the quality described;[23] one such use occurs in what must have been becoming a key passage for the Academic 'inquirers'.[24] Aristotle refers to all the Socratic discussions (in Plato?) as 'zetetic' at *Pol.* 1265a12. But while the 'zetetic' ideal could claim to be Socratic and Platonic, the term 'sceptic' was new to the first century B.C. While I know of no early attempt to call Plato's work, or any aspect of it, 'sceptic',[25] the major division of the dialogues by the time of Thrasyllus (early 1 A.D.) and beyond separates those which are 'zetetic' from those which are instructional (ὑφηγητικός).[26]

This division is important. It is roughly parallel with divisions which we might care to draw between Plato's Socratic-aporetic works and those which do not fall into such a category. The following works would fall into the zetetic category according to Diogenes Laertius (3.49–50):

| sub-species | species: *gymnastic* | | species: *agonistic* | |
|---|---|---|---|---|
| | *maieutic* | *peirastic* | *endeictic* | *anatreptic* |
| | Alcibiades I | Euthyphro | Protagoras | Euthydemus |
| | Alcibiades II | Meno | | Gorgias |
| | Theages | Ion | | Hippias I |
| | Laches | Charmides | | Hippias II |
| | Lysis | Theaetetus | | |

Of the truly Socratic works only two non-aporetic ones are conspicuously absent (*Ap., Cri.*), and only one work which we would not now regard as Socratic (*Tht.*) is included: but one should not doubt that it was regarded as Socratic during the critical period (100 B.C.–A.D. 50). The aporetic element is generally present, *Gorgias* perhaps being an exception. No aporetic dialogue is missing, unless one includes *Parm.* and

*Crat.* among such works. Albinus, who includes logical works[27] among zetetic (not instructional) works, contrives to regard *Parm., Crat., Sph.* and *Plt.* in the zetetic category; he also omits *Tht.* completely.[28] The classification of Diogenes is clearly earlier, for all dialogues except the unimportant *Atlanticus* (= *Critias*) are given the same sub-species as they receive from Thrasyllus (D.L. 3.58—61). I assume that the division of D.L. 3.49 is also that of Thrasyllus.[29]

What the division of Thrasyllus has succeeded in doing is to give all those Socratic works which do not always seem positively to *teach* (whether ethics, politics, physics or logic), as positive a role as possible. The zetetic works were those most likely to be used to demonstrate Socrates' *aporia* and his confession of ignorance;[30] to give them all a precise role, and a role which *requires* that 'Socrates' should not openly state his own view, was to strike a blow for the more dogmatic view of Plato which is expounded at D.L. 3.51—2: immediately after the sub-division of the dialogues at 49—51. Note that the definition of *dogma* at 51 belongs to a period well before Diogenes writes,[31] and would seem to suit the age of Thrasyllus.[32]

I conclude that the zetetic—instructional distinction was one way of distinguishing between the elements of Plato which might be called 'Academic' and those which might be called 'doctrinal'. Such a distinction would be more readily understandable in the light of a continued Academic ideal of inquiry such as is to be found in Cicero.

The other way of distinguishing between these two aspects of Plato, 'Academic' and 'doctrinal', which could go back as far as the first century B.C., is that which we meet in Sextus Empiricus (*PH* 1.221). Here the terminology used is 'aporetic' and 'dogmatic', until Sextus begins to talk in terms of whether Plato was 'purely sceptic': terminology more likely to have been that of Menodotus than of Academics or Platonists of the first centuries of either era.[33] As we have seen, the term 'aporetic' would be a reasonable description of most of the dialogues of Plato which scholars first labelled 'zetetic', but I suspect that the Academics had no aporetic *ideal. Aporia,* both the ability to puzzle oneself and the ability to puzzle others (cf. D.L. 9.70), was easily associated with both Academics and Pyrrhonists, but in post-Clitomachian Academicism the *aporia* was a means to an end, not an end in itself.[34] Thus, while the Pyrrhonist may well be interested in whether Plato was 'aporetic' in general,[35] the Academic will have been more interested in whether he was 'zetetic': whether he sought without bias the most probable answers to a wide range of philosophical problems.

I have examined several standard descriptions of the 'sceptic', asking in what sense they might have applied to the Academics of the first century B.C. Now it must be asked whether or not the term 'dogmatic' really typified what they objected to in their opponents. The negative answer will have to be given, so long as we consider the sense of the term *dogma* and its cognates during this period; the positive answer is more appropriate if we stick to the modern sense of the term. The Academics objected to the kind of conviction in one's beliefs which prevented one from examining other views with an open mind. For them the ultimate folly was the Stoic requirement that a man should be seen as a sinner if he betrays the Stoic doctrine.[36] The word for 'doctrine' here is *dogma*; that is probably the best translation of the word in the first century B.C.

The Academics could be said to have *dogma* in this sense. In Cicero's *Academica* they are credited with two *dogmata*: (a) at 2.29, they are said to believe that things are non-apprehensible and cannot be 'perceived' and (b) at 2.133, Cicero finds a *dogma* which he and 'Lucullus' share: the doctrine that one should not assent to something which one has not ascertained to be so. In Aenesidemus (Photius cod. 212) it is claimed that the Academics do have *dogmata*, and since the work is addressed to an Academic,[37] the claims cannot be utterly without foundation. An anonymous *Commentary on the Theaetetus* makes similar claims.[38] Thus it is clear that the Academics did not envisage their crusade as a campaign against *dogma* in their sense. Even the Pyrrhonists could find a sense of the word in which they would not object to *dogma* (S.E. *PH* 1.13).

29

More relevant to my present purposes is a distinction between two senses of *dogma* among the works attributed to Galen. At *Medical Definitions* 13 (19.352–3) we read that *dogma* is used in a specific and in a general sense. Textual corruption then obscures the distinction, but there is little doubt that the specific sense was defined as 'assent to an obscure matter',[39] while the general sense was defined as 'assent to an evident matter'.[40] The Academics must have continued to object to *dogma* in that specific sense (cf. D.L. 3.52). But equally their willingness to accept that certain matters were evident, and Philo's allowance that even the sage may occasionally opine (*Ac.* 2.78), would together have made 'assent to an evident matter' quite acceptable. The term did not *per se* imply certainty in what had been decided; for while it was a Stoic ideal that one should not doubt one's *dogma* (*Ac.* 2.27), the term itself did not imply such conviction.[41]

For the study of the term in Sextus Empiricus and his period a recent article by Barnes is valuable.[42] The principal sense of the term for Sextus was undoubtedly something like 'philosophico-scientific tenet', while a secondary sense still of relevance (as it had been for the late Stoa)[43] is that of a 'practical resolution': akin to the political meaning of the term as the 'decree' of a political body, whence Diogenes Laertius (or his source) can see 'dogmatizing' as akin to passing legislation (3.51).[44] In some respects, therefore, a school's *dogmata* were rather like a political party's policy document.

Although the senses of the term in Sextus must not be ignored, they cannot be allowed to dictate the manner in which we seek to understand the term's use in the first century B.C. It is natural, I suggest, that during the many debates on the propriety of *dogma*, on whether Plato dogmatized, and even on whether Pyrrhonists dogmatized (D.L. 9.102–4, S.E. *PH* 1.13–15), the term should have acquired a certain rigidity: a number of clearly defined meanings rather than a semantic range. Since I believe that it was largely Aenesidemus who was responsible for these debates on *dogma*,

I cannot believe that specific senses had been so clearly defined in his own day. Moreover I am reluctant to believe that the term had yet acquired the same consistent 'colour' that Barnes would with reason attribute to it a century or two later.[45]

Cicero's *Academica* give little indication that the word had begun to be a source of great contention. But suppose that it had done? What would Philo's view have been expected to be? We should remember that he was anxious to show that New Academic theory and practice accorded with Plato's. If Plato's epistemology was such as to admit 'the evident' and *dogma* without qualms, then Philo ought to be able to show that the Academy of his own day did not resist these terms in their Platonic sense. Because Plato uses the term περίληψις in the important *Timaeus*, while there is no reason why this should signify less than κατάληψις, Philo must find a sense of the latter term of which he can approve.[46] Because Plato uses the terms 'evident' and *dogma* in the epistemologically important *Theaetetus* (150d6, 203b6, 206b7, 157d2, 158d3), Philo could find a use for them too: in the weaker, pre-Hellenistic sense in which Plato had used them. 'The evident' is allowed as long as it does not imply observable truth; *dogma* is allowed as long as it does not imply an unacceptable level of certainty or commitment.

What *dogmata*, and in what sense, could Philo and the Fourth Academy have accepted? It is reasonable to argue that the traditional New Academy did have certain philosophical tenets in the realm of epistemology, notably the doctrine that nothing is apprehensible[47] (in the Stoic sense at least). If Metrodorus of Stratonicea had argued that this was not a *dogma*,[48] it cannot have been because of his desire to absolve the Academy from all *dogmata*, for he is seen at *Ac.* 2.78 weakening the Clitomachian stance against the permissibility of opinions. It would be strange indeed to allow the sage opinions in defiance of tradition, and then carefully to free one's school from all trace of *dogma* when others had not found it necessary to do so.[49] In fact Metrodorus must have been leaning towards Philo's position on apprehension,

31

which permits some non-Stoic variety. Philo might well have allowed that this stance on apprehension was a *dogma*, *qua* philosophical tenet. But it was *qua* practical resolutions that Philo was most in need of *dogmata*, for the Academy had to compete with other schools in giving practical guidance and in encouraging pupils to lead a rational life. Aenesidemus seems to have been most ready to accuse the Academy of dogmatism in moral matters, and secondarily in matters of cognition (Photius *Bibl.* 170a17—20). Though Philo was not one who would have deliberately set out to construct a set of *dogmata* for its own sake, the constructive role which he gave to moral philosophy (Stob. *Ecl.* 2.39.20ff) did demand certain definite moral assumptions. And he must have needed still more *dogmata* in the weak Platonic sense discussed above.

Then, just as it is misleading to speak of Academics of this period as 'sceptics', it is dangerous to see their crusade as a fight against *dogmata*. It is possible that evidence for such a stance will be sought from Plutarch, *Moralia* 1059a, where the comrade of 'Diadumenus' complains that contemporary Stoics accuse the older (New) Academics of being 'subverters of doctrines that proceed along an orderly path' (δογμάτων ὁδῷ βαδιζόντων ἀνατροπέας). But (1) this is evidence of what the Stoics of a later age thought of earlier Academics; (2) the reference to 'older' New Academics makes it plain that only the Second and Third Academies are subject to such charges; (3) it is plain that the companion regards the Stoic charges as offensive, while even 'Diadumenus' does not view early Academic pursuits as destructive (1059f, 1083a), so that Plutarch does not appear to have regarded the changes as accurate; finally (4) the qualification 'that proceed along an orderly path' greatly reduces the scope of the original criticism, and suggests strongly that even the Second and Third Academies were not charged with being opponents of *dogmata per se*, only of *dogmata* selected by the criterion of compatability with a system. Thus opposition to *dogma* in the old sense of the term was not a stated objective of the New Academy, and not an objective of the Fourth Academics in any way at all.

In conclusion we must insist that the period does not invite, and should not receive, interpretation in terms of the standard sceptic–dogmatic dichotomy. The Fourth Academics must be understood in their own terms.

# CHAPTER 2

# CHARMADAS

In spite of the small amount of information available, the case of Charmadas provides a useful starting-point. He was a pupil of Carneades (*De Or.* 1.45), yet a teacher of non-aporetic Platonic dialogues (*ibid.*, 1.47); a devotee of New Academic practice (*ibid.*, 1.84), yet a willing user of the Platonic distinction between knowledge and opinion (*ibid.*, 1.92) when supporting what was apparently an opinion of his own. He thus shows the three principal trends which might be thought to mark off the so-called Fourth Academy (under Philo of Larissa) from the preceding Third Academy (under Carneades and Clitomachus): (i) no great devotion to the doctrine of 'non-apprehensibility' (ἀκαταληψία), (ii) no personal attempt to live his 'scepticism' and suspend judgment, and (iii) a tendency to adopt Plato, where possible, as the authority for his school and the source of his arguments.

It is thus no surprise to find Charmadas' name coupled with that of Philo of Larissa as a leader of the Fourth Academy in Sextus (*PH* 1.220): οἱ περὶ Φίλωνα καὶ Χαρμάδαν. Elsewhere, whenever he uses such an expression to speak of a particular school at a particular time, Sextus includes only Heads of School.[1] It is not surprising that it has recently been suggested that Charmadas was either joint Head with Philo or his successor.[2] Why else was his name important enough to be included by Sextus? But the question is poorly phrased: Sextus probably knew little of Charmadas (or even of Philo), and may have been unaware of whether Charmadas ever became scholarch. A parallel passage in Eusebius,[3] who is unlikely to be following Sextus, shows that Sextus himself was following some source. That source is most likely to have been Aenesidemus,[4] the founder of later Pyrrhonist scepticism, to whom Philo and Charmadas were surely known personally; for it was probably their barely sceptical attitudes which caused him to pass over the Academy,[5] proclaim himself a 'Pyrrhonian', and point to ways in which the Academy he knew failed to meet Pyrrho's standards.

To Aenesidemus the Fourth Academy was of immediate importance, initially perhaps as instructor, later as opponent. Charmadas' name appears in Sextus because Aenesidemus saw his role in the development of Fourth Academic attitudes as of comparable importance to that of Philo. But he is not mentioned at *PH* 1.235 where the alleged Fourth Academic position is detailed, for it was a work of Philo (almost certainly the so-called Roman Books)[6] which detailed that position.

There it is stated that, for the Fourth Academy, things are apprehensible enough for us to grasp their nature,[7] but inapprehensible in so far as the Stoic criterion of apprehension (the apprehensible presentation) could not be met. In the terms suggested by Lucullus' account of the Fourth Academic position (*Ac.* 2.34), things may be impressed truly and with obvious clarity upon the mind. The kind of certainty which the Stoic requires is still thought to be impossible; the certainty demanded by modern theories of practical certitude was perhaps no longer an issue (except in so far as the dogmatists refused to recognize any such compromise position). It is not likely that this position had been publicly voiced, or even worked out in detail, before Philo wrote his Roman Books, but it was the position into which the Academy had naturally drifted. There is little doubt that Charmadas, pupil of Carneades though he was, came to sanction that position.

An Academic's views (his *sententiae*) are not revealed by public proclamation (*De Or.* 1.84, *Ac.* 2.60), nor even by his failure to argue against certain positions (for traditionally he argued *pro* and *contra* every proposition);[8] they were revealed by his arguing more strongly or more persistently against some positions than against others.[9] Charmadas seems to have engaged in a well-worn debate between Academics and public orators (*De Or.* 1.84ff, cf. 46), arguing that there is no worthwhile oratory which can be divorced from philosophy and from the findings (*inventa*) of the philosophers.

In the course of the debate Charmadas frequently ('saepe', 1.90) argued against the claims of rhetoric to be an art, and displayed signs of positively favouring the contrary view.[10] The cynic will claim that it was very much in the Academy's interests to establish that the intending orator must also be a philosopher; but what kind of philosopher? The arguments used to establish the need for a philosophical rhetoric are based on the need of the rhetorician to acquaint himself with philosophical discoveries ('philosophorum inventa', 1.84), notably in the ethical and political sphere (1.85). Philosophy would not be giving the necessary assistance to the intending orator if it did not offer some hope of discovering important answers. Either the Academy currently (*c.* 103 B.C.) did hold out such a hope, or Charmadas' arguments were not entirely self-motivated: it would be the more dogmatic schools which benefited from his attack on oratory-without-philosophy.

Similar considerations apply when Charmadas argues that any art must be a system of facts: all recognized, thoroughly examined, having a single aim, and never erring.[11] He even argues (1.92) that the subject matter of the orators is doubtful and uncertain ('dubia . . . et incerta'), as if any worthwhile philosophy would dispute about matters which were readily ascertainable; that the orators do not clearly grasp (*tenere*: non-technical) all that they discuss, as if the philosophers often did; and that their audiences are not required to receive knowledge, but only opinion ('aut falsa aut certe obscura opinio'),[12] as if true philosophy supplied more than mere opinion.[13]

Had the Academy been a truly sceptical school of philosophy, then Charmadas' arguments would have given potent reasons for the intending orator to study elsewhere. Unless it were able to supplement its exoteric ignorance with some esoteric teaching (such as Charmadas may have favoured),[14] it would not have been able to offer knowledge, art (rhetorical or other), discovery, or even data which were not doubtful and uncertain. So either (a) Charmadas made no special point of arguing against orators, or (b) he approved of this case against them, or (c) he thought that the Academy could gain from this case against them. But (a) seems out of the question unless Cicero misleads us, while (b) would involve Charmadas in approval of the concepts of art, knowledge, and discovery, and (c) would involve the whole Academy in such an approval. They need not have approved the *Stoic* notion of apprehension, but they did need to acknowledge the existence of cognitive acts capable of yielding a significant degree of certitude — sufficient for the orator to be able to ply his trade in a 'scientific' manner: this would involve true impressions clearly registering with the mind, as at *Ac.* 2.34.

Charmadas, I conclude, approved of Philo's idea of non-Stoic apprehension, and was thus no sceptic. It is therefore highly unlikely that he advocated suspension of judgment. He *conceals* his *sententia* (1.84), but there is a strong implication that he had one. Antonius refers to Charmadas' arguments against rhetoric with the words 'hac eadem opinione' (1.94), and Charmadas is said to indulge in both teaching ('docebat', 1.85) and denial ('negabat', 1.92). His refusal to declare his real views was not a sign of genuine doubt, but an educational device aimed at promoting independent thought on the part of the hearer (*Ac.* 2.7–9, 60).

That Charmadas used Plato is not in itself surprising. Plato was studied keenly by Stoics as well,[15] and the Academy must have felt the need for classic teaching texts. Since he was noted for his oratorical powers,[16] it was natural that Charmadas should have studied the *Gorgias* and adopted it as a text for teaching (*De Or.* 1.47). Crassus studied it with him at around the time when Philo succeeded to the Headship of the Academy (110 B.C.), and it may have been Charmadas' presentation of it which fired Crassus' enthusiasm for the work. The influence of the *Gorgias* on Charmadas is plain from his arguments at *De Or.* 1.87, 1.90, and 1.92,[17] and considerations from the *Phaedrus* too appear at 1.87 (*Phdr.* 271b ff). Seeing that most of what we know about Charmadas comes from *De Or.* 1.45–7 and 84–93, and that there is ample evidence of Plato's influence here, one must surely assume that he cherished his school's connexions with its founder, and that he would have given some support to

37

Philo's thesis that there was only one Academy with a continuous tradition of an essentially Socratic nature.[18]

However important it may have been for the philosopher-cum-orator like Charmadas, the *Gorgias* is not the obvious work for an Academic-'sceptic' to use. It is not aporetic, and much of it depicts Socrates in a highly confident mood, able to speak, with some last-minute reservations, of 'iron and adamantine arguments'.[19] It provided the dogmatic view of Plato with more material than the sceptic view.[20] But much of it is, I believe, reconcilable with a rather optimistic view of Carneadean epistemology, based on the Carneadean criterion of conduct as depicted by Sextus (*Math.* 7.166ff).

Like the Carneadean criterion, the *Gorgias* is very much concerned with persuasion. The Platonic distinction between knowledge and opinion, used in a manner reminiscent of *Gor.* 454c—e by Charmadas (1.92), appears in the dialogue as a contrast between the products of two kinds of persuasion ($\pi\epsilon\iota\theta\dot{\omega}$), belief ($\pi\dot{\iota}\sigma\tau\iota\varsigma$) and knowledge ($\dot{\epsilon}\pi\iota\sigma\tau\dot{\eta}\mu\eta$) (454e3—4); the former is produced by a simple persuasion-process ($\pi\epsilon\dot{\iota}\theta\epsilon\iota\nu/\pi\iota\sigma\tau\epsilon\dot{\upsilon}\epsilon\iota\nu$), the latter by a teaching/learning process ($\delta\iota\delta\dot{\alpha}\sigma\kappa\epsilon\iota\nu/\mu\alpha\nu\theta\dot{\alpha}\nu\epsilon\iota\nu$). True arts will be able to persuade by teaching/learning, but rhetoric is content to persuade only. In Carneadean terms rhetoric would be content to aim at what is apt to be believed ($\pi\iota\theta\alpha\nu\dot{o}\nu$), a true art would aim at what is not only apt to be believed, but also unimpeded and thoroughly thought out ($\pi\iota\theta\alpha\nu\dot{o}\nu$ $\kappa\alpha\dot{\iota}$ $\dot{\alpha}\pi\epsilon\rho\dot{\iota}\sigma\pi\alpha\sigma\tau o\nu$ $\kappa\alpha\dot{\iota}$ $\delta\iota\epsilon\xi\omega\delta\epsilon\upsilon\mu\dot{\epsilon}\nu o\nu$). Study of other passages in the *Gorgias* will reveal the link between the true art and the ability to give an account (465a, 501a): to examine the nature of its subject matter, and to explain its actions. In Carneadean terms it will be able to work things out in detail ($\delta\iota\epsilon\xi o\delta\epsilon\dot{\upsilon}\epsilon\iota\nu$). It is this ability (with subsequent correctness) which separates knowledge from belief in the *Gorgias*, and this makes the work's concept of knowledge explicable in terms of Third Academic theory.[21]

It may not be likely that Carneades would have approved of such an application of his criterion,[22] but that is not relevant here. Once the great man had passed away, his pupils were left to make whatever use of his ideas they thought fit.

The Academy was a free-thinking school, bound by loyalties rather than by doctrine. The plain fact is that belief ($\pi i\sigma\tau\iota\varsigma$) now begins to emerge as a key term in Academic debate, as Witt saw.[23] Antiocheans adopted the terminology of *fides* in Cicero's *Academica*:[24] two kinds of belief ($\pi i\sigma\tau\iota\varsigma$) appear in Clement of Alexandria to parallel the two kinds of persuasion encountered in the *Gorgias*, even though he admits that Greek philosophy had tended to despise belief;[25] and Aenesidemus probably made much use of belief-terminology.[26]

The other Platonic work used by Charmadas in *De Oratore* 1 was the *Phaedrus*. From it he assumes the theme of 271b–d that the scientific orator must know by how many types of speech men's minds can be affected (see 1.87), and by which *type* and in which *manner* of delivery (272a, cf. 277c) particular minds will be swayed towards the required verdict. Also from the *Phaedrus* may come Charmadas' conviction that the truth lies deep ('penitus in media philosophia retrusa atque abdita', 1.87) and its accompanying esotericism (276a–7a, 277e–8b).[27] From the same work Academics may have acquired their concept of the *veri simile* (273b), which is probably how Cicero chose to translate $\tau\grave{o}$ $\epsilon i\kappa\acute{o}\varsigma$, for this term is explained in terms of verisimilitude there. From 272de (cf. *Tht.* 162e8) they may have deduced that $\tau\grave{o}$ $\epsilon i\kappa\acute{o}\varsigma$ is a suitable substitution-term for 'apt to be believed' ($\tau\grave{o}$ $\pi\iota\theta\alpha\nu\acute{o}\nu$). From it Antiochus may have learnt to question the ability to grasp the *veri simile* in anybody who is unable to grasp also the truth (*verum*).[28] Plato's rejection of the orator's criterion of 'what is apt to be believed' ($\tau\grave{o}$ $\pi\iota\theta\alpha\nu\acute{o}\nu$)[29] should not have deterred the successors of Carneades from listening closely to Plato's arguments in the closing pages 'of the *Phaedrus*, particularly when even a Carneades required better than this in decisions of importance if time allowed adequate reflection on the issue (S.E. *Math* 7.184–7). It could be claimed that Plato's concept of knowledge ($\epsilon\pi\iota\sigma\tau\acute{\eta}\mu\eta$) in the *Phaedrus* is indeed much closer to the Carneadean complete criterion than it is in the *Republic* or *Timaeus*, and that it would remind one rather of the *Gorgias* and *Meno*, where knowledge is not utterly separate from right opinion, but rather the result of right opinion backed by methodical confirmation-processes. These confirmation-processes may not seem to us to be closely akin to Carneadean διεξόδευσις, but that is not so clear as to deter an Academic from arguing for close kinship. Plato's comments on what is 'apt to be believed' were too important to be missed, particularly the identification of it with 'the probable' (τὸ εἰκός), for this showed Plato to be content with weak criteria in his treatment of the physical world in the *Timaeus*.[30]

Carneadean 'scepticism' has thus been merged with a new and critical treatment of Plato, and it fades gradually into the background as the importance of Plato increases in Charmadas' time. Charmadas is probably not an important figure *per se*, but was nevertheless part of an important trend. And he *may* be the source of important Platonizing passages in the rhetorical works of Cicero.[31]

# CHAPTER 3

# FOURTH ACADEMIC EPISTEMOLOGICAL DOCTRINE

## i A Fourth Academic orthodoxy?

If the Third Academy, that of Carneades and Clitomachus, had been my object of investigation, then it might not have been legitimate to speak of 'doctrine' at all. One would be studying themes, arguments, and schemata rather than *dogmata* or *placita*. Even so, Clitomachus was prepared to speak of the views which Carneades favoured (*Ac.* 2.99) or which the Academics favoured (*ibid.*, 103), using the verb *placere* (i.e. the Greek ἀρέσκειν). It is not, therefore, surprising that we find references to Academic doctrines in the b-column of the Aetius *Placita*, in Aenesidemus, in the anonymous *In Theaetetum*, and in Cicero's *Academica* (2.32–6). In all these cases it appears to me that the Fourth Academy is a likelier source than the Third.

The range of these reports extends to cover the sensations, apprehension (κατάληψις), the evident (τό ἐναργές), and doctrines (δόγματα), and they may be combined to yield a reasonably coherent picture of what might be called Fourth Academy Orthodoxy. One must, however, bear in mind that there could be no orthodox position without the sanction of a Head of School. Since one can probably assume that Clitomachus would have objected to the content of most of these reports,[1] the Head of School in question would seem to be Philo of Larissa. The reports cohere with what we learn of his beliefs from Sextus and Numenius, and these beliefs would seem to be those of the Roman Books.

It seems to be highly improbable that Philo attempted to give a clear written account of Fourth Academic epistemology before the Roman Books. If he had done so, then *either* those books would not have come as such a shock to those who knew Philo well (*Ac.* 2.11); *or*, if the earlier account had been much more conservative than the Roman Books, (a) it is

41

a surprise that we do not hear of it from his opponents,[2] and (b) it is in any case unlikely to have been the source of the seemingly innovative *placita* in the b-column of Aetius and elsewhere. Therefore one must give careful consideration to the possibility that the Roman Books themselves became a handbook of Academic theory.

It is easy to imagine the influence of these books on Plutarch, who clearly considered himself 'Academic', wrote on the Philonian One-Academy thesis, and retained Academic 'scepticism' as a tool rather than as a means of expressing significant uncertainty. Likewise it is easy to imagine their influence on anon. *In Tht.*, who displays similar attitudes. It is natural to imagine that Aenesidemus adopted them as the Academic creed, for their mildness would have enabled him to maximize the conflict between Academic and Pyrrhonian views. And it is quite proper to assume that, after Aenesidemus, most of those who *elected* to call themselves 'Academic' rather than 'Pyrrhonian' would have done so because they had greater respect for a mild Philonian fallibilism (along with allegiance to Plato) than for geniune scepticism. Among these we may perhaps include Eudorus of Alexandria.[3] Thus Philo's Roman Books could be expected to be handed down, particularly in the crucial centre of Alexandria, whither they had arrived with great rapidity and where both Aenesidemus and Eudorus apparently functioned, as the genuine Academic alternative to Pyrrhonism.

Some may find it difficult to believe that the same books which seemed heretical to Antiochus (*Ac.* 2.18), and which were said to indulge in outright lies (*ibid.*, 12 and 18), could ever have become an authoritative text; particularly as they do not seem to have won the complete approval of Cicero,[4] Cicero's 'Catulus',[5] or Heraclitus of Tyre (*Ac.* 2.11). But against this should be set the fact that it was with this work that Philo made an impact, that the Fourth Academic position given by Sextus (*PH* 1.235) appears to be that of the Roman Books, and that outright lies must be false claims of a factual nature, not poor philosophical theory. In my view the lies obviously pertain to the misrepresentation of the Carneadean position, the scepticism of which was played down by Philo sufficiently to attract protests from Cicero's 'Varro' (*Ac.* fr. 1).[6] Moreover Philo would scarcely have written anything that *any* reader could recognize as lies, and the fact that Antiochus could have claimed that he was lying proves only that there was a heated dispute. But we know that there had been important differences among interpreters of Carneades already,[7] and there was no way of verifying Carneades' views. Whatever Philo had written about the Academy of the second century, it could not have been so obviously wrong as to threaten the credibility and authority of the work as a whole. For some, those who were attracted towards Academic fallibilism out of a love of Plato rather than a loyalty to Carneades, and who saw Socrates rather than Carneades as the archetypal Academic, Philo's failure to present an imposing picture of Carneades may well have seemed a strong point, not a weakness.

Apart from Cicero's insistence that one should not assent to what one had not apprehended (*Ac.* 2.133) and that Zeno's definition of apprehension was correct (2.77), I can find no obvious way in which his epistemology diverges from that of the Roman Books. He disagrees also on the interpretation of Carneades (2.78). But he does not press the doctrine of non-apprehensibility beyond the denial that things can be apprehended in the Stoic sense.[8] In the *De Finibus* he goes so far as to assert that he, *qua* Academic, had no quarrel with the Peripatetic notion of apprehension (5.76). It is highly likely that Philo's milder 'scepticism', tempered by common sense, would have appealed to Cicero, who occasionally found his Academic connexions an embarrassment.[9] After all Cicero's studies with Philo date from a period when he must have held the doctrine of the Roman Books.[10] He does not even give a clear indication that Heraclitus of Tyre rejected any element of Philonian *doctrine*, only that he saw it as innovatory (*Ac.* 2.11); and his conservative character 'Catulus' disagrees with Philo on questions of emphasis rather than of substance.[11]

Bearing in mind that Philo may have been the origin of a late Academic orthodoxy, I shall examine the details of reports concerning Academic doctrine and consider them in the light of what we know of Philo. In particular it should be asked how far the 'Academic' doctrines could also be attributed to Plato, since the Philonian One-Academy doctrine demanded that there should be no substantial difference between later Academic teaching and that of Plato.

## ii Sensation

Our reports of Academic epistemology which relate to a Fourth Academic position concern three main topics: sensation, the evident (τὸ ἐναργές, *perspicuum*), and apprehension (κατάληψις, *comprehensio*). The four doxographic reports from the b-column of Aetius are all relevant to the senses. There is a theory of vision (403b8–11), a statement that the senses are *healthy* (for we do receive from them true impressions), but *not accurate* (396b17–19), a denial that the senses are either apprehensions or assents (396b5–7), and a claim that the sage is recognized by reason rather than by sensation (as the Stoics thought) at 398b24.

The theory of vision attributed to them is less than exciting: a stream of rays leaves the eye for the object, and returns again to the sight. Though there are complications with the attribution of the doctrine to Academics,[12] it is probably correct. The main point would seem to be that the Academics concerned disagreed with the type of theory of vision proposed by Leucippus, Democritus, and Epicurus, in which images penetrate the eye, having originated with the object (403ab2–4). The Academics prefer a view closer to that of Plato's *Timaeus* (45b ff), where the visual ray from the eye is the primary agent of sight.[13] No doubt they found it useful to emphasize a subjective element in vision, claiming that the eye plays an active rather than a passive role, thus giving greater scope for error to arise.

The claim that the wise man is recognized by reason rather than sensation need not delay us long. It clearly stems from anti-Stoic polemic,[14] and it is no accident that this entry immediately follows the report of the Stoic claim that the sage can be recognized by sensation. While it may be an example of an appeal to the evident and to established belief, such as the Fourth Academics were prepared to make when opposing the Stoics, it may also be linked with the revival of Platonism: the sage is really only a theoretical entity,[15] an ideal concept or archetype, and as such he must be an object of reason.

The doctrine that the senses are neither apprehensions nor assents is to be expected from an Academic. If the senses were apprehensions in the philosophical (Stoic) sense, then such apprehension would be not only possible but also natural, normal, and extremely common: a totally unacceptable doctrine for an Academic. If they were assents then there would be no sensation of those things concerning which the Academics suspend judgment.[16] Once again the doctrine attributed to the Academics would appear to be related to their disputes with the Stoa. But in this case a third position is given, and is attributed to the Peripatetics (396b8–10); while the senses are not in themselves assents, they are *not without* assent. The 'not without . . .' formula is prominent in the epistemology of the *Didascalicus* (4, p. 156, 5, 6–7, 8, 9 Hermann), in which Antiochean influence has been suspected.[17] It surely occurred too in the Greek original of *Ac.* 1.24: 'neque enim materiam ipsam cohaerere potuisse, si nulla vi contineretur, neque vim sine aliqua materia'. Both the phrase itself, and this particular example in Aetius, are reminiscent of Antiochean attempts to arrive at compromise positions. It also agrees very well with the Antiochean view of the relationship between sensation and assent, as seen at *Ac.* 2.19–21 and 37–8.[18] It ought to be no surprise that Antiochean doctrine should be labelled 'Peripatetic', for Antiochus' two most respected admirers, Cratippus and Aristo Alexandrinus, 'became' Peripatetics.[19] Furthermore Cicero allows an Antiochean to expound the allegedly 'Peripatetic' ethical theory in the fifth book of *De Finibus*. Of the five references to 'the Peripatetics' (as opposed to Aristotle or Heraclides *plus the rest* of the Peripatetics)[20] in Aetius, all relate to epistemology and all are confined to the b-column, as are all the Academic entries. Both sets of entries probably have the same origin, after the age of Philo and Antiochus.[21]

It must also be pointed out that the Academic refusal to consider sensations as assents or apprehensions is a natural consequence of the Philonian One-Academy doctrine, for it would be difficult to see either Platonic or Xenocratean sensation as an act of assent *per se*. A fragment of Porphyry attributes to both the ancients (= Old Academy etc.) and to the (New) Academy the view that sensation is just the bare sense-presentation, while all assent to such presentations can be freely given or withheld.[22] The *Theaetetus*, which must have been the single most important work for the New Academy,[23] appears to exclude any propositional content from sensation itself (184c—6e), for which reason it seeks for knowledge rather in the realm of correct opinion (187a ff). Xenocrates' theory that all sensation is true (S.E. *Math.* 7.147—9) also seems to exclude all propositional content, along with error and opinion, from sensation itself. Thus Old Academic, as well as New, required denial of the Stoic doctrine that sensation is an act of assent.

The Academic claim that the senses are *healthy* but not *accurate* does not at first seem striking. It becomes striking when one realizes that it follows a report that Pythagoras, most of the later Presocratics,[24] and Plato regard the senses as false.[25] Because it follows this report,[26] the Academic entry sounds very like an attempt to show that the Academics are comparatively fair to the senses. One suspects that the Pyrrhonist Aenesidemus attempted to portray his contemporary Academics as milder than Plato,[27] but the One-Academy doctrine ought in theory to have claimed that both Plato and more recent Academics had a similar attitude towards the senses. Moreover it would have been far less objectionable to claim that Plato regarded the senses as healthy (potentially) but inaccurate, than to claim that he thought them 'false'. And even though there are at times indications in the *Academica* that *Philo* may have thought that certain Presocratics were taking a bolder sceptical line

46

than his own school,[28] we have no indication that he thought Plato was more outspoken than he,[29] and we certainly have no reason to believe that he took Pythagoras for a predecessor of 'scepticism'.[30] The inclusion of Pythagoras among those who saw the senses as 'false' is surely the product of a tendency, first seen in Posidonius,[31] to see Pythagoras as the source of Platonic works such as the *Timaeus*,[32] the *Phaedo*,[33] parts of the *Republic*,[34] and the *Parmenides* (second part).[35] That tendency appears clearly in the Academic Eudorus.[36] It is equally clear in the Aetius doxography.[37] It is reasonable to suppose that the doxographer wrote a short time after Eudorus, and that the attitude towards the relative degrees of distrust of the senses in Pythagoras, Plato, and New Academy is Eudoran rather than Philonian.

I doubt, however, whether Eudorus himself could have been the source of the Academic position described. It is not known what authority Eudorus might have had, but it seems highly unlikely that he should have been the Head of any 'official' Academy.[38] It is doubtful whether any study which he might have pursued under any prominent Fourth Academic could have been extensive.[39] Surviving remains suggest that he may in fact have had closer links with the school of Posidonius.[40] Thus he could not claim the title 'Academic' as a right, by virtue of having studied with the school until a mature age, as was clearly required of one who was to make definitive statements on Academic doctrine.[41] He adopted the title because he found his views coinciding with the position now regarded as the true Academic position. This was virtually all that one could do after the collapse of the great philosophical schools, so that the terms 'Stoic', 'Academic', and 'Peripatetic' came to indicate one's philosophical *preference*[42] rather than one's course of study.[43] Already the 'Academic' label was not one which would be assumed by a true sceptic, not because Antiochus had won the Academy over to dogmatism,[44] but because such people now had the choice of Pyrrhonism. Since Aenesidemus[45] the Academic position, in Alexandria at least, had to reject the extremes of both dogmatism and doubt, looking back to Philo of Larissa for a definitive Academic policy.

Thus I assume that Philo is the ultimate source of the doctrine that the senses are (potentially) healthy, but not accurate. There can be little doubt that his Roman Books had a good deal to say about the senses,[46] and that, in the course of complaining that they lacked precision, he also had to defend himself against Middle Stoic and Antiochean charges that Academics 'rob themselves of their own light' in rejecting the evidence of the senses.[47] The extent to which Academics were prepared to accept sense-evidence had to be clearly indicated. Given this need, it is not surprising that Philo should have talked of the *health* of the senses. Antiochus places great importance on their being healthy ('sani . . . ac valentes', *Ac.* 2.19); he also suggests that his opponents rely too much on the examples of dreamers, madmen and drunkards (*Ac.* 2.53). These are the tactics of men who have little complaint to make of sound and wakeful faculties. Since a large part of Philo's educational programme was directed towards the removal of false opinions 'by which the mind's faculties of judgment are made sick',[48] one realizes that he too found little fault with our powers of cognition when healthy: and it is scarcely conceivable that he did not include sensation among the mind's faculties of judgment.[49]

In Aetius the *reason* which is given for the view that the senses are (potentially) healthy is that we receive true presentations through them. The existence of true presentations is certainly admitted by the New Academics of Cicero's *Academica* (2.34–6, 40, 111 etc.), and there is no doubt that it was admitted by Philo himself. And, just as Aetius seems to link truth and health in Academic epistemology, so did Philo in the passage referred to in the last paragraph.[50]

But was *health* enough for Philo? Its ability to provide us with true presentations certainly proves that we should not slander healthy sensations and healthy sense-organs, but were there not cases when more was required? Cicero answers this very question at *Ac.* 2.80: we should like to be able to see further, particularly through dense media; we should like to discern the slow motion of distant ships; we should like to be able to judge the size of the sun; we should like to distinguish identical twins, hairs, grains, imprints in wax. All this amounts to the complaint that the senses are less than accurate, or at least less accurate than we should wish; it is thus the same complaint that Aetius' Academics offer. Though we cannot be sure that Cicero is following Philo at *Ac.* 2.80ff, we can at least claim that the attitudes towards the senses found in Aetius' report were current in the Academy that Cicero had known. We can claim, though with less confidence, that those attitudes would not have been prevalent in Carneades' time, and the source of the report was not Clitomachean.[51] We can be almost certain that the report was not envisaged as a report on Old Academic doctrine, for Plato's view is reported to be more extreme (396b15−16). Thus Aetius' Academics are what Antiochus would call 'New Academics', and very probably post-Clitomachean Academics. Since there is some affinity between their doctrine and Platonic theory, it is probable that their ultimate source is Philo's attempted reconciliation between Plato and his own school.

### iii Evident or obvious clarity

Though Carneades had reportedly claimed that the basis of any dogmatic epistemology had to be our experience of evident or obvious clarity (Latin *perspicuitas* = Greek ἐνάργεια),[52] and though Clitomachus assumed that Carneades' attacks on the notion of such clarity were confined to a strong sense of the term,[53] there can be little doubt that an orthodox Carneadean would not have embraced the concept with any enthusiasm. Like the term 'evident', by which we will henceforth render it, the Greek ἐναργής strongly suggested a quality which excluded the possibility of error. Just as what is 'evident' or 'obvious' is not expected to admit error, so neither was any presentation which the Greeks could call ἐναργής. Consequently the Epicureans made much use of the concept as a foundation of their epistemology, and for similar reasons it came to play an important part in the debate between Antiochus and Philo.

Antiochus claimed, as is shown by *Ac.* 2.34, that the

Academics of his own day were abusing terminology by (a) admitting that some things were evident, and (b) persisting in the claim that nothing could be apprehended with certainty. For Antiochus, if $x$ is evidently $F$, then all doubt that $Fx$ is removed and that proposition is truly apprehensible. Clearly the Academics did not agree; for them the term did not have the necessary overtones of infallibility. The best example known to me of this weaker use of the notion of the evident may perhaps come from an earlier work of Antiochus himself, written before his break with Philo.[54] At S.E. *Math.* 7.143 the epistemological theory attributed to Plato demands more than evident clarity: 'But evident clarity is not in itself sufficient for cognition of the truth; for the fact that something appears evident does not mean that this thing also truly exists; there should be present some faculty of judging what only appears, and what, in addition to appearing, actually exists in truth . . .' From Sextus and Cicero it would seem that the Academics refused to give up the idea that under certain conditions, however limited, a false presentation could arise which seemed just as evident as any evident true one.

Faced with such a theory the later Antiochus asks what help this kind of evident clarity could be. For him the Academics still destroy the basis of colour, body, truth, proof, sensation, and evident clarity, because they still insist on the occasional presentation which, though false, will appear just as evident as a true one. But his view would not have attempted to be fair to Philo's. It is clearly the *occasional fortuitous presentation alone* which, while false, has all the clarity of an evident true one. It will be produced by abnormal conditions, such as insanity or drunkenness in the perceiver or the appearance of a forgotten identical twin. But with continuous observation over a period of time, and with a number of observers, it is possible to guard against the occasional fortuitous experience. Hence Philo's move towards practical certitude is said by Numenius to have been prompted by the evident clarity and *agreement* of our experiences.[55] Agreement here appears to cover both the internal consistency of the individual's experiences and the similarity between the experiences of a number of individuals concerning any given object or set of objects,[56] particularly the latter. In the third book of Cicero's *De Natura Deorum* the Academic 'Cotta' propounds a theory of the evident according to which people agree on matters which are really evident (*ND* 3.9–11): 'evidens de quo inter omnis conveniat' and 'hoc perspicuum sit constetque inter omnis'. Even though what appears evident to a given individual may be false, it is usually possible to check whether others have received a similar evident presentation; even though what appears to me to be evident at a given moment may have no truth, it is generally possible to detect some conflict with other evident impressions that I have received over a period of time. Agreement and consistency offer a check against the occasional fortuitous presentation, and with the aid of this check whatever appears evident can provide a reasonable foundation for practical certitude.[57]

The link between agreement and evident clarity seems also to have been acknowledged by Antiochus, for not only does it appear to be recognized at *Fin.* 5.55, but it is also implicit at *Ac.* 2.38 – where evident presentations are supposed to win our *inevitable* assent. Thus all who receive evident presentations concerning the nature of a given object must necessarily assent to them, and, since Antiochus thought that evident clarity entailed truth, all would assent to the same true proposition, indeed to the same true presentation, about that object.

Problems then arise concerning the deep disagreement among philosophers. Have they not received such presentations; or have they somehow withdrawn their assent in retrospect? A possible Antiochean answer appears at *Ac.* 2.46: disputes arise when one or both parties (a) do not fix their minds firmly enough on what is evident, and (b) are misled by sophistic problems so that they pass over the truth of these evident presentations. As the previous section also shows, the problem is not one of failing to give our initial assent to what is evident, it is rather our failure to abide by that initial assent and continue to trust in its authority.

But the orthodox Academic could give no such answer, since he would believe that no isolated impression was sufficiently authoritative to be trusted for ever. For him disagreement arose because evident clarity was not to be found among those things which the philosophers debated. It was in these areas that Carneades was concerned to deny the possibility of knowledge (according to the Philonian view at Aug. *c. Acad.* 2.11), while he did not try to question facts upon which we all agree. Anon. *In Tht.* col. 70 also appears to suggest this answer to the problem of disagreement.[58]

The anonymous writer preserves another feature of Academic thought concerning the evident: they approved of the notion that certain things, e.g. physical growth, were evidently clear, but believed that one should not try to demonstrate such things, for contrary arguments will always appear. Some perhaps, like Galen or Clement later, adopted evident propositions as the basis of all demonstration, the point from which one must begin.[59] And so it would be fruitless to try to demonstrate things which had to provide the starting-point of all demonstration. Cicero's 'Cotta' also objects to the notion that what is evident can be demonstrated: 'perspicuitas ratione elevatur' (*ND* 3.9).

A further feature of Academic theory on this subject is that not only things evident to the senses, but also things evident to the intellect were admitted. This is clear from Aenesidemus' criticism of Fourth Academic epistemology at Photius *Bibl.* cod. 212, p. 170a37–8, where his argument will not work unless they assent to the proposition that certain things can be grasped evidently in accordance with sensation or intellection.[60] The dual theory operates repeatedly in the works of Galen.[61] It also appears in the Antiochean account of Peripatetic epistemology at S.E. *Math.* 7.218, though, as is expected from Antiochus, all intellectual cognition is there carefully traced back to origins in the senses; Antiochus was less able, it seems, to envisage a truly independent second category of evident.[62]

The material on evident clarity certainly concerns Philo,

but only in Numenius is it linked by name with Philo; and though it is here specifically related to Philo's drift away from scepticism, it is still not clear that it had any special relation to the Roman Books. Moreover there is no indication at *Ac.* 2.34 that the theory of evident truths impressed upon the mind was *either* confined to Philo *or* a special feature of the Roman Books. If it is remembered that similar theories on evident clarity, and on its being a necessary but insufficient condition of knowledge, had, if I am correct, featured in a work of Antiochus written under the auspices of the official Academy and before the Roman Books, it will not be surprising that the theory is not seen as being peculiar to Philo. The material in anon. *In Tht.* is again not related to any Academic in particular, but this does not mean that Philo is not the immediate source; he could, after all, have been expected to represent the doctrine of those books as the doctrine of the entire Academy, not just in his own day but from Plato's time on.

### iv Apprehension

The particular feature of Fourth Academic approaches to apprehension is that they consistently maintain that it is the Stoic theory of apprehension which they cannot accept. Besides a number of relevant passages of Cicero's *Academica* (2.18, 77–8, 112–13) and also *Fin.* 5.76, we have the supplementary evidence of Augustine (*c. Acad.* 2.11), of Aenesidemus,[63] and of Sextus (*PH* 1.235). Only the last passage mentions Philo by name as one who tried to limit the scope of the non-apprehensibility doctrine, and even here the periphrasis 'those about Philo' is used; for Sextus does seem to be attributing the doctrine to the Philonian Academy as a whole.[64] But I think it is necessary to regard the Roman Books as the principal text for a limited non-apprehensibility doctrine.

That the Roman Books claimed that 'non-apprehensibility' should not be regarded as an Academic *dogma* is fairly certain from Augustine *c. Acad.* 3.41:

Philo — homo circumspectissimus, qui iam veluti aperire cedentibus hostibus portas coeperat et ad Platonis auctoritatem Academiam legesque revocare — quamquam et Metrodorus id antea facere temptaverat, qui primus dicitur esse confessus non decreto placuisse Academicis nihil posse comprehendi, sed necessario contra Stoicos huius modi eos arma sumpsisse — . . .

Here the claim that 'non-apprehensibility' was not a *dogma*, in which Metrodorus of Stratonicea had anticipated Philo, is seen as a part of the One-Academy thesis of Philo's Roman Books (*Ac.* 1.13). This explains well why Antiochus reserved his special wrath for the Academics' unwillingness to have doubts about what he continued to regard as their *dogma* (*Ac.* 2.29); for his *Sosus*, Cicero's source, was replying directly to Philo's attempts to escape from commitment to non-apprehensibility (cf. *Ac.* 2.18: 'eo quo minime volt revolvitur' and 'eam definitionem [sc. 'comprehensionis'] quam Philo voluit evertere'). The fact is that in the Roman Books Philo had denied that the Academics were totally ('omnino')[65] in favour of doctrine usually regarded as Academic (*Ac.* 2.12); this denial, either alone or together with similar claims, provokes the accusation of lying which follows. It is tantamount to heresy in Antiochean eyes, and for this reason alone it can safely be attributed to the Roman Books.

As the passage from Augustine shows, Philo's allegedly heretical work was not original in claiming that there was no real *dogma* of non-apprehensibility, or that the issue had been raised as an anti-Stoic device. Indeed there was an extent to which both claims must have been true, much depending upon the exact sense in which the word *decretum* (= *dogma*) is meant. Philo's heresy consisted rather in the claim that there could be a sense in which the Academics would admit the possibility of apprehension. It is too frequently claimed that the debates which prompted Cicero to write the *Academica* were concerned simply with the possibility or impossibility of apprehension, but, besides excellent external evidence in Sextus and Aenesidemus, even the internal evidence is sufficient to show that there was an important third position. The latter part of 2.18 shows quite clearly that Philo (a) rejected the Stoic definition of an apprehensible presentation, and with it the whole Stoic notion of apprehension; (b) that he very much wanted to retain *some* notion of apprehension; and (c) that Antiochus insisted that the Stoic definition was essential for *any* valid notion of apprehension. But it does not show that Philo had come to agree with him. Cicero himself, claiming Arcesilaus' support as well as Zeno's, did agree with Antiochus (2.77), but only in a passage where his differences with Philo and Metrodorus are acknowledged (2.78).

If Philo wanted to evade the Stoic definition of apprehension, what did he intend to put in its place? Cicero gives the impression that he *weakened* the definition,[66] and also that the dispute concerned the final words in particular, omitting any polemic over the initial part. All debate seems to have concentrated on the words 'quale esse non posset ex eo unde non esset' (2.18),[67] or the alternative 'quo modo imprimi non posset a falso'.[68] According to 2.112 the Peripatetics do not require such a condition for apprehension, and according to 2.113 neither did the Old Academy. The only conditions needed by Zeno's predecessors seem to have been an imprint in the mind and the truth of that imprint ('quod impressum esset e vero'). But these 'Peripatetic' conditions from 2.112 are obviously being met by the Academics criticized at 2.34, who believe in something self-evident, true, and impressed upon the mind. They do not call it 'apprehensible', but, to the extent that the Peripatetics and Old Academy believed in apprehension (2.113), so do they. They resist only the Stoic notion of apprehension; the fact that Antiochus represents them as resisting just 'apprehension' stems from the fact that Antiochus will admit no other kind, for 2.33—4 makes it abundantly clear that the one thing which these Academics oppose is *the final part*, i.e. the specifically *Stoic* part, of the Stoic concept of apprehension:

> hoc se unum tollere, ut quicquam possit ita videri ut
> non eodem modo falsum etiam possit ita videri.[69]

All else they concede, and, unlike Antiochus, they believe that it is a considerable concession.

But *towards what* was this thought to be a concession? Antiochus is quite right to observe that it is not a concession towards the absolute personal certainty which he demanded; and it is surely true that the one thing which nobody who professed to follow Carneades could allow was this brand of certainty. If certainty were to be found then the Academic educational methods would be redundant; simple dogmatic teaching was all that was required. In fact it was just a concession to common sense, designed to give meaning to a number of cognitive terms which would otherwise be redundant. A more positive scepticism would deny any meaning to terms such as 'knowledge', 'apprehend', or 'skill'. But recent Academic willingness to accept the value of our 'common notions',[70] as well as the significance of everyday language,[71] meant that some significance ought to be found for these terms. It was not their non-technical application to which he objected, only the way in which they were used by certain philosophical groups. Absolute personal certainty was not a necessary part of these concepts, even though they did imply *both* correctness *and* sufficient confidence in one's beliefs. The Academics believed that a true, clear and seemingly evident impression in the mind produced such confidence.

The critic may well claim that it would be gross misrepresentation on the part of Antiochus to represent these Academics as distinguishing between *things evident* (possible) and *things apprehensible* (impossible), if their attitude to apprehension was as I have indicated. But there is no doubt that this is precisely how the Academics' distinction would have seemed to Antiochus. In his eyes definitions could, indeed ought to be, correct and true (*Ac.* 2.43); above all, like Cicero (2.77), he thought that the Stoic definition of an apprehensible presentation was *correct* (2.18, 33–4), and is thus able to regard Zeno's definition, along with the rest of his innovations, as a *correction* of Old Academic and Peripatetic theory (1.43).[72] The Academy's refusal to acknowledge the existence of anything conforming to that definition was thus seen to be a denial that anything apprehensible existed, whether or not the Academics *meant* to deny it. Furthermore it was in his interests to continue to represent the Academy as opposing the very idea of apprehension. And finally it should be kept in mind that prior to the Roman Books all Fourth Academics had probably represented their distinction as being between the evident and the apprehensible.[73] Antiochean theory is not aimed directly at the Roman Books at 2.34.[74]

From this it appears that a careful reading of the *Academica* will show how Philo rejected the extreme non-apprehensibility doctrine in favour of the view that apprehension, more modestly defined than by the Stoics, was possible. It will also show that this was thought to be a departure from the previous Academic stance by Antiochus and Cicero alike. Antiochus, as Augustine shows,[75] held that the characteristic of Academic philosophy was the habit of treating its suppositions as non-apprehensible. Sextus Empiricus (*PH* 1.3) agrees, believing that the Pyrrhonist alone treats things as neither apprehensible nor inapprehensible. No doubt Sextus' views have been moulded by that other opponent of Philo, the architect of the new Pyrrhonism, Aenesidemus. But Sextus sees the Fourth Academic position in a much less simple light, thus virtually confirming that Philo introduced innovations such as we have assumed: 'Philo's school says that, to the extent required for[76] the Stoic criterion (that is to say the apprehensible presentation) things are non-apprehensible, but, to the extent required for the nature of things themselves, apprehensible.'

The initial part of the statement is clear enough, and serves to confirm what Cicero causes us to suspect, that Philo confined his denial of apprehensibility to the Stoic sense of the word, moulded as it was by their concept of an apprehensible presentation. The latter part is more troublesome, and I have tried to preserve some of the ambiguity which I detect in the Greek. Does Philo mean (a) that things are apprehensible in their own right, but that we are incapable of apprehending them in the absence of the Stoic criterion? Does he mean (b) that the nature of things is not such as to require that they be apprehended by the Stoic criterion? Or does he mean (c) that we can penetrate appearances and grasp the nature of things without the Stoic criterion?

I think that (a) is unlikely. Philo could scarcely have made any very definite affirmation to the effect that things are apprehensible in themselves at the same time as denying that men can apprehend them in any sense of the term. What right would he have to claim that things are apprehensible if he were not able to apprehend them? In spite of the efforts of David Sedley to link such an interpretation with Philo's view of the *Timaeus*,[77] it is not easy to see how Philo could have reconciled position (a) with his One-Academy thesis. It is made clear in many Platonic dialogues, the most popular among them,[78] that Plato does not believe that the ordinary things of this world can be objects of infallible cognition. Although Plato does put some blame upon man's own cognitive weaknesses, it is clear that the objects themselves are just as much to blame. This is the position of Cicero too, who speaks of the obscurity of things themselves as well as the infirmity of the sensations (*Ac.* 1.44, 2.7): if the emphasis usually fell on the latter, this is scarcely surprising, for who could discuss the intrinsic faults of sense-objects in much detail when he does not believe that he can grasp their nature with any certainty? And natural science was surely admitted to be an extremely difficult subject.[79]

If one were to assert that things are of an apprehensible nature, but that man is unable to apprehend that nature, one would be suggesting that they are able to be apprehended by a being so constituted as to be capable of such apprehension. By a God perhaps?[80] But then (i) how does an Academic justify such judgment about a God's cognitive abilities, and (ii) how does God manage without the Stoic criterion? For (ii a) if God can only apprehend $P$ without the Stoic criterion, then $P$ is only apprehended in a non-Stoic sense; while (ii b) if God does possess the ability to judge by the Stoic criterion, then it was inaccurate to claim that things were not apprehended by the Stoic criterion. One must add that Sextus' words do not refer either to man or to any other creature, nor do they contain any reference to the weakness of our senses.

Another way of defending position (a) is to say that things are sometimes apprehensible, in so far as things (propositions, presentations) may be true.[81] But it is very odd to say that all truths are apprehensible, and even more so if (i) the Stoic sense of apprehension is being applied, and (ii) one is denying that things may be apprehended by the Stoic criterion.

Thus position (a) involves position (c), for if things are apprehensible to any kind of being or because of any property such as truth which they may possess, they have still been declared to be non-apprehensible according to the requirements of the Stoic criterion, and *some other sense of apprehension must apply.*

Position (b) also reduces to position (c). For if nature does not require that we possess the Stoic criterion, then either (i) nature does not require that we should apprehend, or (ii) it requires that we should apprehend in a non-Stoic sense. But if (i), then it would be absurd to call things apprehensible simply because they do not need to be apprehended, while if (ii), then Philonians believe that nature is apprehensible in so far as it is enough that we apprehend things in a non-Stoic manner.

If it is enough that we apprehend things in a non-Stoic sense, and things are, in consequence, apprehensible, it must surely be the case that the nature of things is *to this extent* open to us to grasp. And this no doubt follows from the admission that we receive true and self-evident impressions concerning a wide number of things.

Had our text of Photius' *Biblioteca* cod. 212 been reliable, then there is no doubt that we should receive confirmation that the Philonians took this view of apprehension. Photius reports his impressions of the eight books of Aenesidemus' *Pyrrhonian Logoi.* We are given a fairly full account of the first portion of book 1, in which Aenesidemus sets forth the difference between his own revived Pyrrhonism and the practices of the Academy. This work is addressed to L. Tubero, an Academic of the same sect (αἵρεσις) as the writer.[82]

It is important that the *Academic Index* uses this term for a philosophical orientation *within* the Academy as a whole.[83] It is most unlikely that Aenesidemus had meant to say that he had studied in the same 'school' or 'class' as Tubero, for this would involve an anachronistic organizational sense of the term:[84] he refers rather to a similarity of attitude between Tubero and himself on an issue which had split the Academy: 'of those from the Academy one who took his own side'.

One would like to know what this issue was concerning which Aenesidemus and Tubero had taken the same side, and it is natural to assume that it was linked with the only major dispute within the Academy of which we are aware: the split between Antiochus' neo-dogmatists, and those who adhered to some degree of 'scepticism'. Whether Aenesidemus envisaged just two sects, or whether he was saying that both he and Tubero were genuine sceptics as opposed to Philonians, is not clear, though the latter possibility seems less likely.[85]

Whether Aenesidemus hoped that Tubero would become a convert, a patron, or a mere sympathizer, one may assume that he did not grossly misrepresent the 'official' Academic position, for it would have been foolish to misrepresent the position of the dedicatee's own school. Thus Photius, if he reports Aenesidemus accurately,[86] is good evidence for the views of Tubero's school: the Philonian Academy.

Lines 170a29–30 (ἅμα τε φάναι κοινῶς ὑπάρχειν καταληπτά: 'and at the same time to say that there are things which are apprehensible in a general way' or 'in a general sense') would, if they were reliable, agree with the position which we have outlined above. Though I acknowledge that the text is at fault, I have attacked Hirzel's emendation ('non-apprehensible' for 'apprehensible') elsewhere,[87] and made suggestions, partly inspired by Glucker's emendation,[88] concerning the text which ought to have been read, judging from the subsequent explanation of the point being made. It appears that Aenesidemus had argued that, since the

Academics continued to express doubts about $P$ and $-Q$, it followed that they did not know (γιγνώσκειν) $P$ and $-Q$. But if $P$ and $-Q$ were unknown (ἀγνοεῖται), they must be admitted to be non-apprehensible. Whereas it they were self-evidently apprehended, they should be admitted to be apprehensible. The Academics are therefore accused of making things *entirely* non-apprehensible (by their insistence on doubt, and thus on absence of knowledge), but apprehensible *in a general sense* (by their acceptance of the existence of evident impressions).

The accusations agree with other details of the passage which throw light on the Academic attitude to apprehension. For 169b42–170a3 strongly suggested that the Academics did attempt to distinguish between ways in which certain things were apprehensible for certain people at certain times, and ways in which they were not. Again 169b25–6 holds that non-Pyrrhonists in general fail to realize that their apparent 'apprehensions' are illusory, while at b28–9 the realization that one has apprehended nothing is apparently a distinguishing mark of a Pyrrhonist. No suggestion that Academics might agree with Pyrrhonists on this issue is apparent, and it must be presumed that Aenesidemus includes Academics among those who think that they apprehend things. The Academic rejection of the Stoic criterion is alleged to be the full extent of their 'scepticism' (170a21–2). Moreover, Aenesidemus' attempt at 170a33–8 to justify a sharp dichotomy between apprehension and non-apprehension suggests that his opponents resisted so clear a division and aimed at finding some intermediate compromise position.

Aenesidemus' criticism is in fact invalid. The Philonian's continued doubts were based upon man's failure to know what he knew: to be certain that he had grasped something accurately. If the term employed by Aenesidemus, the non-technical γιγνώσκειν, implies *knowledge of knowledge*, then the absence of such cognition (γνῶσις) does not entail the absence of Philonian apprehension. Whereas if the term does not imply knowledge of knowledge, then there is no ground for insisting on certainty. Philonian doubts only implied the absence of knowledge of knowledge, and its absence could not be said to entail the complete absence of apprehension; hence there is no conflict with the Philonian theory that things are, in a meaningful sense, apprehensible.

The idea that things may be apprehensible 'in a general way' or 'in a general sense' is interesting. The general sense would no doubt have been opposed to the philosophical sense (determined of course by the Stoics), giving some point to the ordinary man's belief that he can apprehend things. It was essential for the Academy to respect the existence of an ordinary concept of apprehension now that it was attaching significance to man's common and natural notions.[89] Consensus of opinion could not be ignored; men thought they apprehended things. It is no surprise then to find in [Galen] 14.685 (Kühn) the notion of 'human apprehension', sufficient for the medical art, insufficient for knowledge.

## v 'Dogmata'

The Academic adoption of a new[90] notion of apprehension allowed them to escape from the frightening alternatives of accepting Stoic epistemology or teaching nothing. Teaching could now be based upon apprehensions in the general sense, 'human apprehensions'. Teaching in turn would lead to *dogmata* in the contemporary sense of that term discussed in chapter one. As a result anon. *In Theaetetum* can claim that the Academics, with very few exceptions, had *dogmata*: the same ones as Plato on the principal issues.[91] There is no reason to suppose, with Glucker,[92] that the writer has simply forgotten how long the Academy had remained dominated by 'sceptical' influences, and that he is referring to Old Academics and the Antiocheans. The phrase 'those from the Academy' at 6.30 and 70.14 clearly refers to the New Academy, and the reference to 'the other Academics' here at 54.45 must have a similar sense, particularly as it is used to pick up the description of Plato as 'Academic' (*qua* non-dogmatic) at 54.40. There can be no doubt that the anonymous writer is claiming that even the majority of (so-called) New Academics had similar basic doctrines to those of Plato. The claim is actually linked with a statement that there is only one Academy: Philo's Roman-Book thesis. Thus the writer's thesis can scarcely be that the 'sceptical phase' was a mere fleeting aberration.[93]

Two questions concerning the anonymous writer's treatment of the One-Academy theme immediately come to mind: (i) what doctrines are New Academics supposed to have shared with Plato, and (ii) which New Academics are excepted? The former question must be treated later,[94] but the latter may be discussed briefly here. Some believed that the Academy of Arcesilaus still continued to teach Platonic doctrine esoterically (S.E. *PH* 1.234), and since the 'some' must be the Philonian school (the only school with the motive to make such a claim, being linked with esotericism elsewhere),[95] it is clear that anon. did not have to acknowledge that Arcesilaus was an exception. It was Carneades and Clitomachus who presented him with difficulties, particularly since the latter claimed that even he was not aware of the views of the former (*Ac.* 2.139). Though Carneades might be credited with *views*, I do not think it likely that he could be credited with *dogmata* unless he revealed them in one way or another — particularly by a Philonian, who had to deny that the non-apprehensibility theory was an Academic *dogma* (Aug. *c. Acad.* 3.41). Thus Carneades and Clitomachus were the exceptions who had no '*dogmata*'.

The claim that Philo's Academy 'dogmatized' on many issues is to be found in Aenesidemus at Phot. *Bibl.* 170a17: the claim is explained with reference to the following Academic practices: (i) they introduce (*sc.* as meaningful terms) virtue—folly,[96] good—bad, true—false, probable—improbable, being—not-being, etc.; (ii) they give firm definitions of many other things, (iii) they persistently dispute only the concept of the Stoic criterion. Thus the 'dogmatism' (mentioned also at 169b39) is based rather on the willingness to accept concepts and distinctions whose validity the Pyrrhonist would dispute than on outspoken statements. The Academic habit of speaking in terms of Stoic concepts and using Stoic definitions is well known.[97] And though the claim that the Academics 'define many other things' (ἄλλα τε πολλὰ βεβαίως ὀρίζουσι) may be used in its wider Pyrrhonist sense of 'positively affirm' something,[98] it is more natural to understand the normal sense of 'define' here. But to accept the concept of an $x$ is not far from agreeing to the existential statement that at least one $x$ exists; and such existential statements can legitimately be seen as doctrine.

One such existential statement that Aenesidemus complains of is the statement that apprehensible things exist (in a general sense of that term) at 170a30, an example of positing something (τιθέναι τι) in Aenesidemus' eyes. And in this case what they posit is said to be unequivocally abolished by their continued doubts (or rather by their insistence on continued doubt).

The general statement that the Academics 'are dogmatic, and posit some things without hesitation and reject others without ambiguity' (169b39—40) may be seen in this light[99] — they accept the existence of virtue, truth, even human apprehension, while they do away with the Stoic criterion: the apprehensible presentation. In these cases they neither hesitate nor equivocate.

But there may be another way in which the Philonians are supposed to have posited some things without hesitation while rejecting others unambiguously. We receive the impression from 169b42ff that the Academics were in the habit of suggesting that $x$ is $F$ in relation to time $t$ or to person $p$, but $-F$ in relation to time $t + 1$ or to person $q$. In other words the Academy was attaching a new importance to the relativity of predicates, entirely in accord with its claims to be following Plato, but was failing to realize that this does not imply doubt as to the validity of the proposition $Fx$. Aenesidemus may have pointed out that such expressions as $Fx$ in time $t_1$ and $-Fx$ in time $t_2$ are not a case of hesitation or equivocation, but rather one of two unequivocal statements of an essentially dogmatic nature. Though there may be no direct evidence that the Philonian Academy favoured such statements, which may be seen as a new

Platonic-Heraclitean relativism, this passage strongly suggests as much; and the thesis that it did so would go a long way towards explaining the importance of Heraclitean relativism in anon. *In Theaetetum* (columns 63–8), in Aenesidemus himself, and in Philo of Alexandria.[100]

In spite of Aenesidemus' charges of 'dogmatism' in the Academy we do not receive the impression that his principal opponents embraced it. They merely slipped into it. He does not suggest that the Academy would have officially embraced the doctrine that 'all things are governed by fate' or 'knowledge is the goal of life' (questions debated by philosophers), but rather that 'virtue exists', 'truth exists', 'water is good for fish to live in but bad for men': the kind of assertion with which few men would find fault.

When it came to matters debated by the philosophers the Academic rule, even in Aenesidemus' eyes, was to go on doubting and disputing, as is plain from 170a32–3.[101] These lines agree with the thrust of 170a26–8, where it is emphasized that Pyrrhonist persistency in doubt yields consistency too, while it is Academic *lapses* into confidence (as when claiming that things are apprehensible in a general sense) which have produced inconsistencies. Since 'dogmatic' tendencies are treated as a deviation from the Academic code, the code itself must still (in theory) demand doubt and hesitation.

In Cicero we have little evidence concerning dogmatic tendencies, but what we have points in a similar direction. There were indeed occasions when Academics affirmed or denied something, where they were challenged by listeners curious as to whether they had 'perceived' it, and where they retorted that Stoic 'apprehension' was unnecessary for such statements or denials (*Ac.* 2.35). There was no fear of the charge of *dogma* (*Ac.* 2.29, 133). But the theory behind Academicism still demanded that confident affirmation be avoided (2.8: 'adfirmare vix possumus'), just as Plato had avoided it (1.46: 'cuius in libris nihil affirmatur').

# CHAPTER 4

# ANONYMOUS *IN THEAETETUM*

## i Philosophical stance and date

As we shall become aware, the author (henceforth A) of the anonymous *Commentary on the Theaetetus* (henceforth *K*), belongs to the class of Fourth Academics. That is not to say that he studied with any member of the Philonian Academy (or of any other 'Academy', official or otherwise); merely that he adhered to a position akin to that of Philo of Larissa on the questions of (a) theory of knowledge and (b) history of the Academy. Only a small portion of *K* survives, mostly commenting on passages up to 153e; hence A has only just reached the meat of the *Theaetetus* before the papyrus fails us. Moreover *K* is only one of a number of Platonic commentaries written by A.[1] But his allegiance should nevertheless be plain to those with a knowledge of the terminology of the period: he is a Platonist, who still feels a certain debt to the New Academy (6.29ff, 70.12ff). He also shows genuine interest in the new Pyrrhonism (61.10ff, 63.1ff). He believes in the essential unity of the Academy over the centuries (54.43ff), and, though he sees a positive epistemology in Plato, it is certainly one which avoids the Stoic criterion of knowledge and related Stoic terminology.

Unfortunately such has not been the traditional view of A's philosophical position. Insistence on trying to understand this period in terms of 'scepticism', 'dogmatism', and 'eclecticism' (in defiance of the fact that the thinkers did not see themselves in such terms) has perpetuated views such as those expressed by G. Invernizzi.[2] He argues on the basis of passages which (a) sanction *dogmata* or (b) treat Socratic 'irony' as an educational device which does not reflect absolute ignorance, that *K* is a thoroughly anti-sceptic work (221–2). I find this attitude more than a little puzzling, for (a) neither the New Academy nor Pyrrhonism is treated with anything but respect, and (b) at one point A argues *against* those who appeal to Socratic 'irony' as an explanation of the alleged ignorance of 'Socrates' at 150cd (*K* 58.39—59.2). One must grant Invernizzi that A makes efforts to absolve 'Socrates' from *complete* ignorance, but if 'Socrates' was not being ironic at 150cd, then he was either indulging in outright lies or genuinely aware of his lack of knowledge *concerning the subject under investigation*. In fact A seems to be aiming at a balanced view, devoid of any extreme 'sceptic' or extreme 'dogmatist' interpretations.

Invernizzi's observation that A sees *dogmata* as part of the heritage of the Academy is scarcely relevant, for I have shown (see chapter 3 v above) that *dogmata* were not rejected by the Fourth Academy; indeed A virtually tells us that, when he claims that the majority of Academics (he does not say Platonists!) 'with very few exceptions' had *dogmata*.[3] If he had to except the Fourth Academy as well as the Third and presumably the Second too, he could not possibly speak of 'very few exceptions'. His position is that the Academy had always adopted its 'sceptical' approach as an educational device rather than out of absence of doctrine; that this is the Fourth Academic view ought already to be clear.

My views on A's position will become clearer as the chapter progresses, but some mention should now be made of the date problem. I have now put into print several reasons why I consider it more likely that *K* dates from the late first century B.C. than the mid second century A.D.[4] No single argument could be considered sufficient to establish my position, but the more important ones should be mentioned here.

(1) A believes in the unity of the Academy, and as such would regard himself as an Academic as well as a Platonist, whereas these have become two distinct groups by the mid second century (e.g. Gellius *NA* 11.5.6—8). The use of the term 'Academic' to describe Plato would also have seemed very odd during that period.[5]

(2) There are no signs of the expected Middle Platonist preoccupation with metaphysics-cum-theology.

(3) A's view that the subject of the *Theaetetus* is simple knowledge

67

seems to have been controversial when he wrote, most Platonics preferring to see the *criterion* of knowledge as the subject (fr. 4); but that is unlikely to have been the case after Thrasyllus labelled the work 'on knowledge' early in the first century A.D. It seems more likely that Thrasyllus depends upon *K*. It also seems likely that the early first century B.C. was responsible for regarding the dialogue as Plato's statement on the criterion.

(4) A's text of the *Meno* had an error in the key passage of the work (98a), which emerges at 3.3 and 15.22. The passage is unlikely to have been allowed to go uncorrected in the second century A.D., when there were probably many more texts available.[6]

(5) Second-century authors display comparatively little interest in the *Theaetetus* as a source for Platonic epistemology. But the work was important in the time of Philo Judaeus.

(6) The picture of Pyrrhonism offered by A is consonant with our expectations of Aenesideman Pyrrhonism.

(7) In a list of various types of presentations to which Hellenistic philosophies had appealed no mention is made of 'the most accurate presentation' which Potamo had adopted as his criterion in the Augustan period.

In addition to adducing these arguments I have compared *K* with known Platonists of the second century A.D., and have consistently detected reasons for supposing that none of them wrote it; where their epistemologies are recoverable they exhibit significant differences from *K*. Furthermore *K* is a relatively crude commentary, better placed at the beginning of the traditions of Platonic commentary.[7] It also seems likely that A was unaware of the Middle Platonic debate concerning the interpretation of the prologue,[8] for he takes an attitude which falls between two known positions[9] without giving any hint that the subject was a controversial one. Finally one should mention A's apparent love of adverbs formed from past participles, of which he produces two active and one passive example. A study of indexed authors from Polybius to the third century A.D. has revealed that it is very rarely that active forms of this type outnumber passive forms. I have found two such active forms and no passive ones in Polybius, and two of each in the Septuagint.[10] It so happens that the two which I have found in the Septuagint are identical with the two found in *K*. Of thirteen other authors investigated,[11] only Pollux (three active, and at least twenty-one passive) and possibly Dionysius of Halicarnassus (one or two active, three or four passive) have more than one active form.[12] In Aelian, Diodorus Siculus, Galen, Josephus, Philodemus, and Plutarch, as well as Pollux, passive forms outnumber active ones by at least four to one. If our sample of A's work is anything like representative I should have to allow that in this respect he resembles Polybius, and more particularly the Septuagint (however disparate its authors may have been), rather than later authors.

Though I feel that the weight of evidence lies heavily on my side, I shall avoid assuming that I am necessarily correct about the date, and should not like to think that my case depended upon it. These are not matters which permit certainty. And though my dating strongly suggests Eudoran authorship,[13] it is clearly inappropriate for either me or the reader to take such authorship for granted.

## ii 'Zetesis'

Since one has to judge A's views on the sole basis of his fragmentary comment, one must assume that they are similar to those which he fathers upon Plato: particularly when Plato is treated in a way which might seem controversial or forced, or at a greater length than the original dialogue would warrant. One aspect of his treatment which emerges clearly after a few readings is his treatment of the *Theaetetus* as a 'search' or 'inquiry': a *zetesis* (2.42, 3.20 etc.). As was discovered in chapter 1, inquiry was very much a Fourth Academic ideal. It was an activity with a constructive purpose which was best begun without strong views on the conclusion which would be reached; it could be argued that a dogmatist school did not extend the range of its inquiries sufficiently (e.g. *K* 11.22–4), while Plato was much admired for his willingness to inquire into everything (*Ac.* 1.46). In *K* we find that Platonic inquiries are seen as asking questions, but not as revealing any particular position – so that they made no affirmation, either true or false (59.12–17).

According to *K*, Plato did not always refuse to reveal

himself. He did so, for example, during the 'midwifery section' of the *Theaetetus* (see 55.8—13); 'Socrates' was here speaking openly, but not on the subject of inquiry. If Plato sometimes reveals himself, then it is clear that he is not always engaged in *zetetic* inquiry; there must be other aspects to his work. From 58.23ff it would seem that A associates these inquiries with the Socratic practice of testing people through question and answer, so as to purge them of their false opinions. These processes of purgation were deemed an important part of philosophy by Philo of Larissa,[14] and, besides *K* (2.9—11, 58.33—6), a number of authors who wrote in the Platonic tradition agreed: Philo of Alexandria (*Her.* 247), Plutarch (*Mor.* 1000c), and Albinus (*Prol.* 6, p. 150.17—20 H).[15] But these processes were also considered to be preliminaries, rather than ends in themselves; and A too seems to see Plato's work as a combination of the highly essential *zetetic* inquiry and some more direct method of teaching. The fact that the emphasis in *K* usually falls on the former is due to the character of the work upon which it comments.

As already seen in chapter 1, there was something of a correspondence between Plato the 'inquirer' or Plato the 'instructor' and the 'sceptic' or 'dogmatic' interpretation of his position. That A saw two sides to Plato's work, and that he refused to accept either a strict 'ephectic' or a strict 'dogmatic' view of the master, will come as no surprise. We know from Sextus Empiricus (*PH* 1.221) that some saw Plato as part aporetic, part dogmatic: the aporetic element being found principally in the polemical works and those where Socratic irony is prevalent. We know, moreover, that Thrasyllus' scholarly treatment of the dialogues gave each a class as well as a second name, and that the two principal classes were *zetetic* or 'inquisitive' and *hyphegetic* or 'instructional';[16] *Theaetetus* belonged to the former class. *K*, I believe, belongs to an age before Thrasyllus' work was important, and A is more likely to have influenced Thrasyllus' divisions than to have been influenced by them. There is no attempt in *K* to label the *Theaetetus* (or any other dialogue) with any of Thrasyllus' class-terms, or to contrast its purpose with that of other dialogues; it is likely to be A's work which enabled Thrasyllus to label the *Theaetetus* 'On knowledge' rather than 'On the criterion'.[17]

So 'inquiry' or *zetesis*, is viewed in *K* as just one of Plato's activities, but as an important one. It is not viewed as an exclusively Platonic or Socratic process, for 'Theaetetus' is said to 'inquire' carefully at 12.20. Nor does A appear to be alone in seeing 'inquiry' as the essence of the *Theaetetus* (2.35). But he emphasizes the 'inquisitive' aspect of the dialogues more than some might, and sees Plato as more 'inquisitive' than philosophers of other schools (e.g. the Stoics, 11.25) as did Cicero (*Ac.* 1.46). But it can be seen from 44.48ff that A's view of Platonic 'inquiry' is more positive than that of Cicero's source: ideally it leads from what is less clear to what is more clear; from the more particular to the more universal.

### iii Rejection of the 'ephectic' view of Plato

A's view of Plato appears well thought out, and is not just a colourless attempt to steer a middle course. He reacts against previous extreme views of Plato, in particular against an attempt to show that Plato is *Academic* in so far as he 'does no dogmatizing' (54.38—43). This view has been based in part on such phrases as *Tht.* 150c6 (διὰ τὸ μηδὲν ἔχειν σοφόν), and, to judge from A's comments, 150c4 (ἄγονός εἰμι σοφίας), 150c8—d1 (εἰμὶ . . . οὐ πάνυ τι σοφός), and 150d1—2 (οὐδέ τί μοι ἔστιν εὕρημα . . .) as well. Thus details of the 'midwifery section' of the work had been used by some to show that 'Socrates' made no claim at all to knowledge and wisdom.

My evidence does in fact show that the 'ephectic' view of Plato was highly developed at some stage, and that Platonic texts were closely examined in the search for supporting evidence. Besides the *Theaetetus*, we know that the *Phaedrus* was used to show 'Socrates' unable to affirm whether he is a man or some other creature,[18] while a number of words and phrases in the *Phaedo* had been seized upon as expressing

Plato's doubts about his thesis.[19] The *Phaedo* was also used to show that Plato, though he saw sensation and intellect as man's cognitive faculties, rejected firstly the evidence of the former and then that of the latter (because the senses keep obstructing it).[20] Early aporetic works, such as the *Lysis*, *Charmides*, and *Euthyphro*, were used to show Plato arguing on both sides of the question,[21] while the *Timaeus* was said to leave the truth to the Gods and content itself with the 'likely story' (D.L. 9.72). But the *Theaetetus* was perhaps the most important work of all for this view, and was supposed to show Plato abolishing every explanation not only of knowledge but also of number.[22] I have little doubt that this was because (a) it appears to say that nothing is one (152d2, 153e4, 157a8, 182b3), and (b) it regards the whole as merely the sum of the minimal parts (204a ff).[23]

It will be observed that the view of Plato as an anti-dogmatist at Cic. *Ac.* 1.46 shows no signs of detailed attention to individual texts. The view is presented quite reasonably, without the eristic manner of the more detailed arguments for that view. It seems reasonably clear to me that such arguments were collected and worked out in detail by Pyrrhonists, even though their germ might have been found in the Academy. Aenesidemus, the founder of the revived Pyrrhonism, was a great collector of arguments, who liked to give each argument a number; the ways of proving Plato 'ephectic' which are preserved by the anonymous *Prolegomena to Plato's Philosophy* (hereafter anon. *Prol.*) are numbered clearly 1 to 5. They are pictured as an attempt to prove Plato 'ephectic' (i.e. 'favouring suspension of judgment'), though the term 'Academics' is coupled with 'Ephectics' once (10, p. 2.205.4 H). Yet the 'Ephectics' were the Pyrrhonists in late Neoplatonic terminology,[24] and anon. had distinguished them from the milder 'New Academics' only shortly before (7, p. 202.22–7 H). Moreover, those of the above arguments for an anti-dogmatic view of Plato which were based on *Phaedrus* and *Timaeus* are known to us only from Pyrrhonists.

As for those who tried to prove that Plato was an 'Academic' at *K* 54.50, it is plain that they had used the term in this unusual adjectival sense for some good reason. A would not himself have chosen to use the term in this sense, for he appears to quarrel with them over what the word should mean. They had used it as a rough equivalent of the terms 'sceptic' or 'ephectic' in order to indicate Plato's anti-dogmatic nature, so either the terms 'sceptic' and 'ephectic' were not yet well established, or 'Academic' was meant to distinguish the type of scepticism being attributed to Plato. I suspect that there is some truth in both these explanations. The term is most likely to have been used by one who was interested in the differences between Academics and Pyrrhonians, and it seems to have been Aenesidemus who pioneered this question.[25] Moreover it is very unlikely that A believed that these people were Academics; if he had, he would have to have included them among the 'very few' Academics who had no *dogma*; he would also have had to spend longer refuting their claims, since they would have spoken with some authority. If they were not Academics, they were surely Pyrrhonians.

Such a conclusion is supported by the fact that those who adhere to this extreme view in *K* do appear to be the same group who do so in anon. *Prol*. For the fifth argument there (the second based on the *Theaetetus*) is identical with the one on which A comments, based on the self-depreciating remarks which 'Socrates' makes during the 'midwifery section': 'I know nothing, nor do I teach anything; I just go on puzzling.' Of course we only meet the one argument in *K*, but that is all we should expect in a commentary on this section of the work.

What kind of view of Plato were these extremists trying to put forward? From *K* one is only able to gather that they saw Plato as having no *dogma*, apparently not even in a weak sense, but as 'Academic' rather than Pyrrhonian all the same. From anon. *Prol*. it does indeed seem that he was depicted as Academic rather than Pyrrhonian. The first argument depends upon Plato's frequent use of such expressions as 'it is likely', 'perhaps', and 'as I think' (10, p. 205.8 H). But they indicate a tendency to accept the proposition which they

qualify with a cautious hesitation rather than to adopt a
Pyrrhonist's indifference towards it. Only the Academic
is attracted to one view in preference to another.[26] Moreover the arguments in general are directed towards showing
that Plato sanctions the practice of treating things as
non-apprehensible (10, pp. 205.4, 9, 12, 14, 21, 31, 206.14
H).[27] Only the Academics positively treat things as non-
apprehensible; the Pyrrhonist views even this question with
neutrality.[28]

But if Plato was 'Academic' rather than Pyrrhonian, how
was it that the Pyrrhonists were so interested in demonstrating his nature? Naturally they were interested in pointing
out cases where earlier thinkers had imperfectly anticipated
Pyrrho,[29] and they were probably trying to point to some
aspect of Plato's 'Academicism' which had done so. I feel
that the term 'ephectic' provides the key. It was the adjective
derived from the verb meaning 'suspend judgment' (ἐπέχω),
and should thus mean 'inclined to suspend judgment'. Though
the Fourth Academy were inclined to allow a man to come
to his conclusions, and probably acknowledged that Plato too
had done so on many issues, the Pyrrhonians wanted to use
Plato as an authority for their refusal to judge issues. They
believed that it would be easy to do this if they could show
that he had sanctioned the 'non-apprehensibility' doctrine
(now all but abandoned by the Academy). And in the
*Theaetetus* they detected Plato's refusal to proceed beyond
his *aporia*: 'I just go on puzzling' (*Prol.* 10, p. 206.13); thus
Plato came to no conclusions.

Aenesidemus knew that the examination of both sides of
the question may have very different results: it may lead to
suspension of judgment, but it may also lead to dogmatic
solutions to the problems of conflicting impressions. At
S.E. *PH* 1.210 he sees the initial *scepsis* as a road towards
Heraclitism, to the simultaneous acceptance of opposite
predicates for a given object. The anonymous writer echoes
Aenesidemus' phrase at *Prol.* 10, p. 206.21.[30] But that same
process of *scepsis* (the antithetic comparison of impressions
and arguments)[31] could also preserve the *aporia* and result in

suspension of judgment. One man might use *scepsis* for dogmatic ends, another might 'remain in *scepsis*'.[32] It was important for Aenesidemus to distinguish between early users of *scepsis*, and to see who passed beyond it and who did not.

To confirm this view it is necessary to study S.E. *PH* 1.210—41, where Sextus compared Pyrrhonism with other philosophies, mentioning Aenesidemus' name in connexion with both Heraclitus and Plato. In the latter case our text is at fault, and some have argued that Aenesidemus and Menodotus are depicted as the principal *opponents* rather than the principal *exponents* of the view that Plato is 'purely sceptic' (εἰλικρινῶς σκεπτικός).[33] Much depends upon what these words are taken to mean; in Sextus' time 'sceptic' means 'Pyrrhonian', and no good Pyrrhonist could view Plato as Pyrrhonian in the full sense of the word. But the words are *not* Sextus', for the adverb is not part of his normal vocabulary. Its only occurrence in *Adversus Mathematicos* is part of a quotation from Diodorus (10.114). In the *Pyrrhonian Hypotyposes* it occurs only once outside book 1, at 2.24. The context is enlightening, for at 22 Sextus had used the *Phaedrus* (229e—30a) to show Socrates' ignorance of whether he is a man or not, while 28 denies that Plato defined man 'with positive assurance'.[34] Thus there is a tendency here to see anti-dogmatic elements in Plato as well as Socrates, and to judge from *Math.* 7.281—2 (cf. 141—4) this tendency must belong to Sextus' source — perhaps the same source as he attacks at the end of the previous book. In *PH* 1 the adverb occurs seven times,[35] five of them during the exposition of the Aenesideman 'tropes'; we are left with only 222 (the case under discussion), and 207 (which may well be related).

Thus I see the adverb 'purely' as deriving from those whom Sextus attacks at 1.222, perhaps from Menodotus the Empiric. This would help to explain why the equation of Pyrrhonism with Empiricism is attacked at 236—41, an equation that Menodotus must surely have made.[36] More importantly it would explain why Sextus' opponents at 210—41 appear to be using 'non-apprehensibility' as a criterion of whether a given philosophy is 'sceptic' or not. For Menodotus had almost certainly seen 'non-apprehensibility' doctrines as a mark of 'scepticism': *even when confidently held.*[37] Cyrenaicism, true Academicism, and Empiricism had thus been *equated* with 'scepticism' (215, 220, 236), while Heraclitism, Democritism, and Protagorism had been more loosely connected with it.[38] In these latter cases *scepsis* had become a road to some dogmatic position, as opposite impressions give rise to the belief that *either* (a) *x* had each of two opposite attributes, *or* (b) *x* has neither of them, *or* (a) *x* has the *logoi* or potential for each (cf. 218).

It seems to me that Menodotus (or some similar Empiric) had provided Sextus with the basic material for this section, but that the material was nevertheless based on Aenesidemus (perhaps without his being fully understood). The material appealed to the authority of Aenesidemus at least twice, at precisely those points where comparisons were most contentious: on Heraclitus (rarely seen as having an affinity with scepticism)[39] and Plato (by Menodotus' day seen mostly as a dogmatist). It was not a complete list of doubting philosophers which was given (as at D.L. 9.71–3),[40] but a list of those who were influenced by opposite impressions. As seen in chapter 1, the use of opposite impressions was 'scepsis' in its early sense, a sense surviving at *PH* 1.8, and it is this sense of 'scepsis' and 'sceptic' that had been employed by those to whom Sextus replies in *PH* 1.210–41. There is good evidence for the importance of opposite impressions in Aenesidemus' philosophy,[41] *particularly* at *PH* 1.210 as U. von Burkhard notes.[42] That *scepsis* had not just been another term for Pyrrhonism in the source material is indicated by telling changes of terminology at points where alleged similarities with Pyrrhonism are *not* related to the antithetic comparison of impressions and arguments.[43]

The meaning of the phrase 'purely sceptic' at *PH* 1.222 may now be clarified. Whereas Heraclitus and others were partially sceptic, because they began with Aenesideman *scepsis*, some were purely sceptic because they never abandoned that *scepsis* by constructing a dogma to explain the opposite impressions. If *x* is 'purely sceptic' then he also has no *dogmata* (as at *K* 54.42—3) and to this extent he is also inclined to suspend judgment (as in anon. *Prol.* 10). Moreover 'pure scepticism' is naturally accompanied by the general feeling that things are non-apprehensible (as in anon. *Prol.* 10). Thus the anti-dogmatic view of Plato at *K* 54, at anon *Prol.* 10, and at S.E. *PH* 1.222 is all one thesis: 'purely sceptic' is just another way of saying 'non-dogmatic' or 'ephectic'. It seems to me that the original purpose of the comparison (in *PH* 1.210—41) between those philosophies which used *scepsis* had been to find out which were truly 'ephectic' and which resulted in *dogma*. Thus when Sextus introduces this section he describes its purpose as 'to discern more clearly the *ephectic* discipline' (209). The term 'ephectic' must come from source material, for it is otherwise only found at *PH* 1.7 (in a discussion of names for Pyrrhonists), at *Math.* 11.152 (where the context deals with the merits of 'suspension of judgment' and so requires the term), and at *PH* 2.9—10 (where I suspect the continued influence of the same source material).[44] Note too that *PH* 2.10 speaks of the 'ephectic' thinker *remaining* in the 'sceptic' state of mind.

It may seem to the reader that this lengthy digression on the sceptic view of Plato was unnecessary, but it is only by an understanding of the Pyrrhonist thesis that A's position can become clear. He rejects the view that Plato *remains* in *scepsis*, and thus does not see him as 'ephectic'. For A the *scepsis* leads to *dogma*, not only in Plato but also in the great majority of later Academics. Indeed their *dogmata* had followed his on the most important issues. He does not of course mean that they were dogmatic in the modern sense, for he suggests that we may see Platonic *dogma* in the 'midwifery' section where Plato is certainly not being dogmatic. He simply has a positive impression to convey to his reader as a result of certain positive views. A's thesis, therefore, is that there was *both* systematic impartial 'inquiry' *and* positive conclusions from that 'inquiry' in the Academy from Plato's day on: with odd exceptions, but not enough to detract from the fact that the Academy had a single continuous tradition. This is the same One-Academy thesis which I would attribute to Philo of Larissa.[45] The thesis does not deny the fact that Arcesilaus *concealed* his Platonic conclusions from the public, but, like *PH* 1.234, it does claim that he came to Platonic conclusions. It makes allowances for the possibility that Carneades might not have come to conclusions, as even his most intimate pupils were not told of any, but Carneades remains a rare exception.

That A saw Plato and the New Academy as proposing the same doctrines on important questions raises the issue of what were the most important questions. A speaks of the 'most fundamental doctrines' (τὰ κυριώτατα τῶν δογμάτων, 55.4–6), and Antiochus would appear to have identified these with one's answers to the problems of the 'end' and of the 'criterion' (Cic. *Ac.* 2.29). A promised to demonstrate the identity of fundamental doctrines in *K*, so that they must be issues which the *Theaetetus* gave him the opportunity to raise. Certainly it allowed him to raise the problem of the criterion (see 2.21–3), and, if likeness to God is his 'end' as seems likely,[46] then he would discuss this issue in relation to 176a–c. We will discuss A's attitude to the 'criterion' shortly, but we must briefly consider how he could possibly have regarded 'likeness to God' as a New Academic 'end'.

Firstly one must note that Eudorus of Alexandria, whom I regard as contemporary with, if not identical with A, saw the assimilation-process as belonging primarily to our powers of reasoning.[47] Similarly Cicero, speaking from the Fourth Academic standpoint, had seen Plato's goal as an intellectual one, similar to that of Erillus (*Ac.* 2.129).[48] But the issue would appear to have been regarded as a complicated one for Plato, by Cicero,[49] by Antiochus,[50] and by Eudorus.[51] Eudorus seems to have been thinking in terms of the perfecting of our reasoning powers (by assimilation to the heavenly God)[52] rather than simply of knowledge. It could be argued with some plausibility that the New Academy also aimed to perfect our intellectual powers, and there is certainly no good reason to assume that suspension of judgment was ever a declared 'end' of the New Academic philosophy.[53] As far as Cicero was concerned (*Ac.* 2.7) the Academic discipline aimed at either the truth, or the closest possible approximation to it: which might be described as 'assimilation to an omniscient divinity as far as is possible'.

## iv Flux and relativity

Another doctrine which A probably saw as common between Plato and the New Academy is that of the flux and relativity of things of this world. He discusses the Heraclitean and Protagorean doctrines at 62.7ff (virtually to the end of the extant part of *K*), and regards relativism as a consequence of the flux doctrine (63.48–64.36). This is perhaps not the *only* way that relativism may come about, for 63.1–40 does not connect flux with Pyrrhonist relativism (which is admitted to be different, 63.1); but it is seen to be the way in which Protagorean relativism has emerged, as also in Sextus' source-material for *PH* 1.217–19. Just as Sextus' sources see a positive doctrine about the nature of matter emerging from Protagoras' awareness of opposite impressions, a doctrine not shared by Pyrrhonian relativism; so A sees Plato passing beyond the initial answer of 'Theaetetus' (which as yet has a Pyrrhonian quality, 61.10–46), to a fuller Protagorean position which differs from it (62.8–12, 63.1–4). Thus those whom Plato follows (including Heraclitus, Democritus,[54] and Protagoras), go beyond opposite impressions and come to positive conclusions about the nature of matter, as in the source-material of *PH* 1.210–41. They thus have *dogma*, and this *dogma* may well be one which A attributes both to Plato and to the New Academy.

What evidence could A have produced to support the conclusion that the New Academy believed in the flux and relativity of the things of this world? That which we have is chiefly derived from Aenesidemus. When speaking of the 'dogmatic' expressions which Pyrrhonists (*as opposed to Academics*) avoid, he launches into the following string of examples:

No one of them at all has ever said either that all is inapprehensible or that it is apprehensible; but still they have called them no more of this kind than of that, nor sometimes such and sometimes not such, nor *such to one man, not such to another, and to another quite non-existent*; nor again that all (or some) things are within reach or beyond reach, or within reach at one time but not at another, or for one man and not for another; and indeed (he describes things as) neither true nor false, neither persuasive nor difficult to believe, neither existent nor non-existent, but just the same, so to speak; no more true than false, or persuasive than difficult to believe, or existent than non-existent, or then such but then such, or for him of this kind but for him of that kind.                              (Photius *Bibl.* 169b42–170a11)

The words italicised, with their notion that even existence may be relative to the individual, are clearly reminiscent of Protagoras' famous principle that man is the measure of all things, both of their existence and their non-existence.[55] This is broadly true on any interpretation, but particularly if the 'such . . . such' is meant to pick up 'inapprehensible' and 'apprehensible', rather than being used purely in a general sense, as attributes $F$ and $-F$. The whole passage suggests that the Academy were particularly prone to seeing attributes of various kinds as relative both to the individual percipient and to the time of perception. Aenesidemus accuses the Academy of reading differences in the way we perceive things as differences actually belonging to the objects (or presentations) themselves; Academic *scepsis* is leading towards an ontology. Hence all the terms used (with the exception of 'within reach' (ἐφικτός) which could still have the epistemological *application* of 170b11) are epistemological or ontological.

The apparently Protagorean relativism is not difficult to reconcile with Fourth Academic claims to follow Plato, for (a) they could claim that the *Theaetetus'* discussion of Heraclitism and Protagorism did offer Plato's real view of the world of phenomena, and (b) this relativism could be used to offer an explanation of Plato's attribution of a limited reality to the things of this world.[56] The apparent readiness to concentrate on that which is relative to the percipient or to a given time recalls Heraclitus' work on opposite attributes concurrently applicable[57] and on flux, and the Heraclitean aspect of Plato's treatment of the physical world must have been obvious enough to the Fourth Academy. Since Plato uses this Heraclitism as a means towards rejecting knowledge of the physical world (cf. *Crat.* 440a–c), it might have seemed attractive for the Fourth Academy to pay it particular attention.

Cicero's writings give one no reason to suppose that the Academy which he knew was particularly interested in either Heraclitus or Protagoras, but Academic interest in them would assist in explaining Aenesidemus' so-called Heraclitean doctrine and his strong emphasis on the relativity of our cognition.[58] The latter was certainly foreshadowed by the Academy (see *Cic. Ac.* fr. 9), and I have suggested elsewhere that the Aenesideman view of Heraclitus was based in whole or in part upon the Academic view of him.[59] Cicero probably knew of the attempt to make air rather than fire the first principle for Heraclitus,[60] while it seems to me that the Aenesideman account of Heraclitean 'truth' depends upon an epistemology attributed by Antiochus to Heraclitus.[61] Rist saw Aenesideman 'Heraclitism' as related to his (alleged) Academic background,[62] and Burkhard's theory that the interpretation is invented in order to refute the Stoic one does not in any way reduce the chance of an Academic origin, for it was the Academics rather than the Pyrrhonians who saw the Stoa as the special enemy. It has often been observed that Sextus avoids giving the impression that Aenesidemus *personally* held the doctrines which he attributed to Heraclitus, and strange interpretations are generally the product of personal beliefs; it thus seems unlikely that these are the product of Aenesidemus.[63] I suspect that they are particularly associated with him because he had used 'Heraclitus' as a character arguing against the Stoics in some lost work.[64]

The Second Academy evidently showed interest in Heraclitus, for Plutarch (*Mor.* 1121f) suggests that Arcesilaus made appeal to him, apparently regarding him as a predecessor of his own (along with Socrates, Plato and Parmenides). It should be noted that it was in the time of Arcesilaus rather than that of Aenesidemus that Heraclitus was a key figure for the Stoics.[65] Equally important is Academic use of the Heraclitean flux-theory in order to challenge the assumption that things remain the same while they grow; both A (*K* 70.12–26) and Plutarch (*Mor.* 1083a–c) knew of these challenges.[66] Both authors believe that the Academics were not seriously opposed to the notion of growth, and Plutarch represents their difficulties as real problems besetting those who looked for an answer (1083a). For him the premises used in the anti-Stoic argument were adopted by the Academics too: (i) that particulars are all in flux, giving off and receiving particles of matter; (ii) that the types of matter constituting them do not remain quantitatively the same during this process; and (iii) that such change is better described as coming-to-be and passing-away. Again it appears to have been the Second Academy which adopted this Heraclitean line, but both A and Plutarch demonstrate that later Academics either revived or continued this interest in *both* the Academic argument *and* the flux-doctrine itself.

Thus, in addition to there being adequate evidence for linking the Fourth Academics with Protagorean relativism, there are grounds for believing that they also used Heraclitism, including flux-theory, which both A and the source for *PH* 1.217–19 view as the natural accompaniment of Protagorism. Just as A could plausibly claim Plato's support for the Heraclitism/Protagorism of *Theaetetus* 151e ff *as applied to the world of our senses*, he could plausibly claim New Academic support as well. I do not claim that such an appeal to the authority of the Academy (even the Fourth Academy) would not have been based upon a very one-sided view of the nature and purpose of Academic philosophy: rather that A could view his own style of Platonism as operating within a more recent Academic tradition.

## v A's criteria of knowledge

A's epistemology is very much based upon Plato's *Meno*, and the *Theaetetus* is interpreted with an eye to the *Meno*. The earlier work is perhaps seen as supplying the *dogmata* which lie beneath the surface of the Theaetetus' non-dogmatic 'inquiry'. Certainly the *Meno*'s theory of 'recollection' is seen as a *dogma* which should be read into the 'midwifery' episode (47.48—48.11, 52.44—53.36, 55.26—57.22). And *Meno* 98a is believed to supply the correct answer to the question which the *Theaetetus* asks (2.52—3.21), the question of what constitutes simple knowledge (cf. 15.2—26). Reference is made to the *Meno* at 28.43 and 56.27 as well as 15.20, but it seems that A had not commented upon the work. He was intending to speak at length about the theory of 'recollection' in a commentary on the *Phaedo* (48.10). One might well ask why A comments on the *Theaetetus* rather than on the *Meno*, if the latter work contained Plato's basic epistemology; I suspect that the answer is that the *Theaetetus* was a controversial work at the time (see col. 2), and that A felt that it was in need of reinterpretation; and it may also be significant that both the *Theaetetus* and the *Phaedo* (on which A is about to write) had received considerable abuse at the hands of the Pyrrhonists (see section ii). It was in A's nature to wish to correct such abuse and to steer away from all extremes of interpretation.

It is clear that A believed in the pre-existing soul, and believed also that it had access to clear knowledge in this prior existence (53.3—8, 57.26—42), but that he saw grave impediments to the recollection of that knowledge in this life: some recall nothing at all (53.31—6) and do not appear to be 'pregnant' with embryonic knowledge (57.23—39). Thus A does *need* an epistemology, for knowledge is very far from being automatic. The *Phaedo*'s theme that the body is inclined to hinder the reawakening of one's intellectual faculties in this life is clearly present (53.23—5), though character and quickness of mind are likewise relevant (53.25—31). The knowledge-giving process is thus seen by A not as a mechanical response of the mind to various data which it receives, but rather as a movement towards accurate judgment coupled with unshaken confidence (2.26—32) in the face of the difficulties presented by our human circumstances.

The material which awaits 'recollection' would appear to

be man's 'common notions' (47.42ff). These require careful analysis or 'taking apart at the joints' (46.44, 56.36) before they can yield knowledge, and the search for a definition apparently assists such a process (23.5–12, cf. 46.34–47.7). Prior to this process the 'common notions' have a more obscure role to play, for traces of them (traces, I assume, of some universal knowledge awaiting recollection) have practical effects on our conduct (46.45–9). Here we appear to have A's interpretation of the *Meno*'s explanation of political virtue in terms of right opinion (99b ff): the Platonic ideas which we should ideally 'recollect' exercise a hidden and less rational influence over the good politician. The *Meno*'s 'divine portion' by which political virtue comes is no longer pot luck, but rather a spark of immortal knowledge within us, an unarticulated intelligence. This strongly suggests that A was using a text with the same emended reading of 99e6 ('occurring by divine portion ⟨not⟩ without intelligence') as that of Clement of Alexandria.[67] The 'not without' expression appears to have been a popular device in Platonism from the time of Antiochus, '*x* is not without *f*' being a way of compromising between *Fx* and −*Fx* (e.g. K 73.10), and the emendation may have been designed to accord with Antiochean doctrine.[68]

Textual emendation in A's copy of the *Meno* had occurred at 98a3–4 too, the phrase 'by reasoning of a cause' (αἰτίας λογισμῷ) having become 'by cause of reasoning' (αἰτίᾳ λογισμοῦ, 3.3, 15.23). A is unlikely to have misremembered a phrase so important to his case, and his interpretation of the passage at 3.3–7 gives full weight to the notion of the cause and cannot itself have prompted the emendation. Whoever invented the emendation seems to have thought that *reasoning alone* could act as cause of the conversion of right opinion into knowledge (this agrees with what we know of Antiochus);[69] but A believes that the *Meno* offers something more than 'right opinion + an account' (3.15–25), so that the force which converts right opinion into knowledge cannot for him be just reasoning (unless for him λογισμός is substantially different from λόγος), but has to be reasoning *why*.

84

Exactly how A connects our 'recollection' of 'common notions' with discovering *why* P is not immediately obvious; but it is likely that he is influenced by the *Phaedo*, where there is an attempt to use the Platonic Forms as both objects of 'recollection' and causes (100b), causes explaining why *x* must have the property *F*. It may be that the various propositions which 'recollection' is alleged to establish are thought of as being Plato's 'simple knowledge', for this is the case in the Middle Platonic *Didascalicus* (4, p. 155.28−30 Hermann); since the immediate objects of recollected knowledge are the 'natural notions' in *K* as in *Didasc.*, these 'natural notions' would then be the objects of 'simple knowledge' too; and since 'simple knowledge' involves working out *why* (3.21−5), the 'natural notions' would have to be potentially such as to demonstrate *why*. In this case one might expect A to have identified the 'natural notions' with 'simple knowledge' as the author of *Didasc.* does, whereas the two concepts are not discussed in close relation to each other in extant parts of the commentary. In fact, however, no such identification is possible for A; the 'natural notion' can only yield 'recollection' and so become 'simple knowledge' if it is analysed (διαρθρόω) or *simplified* (ἐξαπλόω), a process involving definition by genus and differentia (23.1−12, cf. 46.43−5). In this way the 'common notion' will lead one to an understanding of the Platonic Form, and the genus and differentia taken together will tell us *why* all *x*s must be *F* and all *y*s must be *G*.

Thus in my view A begins with the 'natural notion', not yet knowledge but a dim reflection of pre-existing knowledge. This is unfolded (47.42) and analysed into its parts, with emphasis falling upon the establishment of genus and differentia, until one has risen above the suspicion that a bird has feathers to the awareness that any bird *must*, by definition, be a feathered biped. In this way the 'analysed natural notion', with a supposed grasp of the recollected Platonic Form, becomes 'recollection' by making us aware *why* such and such is the case, and thus ends in 'simple knowledge'. This simple knowledge then supplies the elements of which any 'compound knowledge' (i.e. any science as a whole)[70] may be constituted (15.2—26).

'Simple knowledge' is singled out as the particular kind of knowledge upon which the *Theaetetus* deliberates (2.20, 15.8), and we might legitimately speak of this as elemental knowledge. It is the elements of knowledge that the dialogue attempts to trace; for its later pages are particularly concerned to reject the idea of compound knowables constructed from unknowable simples (202d ff). And the discussion of false opinion at 187d ff, particularly the aviary section (197d—9e), is largely concerned with the problem of how knowledge-elements can become muddled or confused in the mind. It is clear that the dialogue is not asking what a compound science is, and to this extent A is right in seeing it as a discussion of 'simple knowledge' only.[71]

What *criteria* of knowledge can a theory such as A's involve? By what standards can he judge? It seems impossible that he can supply anything which would perform the same function as the Stoic 'apprehensible presentation', but then it does not appear that he sees knowledge in the same light as the Stoic. The emphasis on knowing *why* shows that it is understanding rather than certainty which characterizes 'knowledge' for A, and this appears to have been the case in the *Theaetetus* itself.[72] As an Academic A could not legitimately produce any theory of how certainty is possible, certainly not if that certainty is to extend to matters of the particular objects within the physical world. As in the *Meno* accuracy and permanence are the marks of knowledge (2.28—32, cf. 97d—98a). Knowing *why* seems to yield permanency, since the *cause* is also the *Meno*'s 'bond' (3.22), by which correct opinions may be bound so as to constitute knowledge (98a). Accuracy is rather the precondition if one is to have those correct opinions in the first place.

One cannot really regard 'knowing *why*' as a criterion of knowledge, for we would then require a criterion of knowing *why*. One might propose to regard the fully analysed 'natural notions' as a criterion, but it is not easy to recognize whether one's 'notions' actually do constitute proper 'recollection'.

As A well knew (52.44–53.36), false notions can occur; once again one would require a further criterion.

It is thus no surprise to find that extant parts of *K* see only the 'criterion through which' and the 'criterion by which' as relevant to the *Theaetetus* (2.23–7). The terms are not explained, beyond the mere identification of the 'criterion through which' as a tool (2.25),[73] and it is not even clear from the text whether these two expressions are supposed to have separate or identical reference. The former may seem the likelier possibility bearing in mind Plato's careful distinction between perception 'through' and perception 'by' at 184c. But this may have been a case where contemporary usage conflicted with Platonic usage, in so far as both intellect and senses were seen as criteria 'through which' (or at least as candidates for consideration as criteria 'through which'),[74] while Plato spoke of us perceiving 'by' the mind 'through' the sense-organs (184d3–5). A's usual practice is to explain Plato using contemporary terms and contemporary senses; moreover the contemporary sense *could* be reconciled with Plato if one is prepared to see the intellect as a criterion 'through which' in so far as it grasps certain things 'through itself' (185e). And the expression 'that *by* which we shall judge' may merely show A's willingness to revert to the non-technical language to which Plato refers at 184c.

It therefore seems that A makes the following points at 2.21ff: in investigating knowledge Plato has to examine the criterion, i.e. the criterion 'through which' as through an instrument (such a criterion may be sense-organs, senses, or mental faculties); for it is essential to have that by which we shall judge things, and when this is accurate knowledge may result. A has not yet given any clue as to what the criterion 'through which' may be, either for himself or for Plato, because it is a matter to be investigated as yet. Plato in fact considers the nature of both mind and senses in his quest for knowledge. But the switch to the term 'by which' may indicate that A believes the mental faculties to be the proper criterion of this type. For to act as a criterion *of knowledge* the senses would have to be *accurate*, whereas A seems to imply at 3.11—12 that they do not possess such accuracy, in accordance with Academic doctrine.[75] Thus the proper criterion 'through which' would have to be some mental instrument or organ, such as the 'reason' or *logos* which acts in precisely this capacity in the *Didascalicus* (4, p. 154.13).

Details of A's criteria are perhaps beyond recovery, but one point should be forcefully made: the type of criteria of which he speaks, mental faculties and perhaps their associated sensation-mechanisms, are also the kind of which Philo of Larissa had spoken: faculties which may become more or less healthy, more or less accurate.[76] It is also the commonest kind of criterion acknowledged by Philo of Alexandria.[77] The search for a criterion no longer involved one in the search for an impression which was the guarantee of its own truth. It involved one rather in the search for the most accurate data possible;[78] accurate data demanded accurate cognitive faculties; and, because the intellect could offer greater hopes of accuracy than the senses, the primary search was for the most precise intellect possible. That intellect resides in the heavens; it was up to man to imitate its perfect motions, and assimilate his own mind to it as perfectly as possible.[79]

# CHAPTER 5

# INTERLUDE: ANTIOCHUS IN THE
# NEW ACADEMY

## i Antiochus and Carneades

In *Dionysius* 5 (1981), 78–83, I give grounds for supposing that the work of Antiochus of Ascalon used by Sextus in his doxography of the criterion (all or part of *Math.* 7.89–260) was composed prior to his quarrel with Philo in 87 B.C., and thus in a period when he was still nominally an Academic-'sceptic'. Since such a theory would be of great importance for the history of the Academy if it could be proved, I intend first to take the three passages where Antiochean influence can scarcely be doubted, and to see what can be learnt from them.

Antiochus is first mentioned by name at *Math.* 7.162, where his explanation is given of a Carneadean conclusion that any valid criterion of knowledge would have to be a presentation 'capable of presenting both itself and another object'. It is difficult to believe that Sextus would have turned to this *explanation* of Carneades' demands if he had not been following Antiochus' *account* of those demands. This means that it is safe to see Antiochus as a source from 160 to 165.

Antiochus is clearly impressed with Carneades' account of what a criterion of knowledge would have to be like. It must be sought 'in the affection resulting from evident clarity' (161); the 'affection' (πάθος) must indicate to the mind both itself and the object which caused it, and such an affection must be a presentation. Lucullus' speech suggests strongly that Antiochus continued to agree with all this. Carneades may have doubted whether there was such an affection as could present both itself and the object which causes it to the mind, but Antiochus' explanation of the notion offers the parallel case of light, which presents to the sight both itself and the objects which it illuminates (163). There is confidence in the belief that the presentation must be the leading factor in cognition, and that some presentations are true while others are false (*ibid.*). All this Antiochus continued to believe later.

Moreover the Carneadean arguments claim that reason (λόγος) must derive from or depend on the evidence of the presentation; 'and reasonably so' (καὶ εἰκότως), we are told, since any object which is to be judged must first appear, and nothing can appear without *irrational sensation*. The commentary on the Carneadean theory is coming from a source which jumps from 'presentation' to 'irrational sensation' with such ease that the source must hold that the senses supply the mind with *all* its basic information. The source also works naturally with the reason—sensation dichotomy employed by the New Academy and inherited by Aenesidemus (165). All this would agree with the picture of the anti-sceptic Antiochus which we receive from Cicero.

There is in fact only one item of this Carneadean argument for the non-existence of the criterion of knowledge with which Antiochus would later disagree. Carneades denies the existence of that kind of presentation which would meet his requirements for a criterion: none is true and of such a kind that an exactly similar false one could not be found (164). If such a presentation were found it would be 'apprehensive', and thus would supply the criterion of knowledge; without it there is no criterion, for our mental powers are left impotent without secure observations with which they may work. It is precisely because there can be no criterion without the 'apprehensive' presentation that Antiochus will later argue that the 'apprehensive' presentation *must* exist. He needs the full Carneadean argument in order to prove a single premise wrong by pointing to the correctness of other premises and the unacceptable nature of the conclusion: because knowledge does in fact exist, there must be a criterion of knowledge; but it must be such as Carneades had required it to be; therefore the 'apprehensive' presentation does exist.

All this makes it easier to understand the account of

Antiochus' earlier career at *Ac.* 2.69. Nobody had studied the Academic position longer than Antiochus; he had indeed written *acutissime* on the subject. In fact he had defended the Academic position just as keenly then as he had attacked it in the *Sosus* 'in senectute'. Clearly his career as a philosophical writer had begun during a long period of devotion to the Academy, and he had not displayed any of his later unorthodoxy for some time. This unorthodoxy is associated with his declining years. It may seem a radical change to switch from Carneadean scepticism to a dogmatism of great conviction, but all that was required for that change to take place was a change of heart on the question of whether any true presentation existed such that it could be distinguished from any possible false one. If it did, then a broadly Stoic epistemology had to be adopted.

Unlike Philo, Antiochus did not believe in half measures. The same confidence which characterized his earlier scepticism later came to characterize his neo-Stoic position: not just the same *kind* of confidence, but confidence in the same argument. If no 'apprehensive' presentation exists, there is no criterion of knowledge. That is what Antiochus had accepted for a long time ('multos annos'). But as the conviction grew among milder Academics that there was in fact knowledge, Antiochus re-examined the belief which he assumed to be incompatible with the existence of knowledge, and found the arguments against the 'apprehensive' presentation less convincing. The meat of Lucullus' speech in the *Academica* (47—58) is devoted to demonstrating their inadequacy.

It should, however, be emphasized that Antiochus' change of heart concerning the validity or otherwise of sceptic arguments for the non-existence of the 'apprehensive' presentation cannot have been sudden. *Ac.* 2.70 gives the impression of a concession which was made after a build-up of pressure from outside. Antiochus failed to withstand the 'concursus omnium philosophorum' against a position which the Academy alone defended. If the Academy were indeed tending to use general agreement as a criterion and to spurn 'private opinions' as I have maintained, then this is not

91

surprising. Cicero's concession that there are quite a few other points of contact between groups of philosophers points towards the importance of the agreement-principle in the affair. For once the Academics appeared to be defying popular opinion: the popular opinion that we know some things for certain.[1]

The fact that Cicero mockingly speaks of Antiochus' day of revelation, when the mark of true and false was revealed to him (*Ac.* 2.69), should not be allowed to obscure the thrust of the passage as a whole. The emphasis falls upon Antiochus' *inconstantia*, which questions the authority of his views. The sudden discovery of a new philosophical point, followed by a clear transfer of allegiance to the Stoics, would have given every justification for Antiochus' conduct and made him look like a man who had grasped some philosophical point for certain. But Antiochus took no decisive step, and continued to operate within the Academy. This should occasion no surprise. One's allegiance was not determined by one's opinion on one issue only, however important that issue may have been. The Academic traditionally argued for and against every kind of philosophical position, and arguments defending the Stoic criterion ought to have had some place in theory if not in practice. Then again an individual might legitimately *favour* the Stoic position from a place within the Academy; only the claim to perceive that position as certain truth would consistute rebellion. Moreover there must have been much to attract Antiochus to the Academy; the study of Plato would seem to have been becoming more dedicated, and the criticism of alien views more constructive. Antiochus did not adhere to the Stoic system in such a way that he would abandon criticism of its details, nor would he have wished to join a school which was still officially opposed to Plato. There was much that could be done within the Academy to proceed towards the truth; the closest proximity to it was the official goal of the Academy (*Ac.* 2.7). Why should Antiochus rush to leave?

He did not leave, certainly not for some time after his Stoicizing tendencies had begun to attract suspicion.[2] On the contrary he tried to encourage the more constructive aspects of Academic thought from within, openly striving to divert the attention of his colleagues away from the Carneadean tradition, which he came to recognize as a liability to them too (*Ac.* 2.35), towards the positive (if mild and uninspiring) thought of the 'Old Academics' such as Xenocrates and Polemon, or even to Aristotle. We see that his tactics had succeeded in acquiring for him a band of followers (*Ac.* 2.69), some of whom apparently came with him to Alexandria with Lucullus.[3] Those tactics did not cause bad feeling between Antiochus and a conservative Academic such as Heraclitus of Tyre (*Ac.* 2.11), but they were surely what alarmed Philo into writing his Roman Books which defended the unity of the Academy, *and attacked those who denied it* (*Ac.* 1.13). Antiochus' anger at seeing these books was natural enough, and Cicero's account of that anger at *Ac.* 2.11 so contrasts it with his normal behaviour that I cannot believe that it is in error. Philo was clearly attacking Antiochus' circle, *even though* Antiochus had remained superficially loyal to Philo so far.

It is against this background that we must understand the Antiochean account of Carneades at *Math.* 7.159ff. Antiochus tries to explain Carneades in such a way that his thought provides guidance for anybody wishing to construct a dogmatic epistemology. Carneades is respected, still treated as part of Plato's school, but seen nevertheless as an opponent of all who went beforehand — presumably including Plato, though this is not made explicit at 7.159. If Antiochus continues to be the source at 166ff, as I think must be the case, then he is surely just presenting the official Fourth Academic view of the Carneadean *probabile* (πιθανόν) as a constructive criterion. For, after breaking with Philo, Antiochus denied that it had any role to play, and began to doubt the view that Carneades actually assented to *probabilia* (*Ac.* 2.59). But here there are no such doubts in evidence; of particular interest is the assertion that Carneades *is compelled* to adopt a criterion on the basis of which he may organize his life.[4] This suggests assent to the proposition that a sceptic cannot live his scepticism. The only choice possible is that between practical 'probabilism' and complete certainty.[5] Thus Carneades has to be seen as *advocating* the 'probabilist' approach, the approach adopted by the Fourth Academy, even though there is much doubt as to whether Carneades himself meant his account of choice of action to be a statement of what ought to happen rather than what does in fact happen.

The most important aspect of Antiochean presentation of Carneades' views, however, is his apparent acceptance of the argument that any adequate criterion of knowledge must be a presentation, and must be such as to conform with the Stoic definition. His view as to whether there was such a presentation may well have been wavering. The only way for him to answer the question of whether such a presentation existed was to ask himself whether knowledge, memory, technical skill, and wisdom (all of which must rely on the criterion of knowledge),[6] really did exist. Men assumed that they did; his colleagues assumed that they did; the matter was agreed, indeed evident. Therefore some criterion of knowledge must exist, and therefore there must be presentations such as to accord with Carneades' requirements and Zeno's definition: ones such that their content could never be false.

## ii The 'Canonica'

A striking case of the verb κανονίζω at *Math.* 7.175 may remind one that 'canonic' is the Epicurean term for epistemology. It is found in this role earlier at 7.22. But Epicurean influence had recently intruded into Academic thought, when Metrodorus of Stratonicea began to receive support, including Philo's support (*Ac.* 2.78), for his version of Carneades' thought. Thus we ought not to be surprised that the title of Antiochus' book to which Sextus refers at 7.201 is *Canonica*.

Antiochus had apparently stated in the second book of this work that ⟨while some people attribute powers of apprehension to *logos* and deny that the senses possess such powers⟩ a certain other person, a well-known doctor with some inclination towards philosophy, accepted that the senses had real cognitive power but denied that we apprehend anything at all by reason. Sextus assumes that Antiochus was referring to (a) the Cyrenaic sect and (b) the medical writer Asclepiades. He observes that the latter had abolished the 'ruling principle' and had been a contemporary of Antiochus. It is the kind of comment that would be of interest to his medical readers, but he does not wish to expand upon Asclepiades' views here (7.202). The two paragraphs clearly constitute something of a digression, but it must be asked why Asclepiades' view was mentioned here at all, and in particular why Sextus comments on a passage of Antiochus which does not specifically refer to Asclepiades at all. Clearly something must have brought Antiochus' words to mind here, and it would seem that Sextus had a special interest in Antiochus' views.

But unless it is to be supposed that this unmemorable passage of Antiochus had for some reason stuck in Sextus' memory, there is little alternative to supposing that the *Canonica* is the work which he had been using, to a greater or lesser degree, in other parts of the doxography. The assumption is reasonable enough. The *Canonica* was clearly an epistemological work of more than one volume, and we have come to expect some kind of doxography to be included in the Ciceronian accounts of Antiochus' views.[7] Surely then the *Canonica* would have included a substantial doxography, such as would have served Sextus' requirements here.

There are, however, one or two puzzles for those who wish to see the *Canonica* as a wider source for the doxographic material of *Math.* 7.89ff. In particular 201−2 does not seem to be an integral part of the structure of the doxography. Consideration of Epicurus would naturally follow straight after the account of the Cyrenaic position. The passage marked as being from Antiochus would appear to have been developing the sensation−*logos* dichotomy, used by the Fourth Academy (e.g. *Ac.* 2.79−98) and found earlier in the doxography;[8] but although the Cyrenaic philosophy before

95

and the Epicurean after do attach weight to the senses at the expense of *logos*, there is nothing to suggest that Sextus' source may have emphasized that fact. Antiochus' words would thus be likely to come from a different part of the *Canonica* from any which Sextus might have been using here as his immediate source. A doxography would in any case have been most at home in book 1. The quotation would probably have been taken from the introduction to book 2, in a backward reference to the variety of positions outlined previously.

There is not a great deal to be learnt from the brief quotation from book 2, but a few points should be noted. It is important for the understanding of the Fourth Academy that we should realize that 'apprehend' (καταλαμβάνω) could be used, as here, without any suggestion of an especially Stoic epistemology (cf. Philo at *PH* 1.235); this will help to explain a reference to 'apprehensive reason' (καταληπτικὸς λόγος) at *Math.* 7.144. It is also interesting to see Antiochus making use of contrasting views on the nature of the criterion: is he following the traditional sceptic device of discrediting dogmatist views by pointing out the extent of their disagreement? I think it is more likely that he is attempting to learn a lesson about the kind of dogmatism which would be necessary if one were going to solve the sceptic's objections. A sharp dichotomy between senses and reason is ruinous for the dogmatists' positions. Some (no doubt the Presocratics treated at *Math.* 7.89–140) sought to attribute all cognitive power to reason, others (perhaps the Cyrenaics and Asclepiades) think that the senses do everything and that we can do without reason. Antiochus will eventually conclude that the active mental power pervades the senses and is all but identical with them (*Ac.* 2.30). Could he have been working towards that view here?[9]

### iii Antiochus on Plato

The third passage where Antiochean influence cannot be reasonably doubted is the section on Plato (7.141–4). For the initial interpretation of *Tim.* 28a is supported at 143 by reference to an interpretation of 'comprehensive reason' (περιληπτικὸς λόγος). This in turn is ascribed to 'the Platonics'. There is no question that these 'Platonics' were not the Middle Platonists of the second century A.D. for whom the term περίληψις attracted no special attention.[10] The interpretation of 'comprehensive reason' is also so devoid of ontological or metaphysical considerations that it is clearly late Hellenistic rather than Middle Platonic. Antiochus of Ascalon naturally attracted the description 'Platonic' because he deserted values associated with 'Academics'. In Sextus' day 'Academic' always suggested an allegiance to some form of scepticism, however mild, while 'Platonic' suggested an adherence to some version of Plato's doctrines.[11] Antiochus could be called 'from the Academy' (7.201) with perfect truth, but 'Academic' is a description of him which later authors prefer to avoid.[12] There seemed to be some doubt in Sextus' source at *PH* 1.220 as to whether Antiochus' school, so clearly separate from that of Philo and Charmadas, should be called an Academy at all.[13] Thus Antiochus, the supreme example of a dogmatist who claimed to follow Plato, naturally attracted the description 'Platonic'.

The epistemology so curiously read into *Tim.* 28a is as follows. The 'comprehensive reason' possesses both truth and evident clarity. That is to say (a) reason, in judging the truth, must make evident clarity its starting-point, i.e. its premises must be evident; and (b) evident clarity, since it is not in itself a sufficient guarantee of truth, requires to be judged by reason in order to distinguish what merely appears evidently from what truly subsists. Antiochus' message is that the two forces interlock in all cognitive activity. Furthermore, when the reason judges the truth of the evident information, it requires the assistance of sensation. For it is through sensation that it receives the evident appearance, so as to be able to produce intelligence (νόησις) and knowledge (ἐπιστήμη) of the truth.

Sextus' garbled account is probably an abridged version of what he had read in Antiochus, since the line of thought is

ANTIOCHUS IN THE NEW ACADEMY

less than clear, and he can scarcely have wanted to record at length an interpretation of Plato which would have been laughed at by any Platonist of his own day. It is significant that he does not present the interpretation of Plato on his own authority. He knows well enough that his material is controversial. A full appraisal of *Antiochus'* interpretation must take into account how it could have been related to *Tim.* 28a. Antiochus cannot have quoted that passage and gone on to explain an important concept from it without relating the explanation to the original in some visible manner.

The most obvious feature of the Platonic original is the sharp dichotomy: external *being* is 'comprehended' (περιληπτόν) by intelligence (νόησις) with reason, while *becoming* is opinable through opinion with sensation. The quotation is curtailed at 7.142 in such a way that one would understand *becoming* to be 'comprehended' as well as *being*, weakening the dichotomy to some degree; this is possibly intentional,[14] and not without justification since Plato does apply the term to *becoming* later (28c1, 52a7). Clearly Antiochus does want to get a 'comprehensive' power involved with assessing the evidence of our senses at a fairly elementary level. But how does he explain the fact that Plato does not associate reason, let alone 'comprehensive' reason, with the cognition of things of this world? His own reason has to span the gap between sensation and intelligible truth; Plato's would seem to be confined to the latter realm.

Antiochus' solution is not difficult to reconstruct. In short Plato's 'opinion' (δόξα) which apprehends the visible world in conjunction with sensation is interpreted as 'doxastic' reason. A parallel may be found at *Didasc.* 4 (p. 154.22–9 Hermann), which also interprets *Tim.* 28a. The reason which apprehends *being* is 'epistemonic', while that which apprehends *becoming* is 'doxastic'. This terminology (ἐπιστημονικός–δοξαστός–δοξαστικός) is found at various points of Sextus' doxography, in relation to Xenophanes and Parmenides (110–11, 114), Speusippus and Xenocrates (145–9), and Arcesilaus (157); the adjective *opinabilis* (= δοξαστός) is used when giving the

Antiochean view of *Tim.* 28a at *Ac.* 1.31. So Antiochus had the same tools at his disposal for interpreting the passage as did the author of *Didasc.*

Asked for evidence that Antiochus is using the concepts of an 'epistemonic' reason (operating in the sphere of *being*) and a 'doxastic' reason (operating on *becoming*), one should first point out that it was not in Antiochus' interests to draw attention to the double reason, for he himself was trying to smooth over the dichotomy in the Platonic original. But when pressed one may easily point to significant details in 7.144. Firstly one notes that in judging evident presentations, apparently with the purpose of establishing which clear sense-based evidence may be used as the premises for epistemonic demonstration, reason uses the sensations as its assistant (σύνεργος). In judging such appearances the reason could not, in Platonic or Academic thought, lead to more than a highly probable opinion; it would therefore be thought of quite reasonably as opinion-giving reason; and *Tim.* 28a in fact speaks of opinion (which has to be interpreted as some opinion-giving cognitive process) as joining with the sensations in this-worldly acts of cognition. Plato's 'opinion' is linking up with sensation in the same manner as Antiochus' 'reason'. So Antiochus' notion of sensation as an assistant is based quite simply on the μετὰ αἰσθήσεως in Plato.

Secondly one notes that after the preliminary stage, in which reason has been judging the evident appearances, it goes on to exercise intelligence (νόησις) and knowledge of the truth. Here, I should maintain, we see the Antiochean interpretation of the words νοήσει μετὰ λόγου as 'by formation of universal concepts [cf. 7.217ff] with *epistemonic* reasoning'. After doxastic reason has judged one's sense-presentations, the epistemonic reason is able to *form* and to *build upon* universal concepts. The process is virtually the same as at *Ac.* 2.30, where the mind first operates through the senses, finding the material to be relied upon; from some reliable material it builds universal concepts, which supply the starting-point of logical demonstration leading to knowledge. It is similarly close to the processes described in the account of Peripatetic epistemology at 7.219—25. The four cognitive forces involved (sensation, doxastic reason, epistemonic reason, and concept-grasping) appear together at *Didasc.* 4 (p. 155.31—2 etc.), entrenched in school-Platonism.

The main differences between the position attributed to Plato here and that which Antiochus subsequently adopted for himself are concerned only with the relation of the theory to Stoic 'apprehension'. Later he will argue that evident clarity is absent from all the empty hallucinations of madmen, drunkards, and dreamers; he does so in such a way as to imply that evident clarity is a sufficient guarantee of truth (*Ac.* 2.51 and 45).[15] In this interpretation of Plato it is no such guarantee. Secondly Antiochus in the *Academica* insists that universal concepts, to be of any use, must be built on infallible sensations, i.e. on Stoic 'apprehensions' (2.22); there may well be a similar feeling present at *Math.* 7.144, but it is not brought out. Finally the 'comprehensive' reason which was seen to operate in Plato was described at 7.144 as 'equal to the apprehensive' (ἴσον τῷ καταληπτικῷ). The phrase is enigmatic; to the conservative Academic it would probably have suggested already that Plato was being credited with a Stoic epistemology; to others it may have seemed only to claim that Plato's epistemological force had all the effectiveness of that of the Stoics, perhaps without being open to the same objections. At least it was man's reason and not the presentation upon which the act of apprehension depended. Philo would have little to complain about yet.

What does Antiochus mean by 'comprehensive' reason here? Platonic usage does nothing to justify his assumption that it is a technical term of Plato's. The verb περιλαμβάνειν is frequently used in the dialogues to indicate the process by which a plurality or totality is apprehended as one single form,[16] but it is not a specialized epistemological term. At *Math.* 7.97, in the apparently Posidonian section of the doxography, we meet the common mathematical use of περιληπτικός, but it helps us little. We have to look to the Epicureans to find a technical concept of περίληψις, for περιληπτῶς at *Ep. ad Her.* 40, περιληπτικῷ τρόπῳ (*On*

*Nature*, book 28, 31.5.9 Arr.²), and περιληπτικῶς (*ibid.*, 31.16.1 Arr.²) do have a technical ring. Philodemus *Rh.* 1.2.17, 2.266.5, *D.* 3.15.5–7, and *Piet.* 133.14 also suggest an Epicurean tendency to employ the words at least semi-technically. Unfortunately we do not have an explanation of what they mean for the Epicureans, and the examples given fall short of presenting a single coherent picture of its use.

Lack of a perfect Epicurean precedent should come as no surprise. 'Comprehensive' reason is defined as (a) κοινὸς τῆς ἐναργείας καὶ τῆς ἀληθείας (143) and (b) περιληπτικὸς τῆς ἐναργείας καὶ τῆς ἀληθείας (144). There seems to be a recognition that truth for Plato was separate from the sensations and sense-evidence *as such*, and thus presumably that it belonged to the intellectual plane, for expressions like κατ' ἀλήθειαν ὑπάρχει and κατ' ἀλήθειαν ὑπόκειται (143) as well as ἐπιστήμη τἀληθοῦς (144) are just sufficient to make the reader feel that Plato rather than Epicurus provides the inspiration. Antiochus was well aware that the Platonic *criterion* of truth was removed from the senses (*Ac.* 1.30), and it would have been perfectly natural for him to see Plato's 'truth' itself as something beyond the sensory world. Admittedly 144 speaks of 'the truth in this [sc., evident clarity]', but this need mean no more than that the intelligible truth does manifest itself in evident appearances. Seen in a Platonic context, the 'comprehensive' reason takes on the role of a bridging force between two 'worlds', bringing an awareness of 'truth' into the domain of the senses and premises which are evident (thanks to the senses) into the world of intelligible truth.

Bridging forces are not uncommon in Platonism. While Antiochus' 'perileptic reason' brings truth to sense-evidence and sense-evidence to truth, so Plutarch's *logos* (reason), mixed from Same and Other, becomes intelligible knowledge by *moving* around its *static* object, and becomes sensation by *standing* about its *moving* object (*An. Proc.* 1024f). In effect Sameness must be brought into the realm of Other, and Otherness into the realm of Same (cf. ὁ κοινὸς λόγος at 1025e). Conflicts with other parts of *An. Proc.* suggest that Plutarch must be following a source here.[17]

Another Middle Platonist who tried to make *logos* a bridging force, with reference to *Tim.* 28a, is Severus. He seems to have made *logos* the single cognitive force of the soul, of which intellection (νόησις) and sensation were mere faculties (Proc. *In Tim.* 1.255.5 Diehl); this scheme was presumably intended to act in parallel with his ontology, also based on *Tim.* 27d—28a, which placed τὸ τί as an ultimate category above both being and becoming (*ibid.*, 1.227.15).

Did Antiochus already know of such interpretations of the *Timaeus* which made reason (*logos*) a bridging force between intelligible and sensible spheres? If, as is plausible, those sections of the doxography which reflect Posidonius' views on like-by-like cognition (92—109, 115—19) are not a post-Antiochean addition, then Antiochus himself must have been influenced by Posidonius' picture of the Pythagoro-Platonic world-soul as an intermediate entity, designed to apprehend both intelligible and sensible entities as well as other intermediates (Plut. *An. Proc.* 1023bc, cf. *Math.* 7.119). One notes that *logos* is a most important feature of the Platonic world-soul, and that Posidonius makes *logos* the judge of all (probably for Pythagoreans *and* Platonists) at *Math.* 7.93; it is presumably by virtue of its being or possessing *logos* that the world-soul is thought to apprehend all kinds of 'ideas' (including mathematical form and the forms immanent in matter) at *Math.* 7.119.

The influence of Posidonius has scarcely been proven, and would certainly have been limited. The basic idea that *logos* could be a bridge between the intelligible and the sensible may have been borrowed. Posidonius may have made some use of the term 'perileptic'; for it appears at *Math.* 7.97, and the preposition περί played a prominent role in the traditions of a bridging *logos* known to Plutarch.[18] But that is not to say that he would have had the same concept of a 'comprehensive' reason as Antiochus. The most important influence of the Posidonian account of the Platonic soul may rather have been to establish the importance of the *Timaeus* in Antiochus' mind; other Academics are unlikely to have given the work the same weight as far as its *epistemological* content was concerned.

## iv The Presocratics

Antiochus' view of the Presocratics is of particular relevance because Augustine tells us that he made appeals to the ancient physicists.[19] To have claimed that these thinkers regarded the sensations as trustworthy would have been a challenge to the orthodox view of the Academy, but if *Math.* 7.89ff is from Antiochus he was at least able to present the Presocratic assault on the senses in a context which showed their confidence in knowledge. The emphasis in the sections dealing with Thales to Democritus (89—140) falls on the Presocratic trust in reason, in *logos* of one type or another. The things that they dealt with are described as those whose apprehension is won through the faculty of reason (89), making it clear from the outset that the writer believes in apprehension of such things himself.

Section 90 introduces material on Anaxagoras which Burkhard recognizes as Academic, though it is observed that he is using a sense-based 'trust' ($\pi\iota\sigma\tau\iota\varsigma$) to demonstrate the 'untrustworthiness' ($\dot{\alpha}\pi\iota\sigma\tau\iota\alpha$) of the senses. In 91 a most unhelpful parallel with Asclepiades is noted; it is interesting that Asclepiades is seen to be using sensation as a judging-power, for we read at 201—2 that Antiochus appeared to regard sensation as Asclepiades' criterion. The point of the comparison with Asclepiades had probably been lost when Sextus abridged his source.

After the section on the Pythagoreans (92—109), which is probably influenced by Posidonius throughout, we have a view of Xenophanes which Hirzel recognized as being non-sceptic in character, comparing it with the more rigorously sceptic account of the thinker at 7.49—52.[20] The terminology of 'doxastic' and 'epistemonic' reason has been mentioned above, but one should also note here the equation of 'doxastic' reason with $\tau\dot{o}\nu\ \tau o\tilde{\upsilon}\ \epsilon\dot{\iota}\kappa\dot{o}\tau o\varsigma\ \ldots\ \dot{\epsilon}\chi\dot{o}\mu\epsilon\nu o\nu$. This is virtually to claim that Xenophanes approached the physical world on the same terms as Plato had done in the *Timaeus*: scarcely an indication of deep-rooted scepticism.

The section on Parmenides (111–14) is fascinating, and sees him as in direct conflict with Xenophanes (who is often thought of elsewhere as an influence upon him).[21] It is easy enough to see Parmenides rejecting 'doxastic' reason in favour of the 'epistemonic' variety, but why quote the whole prologue (most of which is irrelevant), missing out the final two lines supplied by Simplicius (which would have been much more relevant, if rather damaging for the interpretation given)?[22] Why go to such lengths to see Parmenides giving importance to the senses of sight and hearing at 112–13? And why then quote B7 which appears to challenge the authority of eye and ear?

The first interpretation of Empedocles may be left aside as Posidonian in detail, but the second again presents matters of interest. Empedocles is credited with the view that *correct* reason is the criterion of knowledge, and that this is divided into two, divine and human. He is supposed to opt for the latter as the criterion, the former being beyond man's reach; while by contrast Heraclitus (127) is supposed to adopt the divine reason, rejecting private human wisdom (131). Thus we are presented with one Presocratic who favoured each of four types of reason: 'doxastic' (Xenophanes, 110), 'epistemonic' (Parmenides, 111–14), correct 'human' (Empedocles, 122–5), and 'divine' (Heraclitus, 126–34). This is important, as it already shows quite clearly how the source is imposing upon the Presocratics those divisions of *logos* which are later to be found in a pedestrian Platonist handbook.[23]

As in the case of Parmenides, the amount of quotation, all from early in the work (Empedocles B2 and B4) and much of it giving only minimal support, is quite striking. Interpretation is rather more credible than in the case of Parmenides. The hand of Antiochus is in my view particularly evident at 124, where it is claimed that, although Empedocles condemns the senses in B2, he is nevertheless prepared to regard the information received from them as reliable *when reason is in control of them*. A distinction between the irrational sensations and rationally-controlled sensations was needed to explain why Parmenides was said to reject the 'trust' ($\pi i\sigma\tau\iota\varsigma$) of the senses at 111, when 112 shows him employing them as guides and instruments *on the path of reason*. Similarly Heraclitus will be found to reject the *irrational* sensations at 126, while giving the sensory pores important work as passages *through which reason can pass* at 129–30. The importance of the distinction may be seen when the last two words of Plato's phrase τὸ δὲ δόξῃ μετὰ αἰσθήσεως ἀλόγου δοξαστόν (*Tim.* 28a) are omitted at 142. It is certainly a strange place for the quotation to have terminated, but *Ac.* 1.31 shows that Antiochus would not have been shy of including the term δοξαστόν. This seems to suggest that he had a positive desire to close the quotation before the term ἀλόγου ('irrational'). For it was not *irrational* sensation which he wanted to see as a necessary cognitive power, but sensation as guided by 'doxastic' reason: sensation made rational. For since 'doxastic *logos*' was the equivalent of 'likely *logos*' (εἰκὼς λόγος, 110, on Xenophanes) it was scarcely a pejorative term; the whole of Plato's much-respected *Timaeus* had, after all, been composed 'in accord with the likely *logos*'.[24] One need not doubt that Antiochus was willing to see the Presocratics condemning *irrational* sensation while approving sensation under rational control; *Ac.* 2.30 shows clearly just how anxious he was to see the mind involving itself in the act of sensation from the very beginning.

I have little further to say about Heraclitus as portrayed in this account,[25] and will conclude by noting that either Sextus or his source seems to have found Democritus' attitude somewhat puzzling. To begin with he appears to be accepting the traditional Academic view of him (135–7).[26] At 138–9 he sees Democritus, like other Presocratics, as one who espouses the cause of reason at the expense of the senses. The most interesting view of him, however, is that attributed to Diotimus at 140. Here the only supporting texts are from Anaxagoras (B21a) and Plato (*Phdr.* 237b), but one suspects that it is the interpretation that Antiochus would have been most interested in (why else place it last?). Democritus is said

105

to have made the phenomena the criterion of the unclear (after Anaxagoras); the notion (ἔννοια) criterion of the 'inquiry' (ζήτησις),[27] after Plato's observation that one should first establish what one is looking for; and the affections criteria of moral choice. Of most relevance to us is the second of these criteria, owing to Stoic and Academic interest in 'common notions' during Antiochus' formative years. For the Stoics the notion actually did fulfil the role of determining what one is searching for, and it was their answer to the problem set by 'Meno' at Meno 80d (see Plut. fr. 215f = SVF 2.104); and this surely shows that the Diotimus involved was not the early (or mythical) Democritean, but rather the Stoic of the late second century B.C. mentioned by Athenaeus (13.611b) and Diogenes Laertius (10.3).

## v Post-Platonic philosophy

The discussion of Speusippus at 145–6 is designed primarily to explain how the 'epistemonic' character of reason can be imparted to sensation too when it is properly trained. The discussion of Xenocrates which follows (147–9) is designed rather to show how he accepted truth as a necessary property of sensation (though not the same kind of truth as can be found in knowledge). Error was banished to the world of opinion, where reason apparently tried to draw conclusions from our sensations. The examples of Speusippean and Xenocratean epistemology were probably carefully selected so as to show a gradually increasing faith in the senses within Plato's school before Arcesilaus allegedly changed things. The value of these passages for the assessment of the Old Academy and its epistemology is consequently limited.

The report of Arcesilaus' arguments is designed to reflect the normal Fourth Academic view that he was only acting in response to Stoic epistemology.[28] It paints Arcesilaus' conclusions as those which the Stoic ought to come to, though not necessarily ones with which Arcesilaus would have disagreed. The presumption that Arcesilaus, like Carneades at 166, had to inquire actively[29] about the moral goal (158), and that he would need some criterion for the purpose, only demonstrates how little the Fourth Academy had sought to justify complete suspension of judgment. They do not seem to have thought that life without assent would be desirable, or at very least they do not appear to have thought that it was possible to be a teacher of philosophy and offer no positive advice on how one should live one's life.

There is much that could be said about the accounts of Cyrenaic and Epicurean epistemology (190–200, 203–16),[30] but I suspect that the report of Peripatetic epistemology (217–26) may be that which best reflects the philosophy of the *Canonica*. This is perhaps not very surprising, for there seems to have been a movement within the Academy towards accepting the possibility that the Peripatetics were broadly correct: correct in saying that there were true presentations clearly impressed on the mind, and equally correct in refusing to add that such presentations ought to be such that they could not be false. Cicero *in propria persona* claims that he has no quarrel with Peripatetic epistemology at *Fin.* 5.76; similar remarks are used at *Ac.* 2.112, though the tone is rather less conciliatory – probably because Cicero (or his source) is trying to present a more orthodox impression, thus avoiding charges of lying about the Academic position (2.98: 'nec vero quicquam ita dicam ut quisquam id fingi suspicetur'; cf. 2.12 'etsi enim mentitur', 2.18 'aperte mentitur'). The Peripatetic position as outlined at 2.112 ('id percipi posse . . . quod impressum esset e vero') differs little from that of certain Academics at 2.34 who admit that there is something evident ('verum illud quidem impressum in animo atque mente'), but deny that it can be apprehended (*comprendi*). Both recognize a truth which is impressed upon the mind, and accept such truths as evident; the only difference is that the Academics, because they are wont to work with the Stoic definition of apprehension, are forced to deny that such an impression is sufficient for apprehension. The difference could be regarded as no more than a terminological dispute. From S.E. *PH* 1.235 and from *Fin.* 5.76 one gathers that Philo at least was not disposed to continue even this quarrel.

And if he were moving towards acceptance of the Peripatetic epistemology, there can be little doubt that Antiochus would have been moving in the same direction.

The main advance attributed to the Peripatetics is the extension of evident clarity to cover intelligibles as well as sensibles. The Platonic division of 'the nature of things' into intelligibles and sensibles is retained, with sensation as the criterion of the latter and intellection (νόησις) of the former (217). But whereas Plato was only seen to be using evident clarity from the senses (141—4), the Peripatetics saw it as a property which could belong to intellection equally well (218: on the authority of Theophrastus). This would of course mean that the Peripatetics effectively used the Fourth-Academic 'criterion' of 'what appears evidently to sensation and intellection'.[31]

The means by which the Peripatetics extended evident clarity to intelligibles was quite simply to see a mechanical process of concept-building, beginning with sensation which was evident, and proceeding via imagination and memory, to νοῦς (= νόησις) and its corresponding potency διάνοια; also to ἔννοια, ἐπιστήμη, and τέχνη (219—24). The purely empirical account of the production of intelligible concepts allows the compelling clarity of the senses to become a property of concepts also. We may find here the roots of Antiochus' insistence in the *Academica* (2.22—6) that infallible sensation is an essential basis for infallible concepts, memory, *ars*, and *scientia*. We also see in this Peripatetic section the quasi-Aristotelian doctrine that sensation comes first τάξει but intelligence comes first δυνάμει, which works behind the scenes at *Ac.* 2.30 and appears in Clement (*Strom.* 2.13.2).[32] We see a clearly Hellenistic view of opinion (δόξα), regarded as a 'yielding' and assent to a sense-presentation (225). And finally, with no warning from what has gone before (except perhaps the observation that intelligence is prior to sensation potentially), we are told that intelligence is the criterion in the role of the craftsman, while sensation is the criterion in the role of his measuring-tool: his *canon*.[33]

Quite obviously, if the source was indeed Antiochus'

*Canonica*, then the identification of the *canon* with the senses must have meant that he was claiming greater importance for the senses than the Academy had been used to allowing them. By this time a prominent Academic view was that the senses were (or could be) healthy enough, but that they lacked accuracy;[34] but here it is implied that they would have to be accurate too if our notions of memory, skill, knowledge, and wisdom were to have any meaning; I suspect that Antiochus found it impossible to believe in any cognitive activity which was not rooted in the senses. But he still adhered to his belief that sensation and mental powers had to be present together, the one being impotent without the other. Though he acknowledged that many had seen only one of the two as the criterion, he probably believed that this was because the forces of sensation and intelligence were so closely linked that they were often seen as a single power: *either* sensation *or* reason.

Antiochus' desire to give the senses and the mind a role to play at all levels (as seen previously in the interpretation of Plato) had probably been the cause of additional difficulties for him. The Fourth Academic 'criterion' of τὰ πρὸς αἴσθησίν τε καὶ νόησιν ἐναργῶς φαινόμενα was fairly obviously meant to regard sensation and intellection as separate, firstly because that is the way in which Plato's authority might be sought for it, and secondly because that is the way it finally comes to be used in Galen.[35] Moreover the Peripatetics are themselves credited with separate criteria, sensation and intellection, for sensibles and for intelligibles. This would have to be twisted a little to yield an Antiochean position. Accordingly there is a shift from using sensation and intellection (νόησις) to sensation and intelligence (νοῦς) in 218 so that intelligence might appear prior δυνάμει to sensation. At 222 intelligence (νοῦς) appears as a special name for the actual thinking of a concept, where one would have imagined νόησις to have been more appropriate. Then at 226 we find sensation and intelligence (νοῦς) as the two criteria, the latter replacing intellection (νόησις); and the two now seem to be joint criteria for whatever they judge, instead of separate

109

criteria for sensibles and intelligibles. And 226, being the overall conclusion of the Peripatetic entry, is (according to my theory) the most reliable guide as to the lessons which the reader had been supposed to learn from the section.

If the source is Antiochus' *Canonica*, then he could still claim, I believe, to have been defending the right of 'what appears evidently to sensation and intellection' to be the basic criterion of knowledge and the starting-point from which demonstration must proceed. Like Galen (*Plac.* 9.778) he could claim on the basis of the doxography presented that such a criterion was acceptable to *everybody* from Carneades to the Stoics themselves. In practice, however, it was not so much this criterion which he was defending (the criterion being essentially two-fold in Philo, to judge from Aenesidemus in Photius (170a37—8), but rather the sensations themselves: not the irrational sensations (see iv above), but the sensations when controlled by reason.

The defence of sensation comes to the fore at the conclusion of the account of Stoic epistemology. Here the reader may feel that the source had agreed with the later Stoics, who had only regarded the apprehensive presentation as the criterion *when it had no obstacle*. In such a case, it is claimed, it would be evident (257) and entirely sufficient to drag us into assent. Then follows a defence of sensation-based dogmatism in general, pointing out man's eagerness to receive the clearest presentation possible, as being the basis of 'the trust of apprehension' (ἡ τῆς καταλήψεως πίστις, 258). At 259 we read that the denial that presentation is the criterion is self-refuting, since appeal could only be made to another presentation; and also that the sensory powers are like a light given to us by nature. Finally appeal is made to the absurdity of accepting the existence of things, and slandering the sense-perceptions through which we are aware of their existence (260).

It would, I think, be wrong for those who regard Antiochus' *Canonica* as the source to see these four paragraphs as a direct attack on his Academic colleagues. They occur within the account of more recent Stoic doctrine, and must reflect geniune Stoic arguments. The chief reason for suspecting our source's sympathy with them is the rhetorical presentation of those arguments and the strength of much of the language. Just as Antiochus had felt earlier (see i above) that there was positive assistance in New Academic arguments for anybody desiring to reach the truth, so one suspects that he felt these Stoic objections to Academic doubt to be worthy of close attention.

An important aspect of the account of the Stoic position is that while great capital is made out of the Stoic inability to arrive at an adequate account of Zeno's doctrine of presentations (228ff), no attack is launched against Zeno himself. Perhaps we are seeing in Antiochus, as in the Middle Stoa, a desire to return to the position of Zeno, coupled with a distaste for much of what was said by his successors, particularly by Chrysippus. Zeno is Antiochus' hero in the *Academica*, Chrysippus is used only by his opponents.[36] And Zeno, of course, was the pupil of an Academic.[37]

It is probably unsafe to speculate about the epistemological stance finally adopted by Antiochus in the *Canonica* on the basis of doxographical reports allegedly deriving from it. *For practical purposes* he could certainly have proposed evident clarity as an acceptable criterion for settling disputes, since he sees all post-Socratic philosophies as recognizing such a criterion. But as a criterion of knowledge, of sure and irreversible apprehension of the truth, he can have had nothing but the Stoic criterion to offer. As in the *Academica*, he must have been ready to admit what Philo was far less sure of: if the Stoic definition of the criterion cannot be established, then 'percipi nihil posse concedimus', 2.18. There is no indication in the doxography that the source thought he could establish the Stoic definition as actually referring to an existent class of presentations; so he may well have found himself condemned to side with the 'sceptic' for the moment. But his obvious confidence in the senses and in man's mental powers make it certain that he would already have been profoundly dissatisfied with such a conclusion. Was not our possession of knowledge and technical skill self-evident? Did we not have natural notions of both, which ought to be quite sufficient to prove at least their existence? And if knowledge and technical skill existed, was it not essential that we should recognize some genuine criterion of knowledge which fulfilled the Stoic requirement?

## vi Concluding remarks

That *Math.* 7.89—260 is rendered intelligible by the assumption that Antiochus is the overall source should not be doubted. But more than mere consistency is required to prove the hypothesis, especially with regard to the section on Presocratic philosophy and the later discussions of Epicureanism, Peripateticism, and Stoicism. Why should the hypothesis be believed?

It should be noted initially that the doxography ends with Carneades' Academy and the Middle Stoa. Developments in epistemology since that date, including the Philonian and Antiochean positions, which were considered important enough to feature at *PH* 1.235, are not mentioned. Middle Platonic epistemology is ignored; so is Potamo's criterion (D.L. 1.21); the epistemologies of the medical schools are usually passed over. It is not because Sextus has no interest in such positions, or because he did not know of them; it is because (i) they were not present in his source and (ii) that source was not added to by Sextus to any appreciable extent. Antiochus' position is not mentioned because one does not include one's own position in a doxography; Philo's position is not mentioned because the source antedates the Roman Books.

While no post-Antiochean author is mentioned, a few persons contemporary with or slightly earlier than Antiochus do feature within the doxography for reasons other than the need to explain their position on the criterion: Asclepiades (91), Posidonius (93), and Diotimus the Stoic (140). There is every chance that they are mentioned because of their importance to the source's contemporary environment, and this gives considerable credibility to the notion of a pre-*Sosus* Antiochean source.

A strong argument against the doxography's having been devised by *any* sceptic is the strongly historicist account of the development of philosophy: Presocratics regard *logos* of some kind as the criterion, but condemn the senses, then Plato chooses a particular kind of *logos* which reconciles the intelligence with the evidence of the senses. The choice of Plato as the bringer of a new regard for the senses indicates that the source sees Plato as a critical figure in the development of an *empirical* epistemology: a view which could only be held by one who had a similar regard for Plato and for empiricism. Old Academics contribute towards this empiricism, while the New Academy introduces problems which the empiricist must confront, playing (for a while) a key critical role. Hellenistic philosophies then complete the rescue of the senses. A good Pyrrhonist should not have so clear a view of the development, indeed the progress, of epistemology; his doubts must extend to historical matters, as Theodosius (D.L. 9.70) showed.

It is interesting that in the course of the doxography no comparison between any position and scepticism is made, nor is any remark made on behalf of the sceptic school. Little subsequent use is made of the doxography, whose themes are never referred to. No critique of individual epistemologies is ever to be presented (apart from Academic material within the doxography), and some views relevant to the future discussion (Dicaearchus, Aenesidemus according to Heraclitus, and Strato, 349–50) are not mentioned in the doxography. Indeed the following discussion could easily have proceeded without any doxography at all, let alone one as detailed as this.

Next one may question why there appear to be discrepancies between this doxography and *PH* 1.210–41, where Sextus does involve himself directly. Why is Arcesilaus viewed as virtually 'Pyrrhonian' there (232), while his 'scepticism' is played down at *Math.* 7.150–8? Why is Plato treated as a controversial figure there (221ff), when one position has been unhesitatingly attributed to him at *Math.* 7.141–4? Why is Protagoras, who had positive views at

*PH* 1.216—19, not treated at *Math.* 7.89—140? Not because Protagoras was earlier said to have rejected the criterion, for Sextus knew that this was only the view of 'certain persons' (60, 64); but rather because Protagoras does not fit into the source's dogma that Pre-Platonic thinkers saw reason as the criterion.

One must reject the view that Sextus' doxography at *Math.* 7.89—260 is original. But could there have been a plurality of sources? This is, I am afraid, most unlikely. Sextus did not need to get history correct; he only needed a general picture of the diversity and range of previous opinion. If one book could provide this, why should he search for more? Antiochus had tackled the opinions of all schools, and it suited Sextus to adopt the doxography of a prime opponent of the sceptics. Plagiarism was a standard practice of the time, attributed by Porphyry not only to Euclides, Democritus, and Proclinus (*V. Plot.* 20) but also to Ptolemy (*Ad Ptol. Harm.* p. 5.7—16 Düring). It was respectable!

Given that one should look for a single source, one from the first century B.C., why choose Antiochus? He is mentioned twice in the doxography, and he was an important epistemologist. Other candidates do not exist. Identifiable Posidonian material (93—109, 115—19) is not of a doxographic character or primarily concerned with the criterion. Pupils of Antiochus would have followed his later views, not those found here. Aenesidemus could have been an intermediate source, but as there is no Pyrrhonist material here, one would still have to demand some source for Aenesidemus. Hirzel (*Untersuchungen*, vol. 3, pp. 493—524) put the case for Antiochus; Sedley has confirmed this view with particular reference to the treatment of Epicurus;[38] the theory works as long as one takes Antiochus to be still nominally a part of Philo's Academy; it should be accepted on those terms.

# CHAPTER 6

# GOD'S THOUGHTS AS OBJECTS OF KNOWLEDGE

## i Finding a role for Ideas

As one continues to pursue the question of Fourth Academic influence on the revived Platonism, one is forced to consider the much-discussed origin of a characteristic Middle Platonic doctrine: that the Ideas are the thoughts of God, his objects of contemplation, existing within his mind rather than without. Scholars have been chiefly concerned about whether this doctrine should be traced back to Antiochus of Ascalon or to Posidonius. One must now widen this inquiry, asking (a) is it possible that the Fourth Academy should have been responsible for such an interpretation, bearing in mind that they were not averse to doctrine, and that the interest in Plato's works was already alive? (b) if Antiochus was responsible for the doctrine, did he arrive at it before or after his split with Philo, and was there any epistemological purpose behind it?

The Ideas had always been objects of the Platonic creator's contemplation, but it is true to say that this was not a pronounced feature of Plato's Theory of Ideas. On one occasion the Idea is actually regarded as a *creation* of God (*Rep.* 597b); this feature could be coupled with its role as object of contemplation to produce the doctrine that it is a thought-invention of God's mind, and hence a very secondary feature of Platonic ontology; but Middle Platonism did not usually regard the Ideas as a secondary ontological feature, nor did it make anything of the suggestion that they were creations of God. On the contrary, it was usual to claim that Ideas and God, together with matter, constituted the three separate first-principles of the universe.[1] This doctrine is found alongside the view that Ideas are thoughts of God in Middle Platonism,[2] but it ill accords with the view that the Ideas must be understood *primarily* as thoughts of God; to understand

115

them thus would be to allow that they have no existence outside the mind of God; this in turn would suggest that they are dependent upon, hence secondary to, God.

The apparent contradiction in established Middle Platonism, which strongly emphasizes that the Ideas are thoughts of God but which still regards them as a separate first-principle, may perhaps be explained in the following way: originally only God and matter were acknowledged as first-principles, as by Theophrastus (*Phys. Dox.* fr. 9), so that the Ideas were consequently *reduced to* thoughts of God; subsequently the status of the Ideas was lifted to that of first-principle, suggesting that they had independent existence, but their status as thoughts of God continued to receive emphasis. The Antiochean account of Platonic first-principles certainly did consider only God and matter in this role (Cic. *Ac.* 1.24); an account apparently influenced by Posidonius[3] likewise deals only with God and matter, finding no substantial role for the Ideas to play in the Platonic universe. Thus, if we see the concept of Ideas as God's thoughts as the work of Antiochus or Posidonius, it is likely that it grew up with a doctrine of only two first-principles, God and matter. At some stage Platonists, though perhaps not the Platonizing Pythagoreans,[4] introduced the Ideas as a separate first-principle, and thus compromised the dependence of these Ideas upon God. As Dillon has shown, this has caused apparent conflict within the system of Atticus, who at one time appears to emphasize the role of the Ideas as plans or patterns made by the creator-God, but who is actually criticized by Porphyry for having regarded them as self-subsisting entities *outside* God's mind, no doubt in accordance with his doctrine that there are three first-principles.[5] It could be claimed that much the same tensions exist within the system of [Alcinous]. In consequence one finds that we lack statements from the Platonism of the second century A.D. to the effect that the Ideas do not exist outside the mind of God, even though the doctrine emerges with Plotinus.[6]

It is to first-century authors, such as Philo Judaeus and Seneca, that we must look if we are to discern anything of the earlier nature of the doctrine of Ideas as thoughts of God. Here there is no doubt that we are confronted with a doctrine of Ideas as mathematical patterns.[7] Mathematical patterns in perpetual existence within a divine intellect inevitably remind one of the Platonic world-soul rather than either the Good of the *Republic* or the Demiurge of the *Timaeus*,[8] of an all-pervading immanent God of the Stoic type rather than of a transcendent divinity. Thus one can have little quarrel with the standard view of this doctrine: that is an attempt to assimilate the Ideas to the principles of seminal reason which combine to constitute the Stoic Logos:[9] rationally-determined pattern elements belonging to the Stoic immanent God in his rational aspect.

If one regards mere syncretism as sufficient justification for the emergence of the doctrine, it is necessary to proceed no further. Ideally, however, one would like to suppose that there was some legitimate philosophical purpose behind the placement of the Ideas within the mind of God. The Ideas had traditionally played both a metaphysical/physical role and an epistemological role, but no additional metaphysical/physical function is facilitated by confining the Ideas to the divine mind; on the contrary, the positive role which they may play in the physical world will be reduced. Only in so far as they hold the attention of the providential divinity can they achieve order on earth; they must operate only via him. There seems to be no room for them to be reflected directly in the material 'receptacle' as in the *Timaeus* (50c ff).

We search then for an epistemological reason for the innovation. It is immediately obvious that the Ideas provide objects of thought for a mind-God,[10] but external Ideas would have been no less suitable an object than internal ones. As objects of *our* knowledge, the Ideas would seem virtually inaccessible when confined to God's mind, except in so far as the divine spark which the Stoics held to be within us could lead us to those same divine thoughts.

At first sight, therefore, the new view of the Ideas as internal thoughts of God could achieve for them no new philosophical purpose. It merely makes certain Platonic entities, which would otherwise mystify the average late Hellenistic or Roman reader, rather more intelligible; in particular it gives them a location. It also accords with certain principles of economy which have long attracted philosophers, and with the desire to have no 'loose ends' within one's tightly-knit system. It *explains away* the Ideas rather than giving them some bold new role.

We must, however, bear in mind that both Philonian and Antiochean Academics professed to be of a Platonic character, and were therefore under some pressure to utilize the Ideas in some way. Cicero gives them a paradigmatic role in a famous passage of his *Orator* (8ff), and Varro, presumably following Antiochus, also used them in the allegorical interpretation of Minerva-Athena's emergence from the head of Jupiter-Zeus (Aug. *CD* 7.28). Varro at least accepts that the existence of the Ideas is dependent upon the supreme God, while Cicero can give the impression that they exist only within minds,[11] whether our minds or God's.

It is interesting that neither the Antiochean nor the Philonian account of Platonic physics which Cicero offers in the *Academica* refers to the Ideas, even though the opportunity to do so is there (*Ac.* 1.24ff, 2.118). The Antiochean account of Platonic epistemology, however, does so explicitly (1.30), while the shorter Philonian account (2.142), being in broad agreement with the other, appears to assume them. Thus I believe that their chief interest was in finding the Ideas an epistemological role, particularly in view of the great importance of epistemology at that time. Their role would thus tend to be confined to the minds of those who grasped them, and this might tend to be thought of as their 'location', as it had been in the Old Academy.[12] From Varro one would suppose that God was their origin, as in Plato's *Republic* book 10 (597bc), but from Cicero's *Orator* one gathers that they were present in other minds besides God's, thus allowing them a place in epistemology. At one point the Antiochean account of the development of philosophy observes that Plato saw something divine about his Ideas (*Ac.* 1.33), apparently making a connexion between Ideas and God, but failing to specify the type of connexion. This lack of concern about the exact relation of Ideas to God tells against those who would see Antiochus as an innovator in the field; he probably did see God as the origin of the Platonic Idea, but there is no hint that he was concerned about their divine origin as much as about man's own ability to grasp universal concepts.

## ii Recollecting the Idea

Put simply, the traditional epistemological role of the Idea was as object of recollected knowledge, the recollection pertaining to an original 'vision' of the Idea while the soul was in its disembodied state before birth. The theory of recollection was known to Cicero (*TD* 1.57) as a way of explaining innate universal concepts, whose existence is also recognized at *TD* 4.53, *Off.* 3.76, and *Top.* 31. He follows the theory of the *Meno* and *Phaedo*, openly identifying Ideas as objects of recollection. Ideas which can be viewed by disembodied souls in general scarcely belong within the mind of a single supreme soul.[13] Does the disembodied soul peer into God's mind? It may not be so strange that God should view what goes on in our minds, but, seeing that we cannot 'view' the internal thoughts of our fellow-men in any sense, it is difficult to imagine us having access to the internal thoughts of God. It was one thing to have access to external objects which God continuously contemplates, but quite another to have access to the inner recesses of his mind.

How then did the disembodied soul have cognitive access to the thoughts of God's mind? Two possibilities present themselves: *either* the disembodied soul is united with God's mind, our small element of divinity merging into the universal divine intellect or *logos*; *or* the disembodied soul is so assimilated to the divine mind that it thinks the same thoughts. The former option seems to accord poorly with the major Platonic dialogues which deal with the fate of the soul after death, for the soul is there treated very much as an individual entity in the discarnate state too: it receives its own rewards and punishments, chooses its own life, and strives to achieve its own *personal* vision of the Ideas (*Phdr.* 248a ff). Only the *Philebus* (30a) might be taken to suggest that our souls are offshoots of a universal rational soul, apt for reunification, and it does not state that such reunification occurs. Not even Stoicism requires the reabsorption of all individual souls at death into their parent, the cosmic divine power.

Thus it is more probable that the disembodied soul was thought to have achieved its intellectual vision of the Ideas by acquisition of the same mental condition as the divine mind: 'great minds think alike'. In this case the Ideas would be genuinely thoughts of God, but they would be (on occasions) our thoughts also, primarily in our discarnate state, secondarily when we free our souls sufficiently from the impediments of the flesh to be able to recollect them in this life.

Behind such a theory would lie the doctrine of the *Timaeus* (41d) that the soul is composed of the same structures as the divine world-soul, though without the same degree of purity. Thus it functions in a similar fashion to the immanent divinity so long as it is free from bodily impediments; similarity of structure and of function will naturally lead it to view the same Idea-patterns, and thus think the same thoughts. But when the human soul is immersed in its body, both the structure and the motions are badly damaged, with the result that we lose nearly all cognitive ability at first (43a ff); in time, however, we have the opportunity to correct the damage and become intelligent (44bc), and to assimilate the motions of our own souls to their kindred motions of the world-soul, thus achieving happiness and the human goal (90a–d).

It is significant that the *Phaedrus*, which tells us most about the discarnate soul's original vision of the Ideas, tells us also that the soul which best follows a God, *and best likens itself to him*, receives the best vision of the Ideas. Bearing in mind that the traditional Middle Platonic goal is assimilation to God, and that when this goal first appears in extant texts it is also related to the Pythagorean injunction 'follow God',[14] one may assume that the revived Platonism would have welcomed the notion that the discarnate soul too relied upon assimilation to a God, or following a God, in order to achieve its supreme vision of the Ideas. A close connexion between the goal of the Platonic philosopher and that of the disembodied soul was clearly desirable, since Plato had gone so far as to describe philosophy as an attempt to free one's soul from the body: a 'practice of death'.[15] Early in the Platonic revival the goal has indeed been an intellectual one,[16] so that the assimilation-process would have led to a cognitive state similar to that of the divine mind imitated: i.e. the Platonic world-soul's heavenly intellect.[17] One has only to allow that some memory-trace of our discarnate God-like thoughts survived into this life, and any recreation of those thoughts, through the pursuit of mental perfection here, may be regarded as an act of recollection.

Indeed it was only traces of the discarnate vision which were thought to survive; early in life they had some bearing upon our conduct,[18] acting like seeds of virtue rather than as Ideas of the virtues.[19] In order to have any intellectual function our memory of the Idea, identified with the Stoic 'natural notion', had to be first awakened, then analysed.[20] Recollection depended upon far more than the mere background memory-trace and the perfection of the mind. The Hellenistic world had talked so long about the mechanical acquisition of universal concepts from basic sense-data that they could not abandon such ideas altogether. Indeed Antiochus seems to have been insistent that this was the only way in which reliable universal notions could arise (*Ac.* 2.21–2, cf. 30); he is able to base his argument for the Stoic criterion in part upon our inability to acquire concepts, memory, knowledge, and art without that criterion (*Ac.* 2.21–7). Thus for him there is no question of fully developed concepts or memories within the soul at birth; he could use only *parvae notitiae* (vague impressions?) of lofty concepts as an innate guide to later knowledge (*Fin.* 5.59), and their role seems to have been moral (supplying the elements of virtue) rather than epistemological. The only way, for him, in which

121

such a trace of innate knowledge could contribute towards the formation of mature universal concepts would have been by subconsciously directing the mind towards the right presentations for concept-building. He relied heavily upon the mind's ability to sort presentations correctly, and it is here above all that he could use an element of latent knowledge. This applies equally to the theory of the *Sosus* (*Ac.* 2.30),[21] and to pre-*Sosus* theory where the Platonic mind was given the job of distinguishing between apparently and actually self-evident presentations (S.E. *Math.* 7.143–4).

Antiochus, however, may not be typical of the new Platonists; one distrusts his tendency to see Platonism as a foreshadowing of Stoicism, as an early and imperfect realization of Zeno's system, which Zeno later 'corrected' (*Ac.* 1.35, 43). One notes, moreover, that his explanation of the Platonic goal of life, as depicted in *De Finibus* 5, is quite incompatible with the Middle Platonic goal of assimilation to God, in so far as it stresses our duty to live in accord with *human* nature, which is bodily as well as psychical (*Fin.* 5.26–45). It is difficult to see how he could have responded to Plato's call towards the vision of the Ideas as long as he made such concessions to the body and to the senses.

This would suggest that if we are to trace the revival of the theory of recollection back beyond *K* (where it appears well developed) we should turn to the Fourth Academy or Posidonius rather than to Antiochus. I do not find Posidonius a likely candidate, since he was under no pressure to follow Plato, and his interest in epistemology is questionable. But is it conceivable that the Fourth Academy, still openly expressing allegiance to Carneades as well as to Plato, could have found a use for all the trimmings of a Platonic epistemology?

Here I must resume where I left off in the introduction. The Fourth Academy, while retaining many doubts about the ability of the senses to supply dependable information, apparently introduced the notion that some things could seem evident to the intellect.[22] They did not deny that things could seem evident to the senses, but continued to claim that the occasional fortuitous presentation could seem evident without in fact being correct. To guard against the occasional fortuitous presentation one needed a number of confirmatory presentations, as in Carneadean theory, all of these, one hoped, being of the evident variety. Our experiences had to be in agreement, the individual's experiences from one moment to the next, and mankind's experiences from one individual to the next. The link between agreement and the evident in Philo of Larissa and other relevant authors is adequately attested.

With regard to sensible particulars it is doubtful whether sufficient agreement can be found. Different individuals must view from different angles and thus receive different impressions; there is no point in viewing an object from the same angle at a different time as objects move and alter, as do attendant circumstances. Presentations concerning individual objects may thus seem evident, but certain verification is impossible. But the individual's sum total of evident impressions concerning a certain kind of object will indeed be instructive; he will be able to build up reliable notions of classes of things, and he will be able to compare his own notions of such classes with others' notions. With reliable notions he may proceed to reliable deductive reasoning and open the door to scientific knowledge. Thus he will distinguish sharply between the knowability of particulars and the knowability of universals.

This opens the door to a return of Platonism, but it still leaves much to be explained, particularly with regard to those concepts which were important to philosophers, the area of Carneades' principal doubts.[23] Those supreme concepts cannot be reached by the normal empirical processes, because there are no sensible particulars able to present us with an *evidently-clear* impression of them (Plato, *Plt.* 286a);[24] such was the concept of equality, employed in the *Phaedo* (74a ff) to demonstrate the necessity for recollected knowledge, other mathematical concepts, and the great moral and aesthetic ideals (justice, beauty, etc.). These then, Plato's 'finest and greatest' (286a5—6) and 'most valuable' (285e4) concepts, are no doubt those of which Antiochus (*Fin.* 5.59) recognizes an innate knowledge-trace ('notitias parvas rerum maximarum'); of which Cicero (*TD* 1.57) recognizes recollection ('tot rerum atque tantarum insitas . . . notiones'). From where could an orthodox Fourth Academic suppose that we could acquire these supreme concepts?

It may be instructive that Cicero, himself an Academic, saw cognitive activity before birth as the *only possible source* (*TD* 1.57); an Academic's scepticism of worldly theories of cognition may well have led him to look favourably upon the Platonic case. He would at least be obliged to argue for as well as against it. His principal doubts would involve the postulation of strange new entities to explain this a priori knowledge. Here, if anywhere, there would be a good case for suspension of judgment. But all the Academic need postulate is the pre-existent Platonic soul in its ideal condition. Modelled on the principles of mathematics, the concepts used by mathematics would be present in it; the virtues and beauty would also be present, as would be perfected cognitive power. The pre-existing Platonic soul was of such a nature as to have cognition of mathematical, moral, and aesthetic ideals, and if all memory were not lost at birth then recollection of these ideals would be possible. No doubt progress towards perfecting our souls in this life would assist recollection by jogging our memories, a process described by Plato in the *Phaedo* (73d). Such a theory could not be dogmatically held by a Fourth Academic, but it could be ardently defended; the Platonic view of the soul was now attracting much attention,[25] and Plutarch was prepared to defend the theory of recollection as the only answer to the problems of epistemology (fr. 215).

Now if the theory of recollection had been revived in this manner, with the intention of avoiding hypostasization of the Ideas, we may see why the Ideas played an epistemological role rather than a metaphysical one in Cicero's *Academica*; why they tend to be confined to the mind, whether God's or ours; why they play no ontological role in the surviving pages of *K*. They are simply present in the ideal structure of soul, primarily and continuously in the world-soul or immanent divinity, secondarily and temporarily in the individual soul. They may be identified with the indivisible essence of *Timaeus* 35a, as by the Posidonians,[26] but this hardly seems necessary. One may call them numbers and shapes in the mind of God, with Seneca *Ep.* 65.7, but one should not forget that they are potentially within all souls, waiting to be recreated and recollected by assimilation to God.

The theory was not even open to the objection of being purely Platonist dogma. The Stoic postulated a divine spark within man, which would assist in bestowing upon him certain desirable qualities characteristic of the divine.[27] He would presumably have some cognizance of the qualities so introduced into his nature. Antiochus of Ascalon employs an innate mini-notion of the virtues.[28] As long as such a God-like element were within us, we should be liable to appreciate certain God-like qualities, whether or not they were described as Ideas. Indeed all the underlying physical or metaphysical theory was a matter upon which judgment ought properly to be suspended: which is why we do not hear as much as we should like about it. But the Fourth Academy was entitled to adhere to the following propositions:

(1)   There are many concepts which this world is incapable of supplying me with accurately.

(2)   I may nevertheless be confident that I have adequately grasped these concepts.

(3)   I thus appear to have confidence in some pre-existing knowledge, which came with my soul at birth.

The above does not constitute a proof that the Fourth Academy introduced either the Platonic Ideas or the theory of recollection. But it must be noted that if it was they who did so, and if they did so in this rather unassuming way, it is an excellent explanation of why the reintroduction of the theories makes no great impression upon our sources: it was as tentative theory and not as established doctrine that they were introduced.

As for the notion that the Ideas were thoughts of God, we have seen reason to believe that it emerged alongside the view that (i) we should imitate God and assimilate our minds to

125

his, while (ii) we acquire our universal concepts by primarily empirical means. Our thoughts can only become like God's by imitation. Such appears to have been the view of Thrasyllus (Porph. *In Ptol. Harm.* p. 12.8–28 Düring). There is a *logos* of the Forms, which constitutes the knowledge and discursive thought of the God who leads the universe, and according to which nature produces everything in the cosmos. That *logos* is seminally present in the universe and is unfolded in the activities of nature: but it is present in scientific speculation, technical products, and the calculations of human wisdom by *imitation* (p. 12.24, cf. 12.13). A reference back to this *logos* at 13.21 ensures that 13.21–14.28 still follows Thrasyllus, and in this passage we find:

(a) a definite relation (at 14.4–5 and throughout) to the philosophy of *Ep.* 2.341c7ff. where knowledge of the Idea is dependent upon the mind's kinship with and likeness to both Idea (342d2) and Good (343e–4b);

(b) a genuinely empirical account of basic concept-formation, which occurs prior to any intuitive grasp of the Idea.

The grasp of the Idea is thus seen more as a crowning religious vision than as part of man's normal cognition-processes; to see into the thoughts of a divine mind is to transcend the human condition.

# THE ACADEMIC HERITAGE

'If there were no Chrysippus, there would be no me.'[1] With these words Carneades gave recognition to the Academy's dependence upon the activities of its traditional sparring partner at Athens. It is no accident that the collapse of the Academy follows the collapse (or at very least the decline) of the Stoic school in the intellectual capital of the Greek world. If Stoicism still flourished for long periods at Rhodes, Alexandria and Rome, the end of the traditional Athenian conflict between two traditional schools marked the end of the New Academy in its critical role. Philo's own theory that the Academy opposed only *Stoic* apprehension served to underline the fact that other opposition could not provide the same challenge as the Stoa. There was not enough common ground between Academic and Epicurean for a good dialogue to develop, nor enough mutual respect. The Posidonian school at Rhodes did not compete directly with the Academy, and does not seem to have been much concerned with the epistemological issues which lay at the heart of the Academic discipline.

When its opposition collapses, the Academy can only embark upon a course of self-destruction. The enemy comes from within, as Antiochus moves over to a Stoic position, at first with reservation, restraint, and even doubt, then openly in the *Sosus* and with new confidence. There had to be arguments on both sides of the question for the Academy to flourish, and their presentation had to be sharp, laced with a fiery rhetoric and more than a little passion. Antiochus provided what the Academy needed, supplying those propositions which could supply fuel for a philosophy of doubt.

Rivalry between the schools of Athens, so long a driving force, gave way to a scholarly, less partisan, study of philosophy: chiefly away from Athens. Even Antiochus' school

127

professed no '-ism', but taught what it saw as philosophy. Posidonius' school was probably the home of scholarly teaching rather than of brilliant invention. Aenesidemus retreated into the inner world of Pyrrhonism, which carefully selected arguments for its own self-centred ends. In such an age the pupil sought for a respected teacher under whom he might study, but he seldom committed himself to unflinching support for the doctrines which were revealed to him. Rather than the teacher's views, he sought for the beliefs of the ancients, and the teacher was expected to interpret and comment upon early philosophical writings. Those philosophies which failed to furnish themselves with ancient precedents for their views might either forge some,[2] appeal to passages out of context, emend texts,[3] or resort to those thinkers whose true views were difficult to assess, whether through obscurity of style or lack of evidence.

Tracing a history of philosophy through this period is understandably a precarious business. Interpreters made less impression than original philosophers, so that few authors have preserved much of interest about the beliefs of these teachers. Original developments were scarce, and not necessarily inspired by the thrust and counter-thrust of argument now that inter-school rivalry was dying. Personal faiths and convictions came to dominate one's thought as increasing numbers of intellectuals came to recognize just how little philosophy had come to solve. Consequently it was not one's philosophy or even one's intellectual powers that won prestige and influence, but rather one's personal conduct and integrity. There can be no confidence that the thinkers of whom we hear most are the best philosophers, and even less that we hear of their distinctive original contributions. A true history of ideas thus cannot be written for this period, and an outline of the development of Academicism between the *Sosus*-crisis of 87 B.C. and the writings of Plutarch will be tentative at best, as befits the lack of documentation.

Academicism could mean different things to different people. In the period between the *Sosus*-crisis and Plutarch, an 'Academic' (when the word is used as a description rather than as a title used by those who had studied at the Academy)[4] was consistently expected to acknowledge that nothing could be infallibly ascertained and to employ the method of argument *in utramque partem*.[5] He would be expected to counter the arguments of Stoic and Epicurean schools in particular, but he was entitled to be a positive thinker with a genuine system of belief.[6] Strong allegiance to Platonic doctrine might also be present, but this depended upon whether one accepted the Philonian One-Academy thesis. In the case of Eudorus, anon. *In Tht.* (if not identical with Eudorus), Ammonius, and Plutarch it would seem that Platonic doctrine was embraced with enthusiasm and defended, and at least two of them accepted the One-Academy thesis.[7] 'Academic' did not consistently mean 'Platonist', but it did so for the Philonian: probably more so than for Philo himself.

In some ways it is easier to understand this period in terms of attitudes towards Plato than in terms of original doctrine. It is difficult to determine whether the Academy had felt more indebted to Socrates or to Plato at the time when Cicero pursued his studies; if anything Socrates seems to have been given the chief credit for its 'sceptical' methods and outlook.[8] Plato himself was being seen as double, partly Socratic, partly Pythagorean,[9] critical and aporetic when under Socrates' influence, cautiously constructive when under Pythagoras'. The received picture of Socrates as a fairly rigorous 'sceptic' meant that where doctrine was clearly observable in Plato's writings, and particularly in *Gorg.*, *Meno*, *Phd.*, *Rep.*, *Phdr.*, and *Parm.*, and above all in *Tim.*, that doctrine was likely to be attributed to Pythagorean influence. This tendency is visible in Posidonius, Eudorus, anon. *In Tht.*, and Numenius,[10] as well as in the doxographies and Ps.-Pythagorean writings.[11]

There was thus an obvious choice available to those who wished to follow the principal Middle Period doctrines of Plato: they might claim to be Academic or they might prefer to be called Pythagorean. Whether it was yet open to one to use the term 'Platonic' as a brand-name for one's philosophy is less clear; such descriptions are encountered in anon. *In*

*Tht.* and in an epistle of Apollonius of Tyana,[12] but there is nothing to suggest that the term had already become a sect-title. In the former case it may well be used generally for all Platonic *interpreters* (a sense found in Proclus),[13] while the heading of Apollonius' epistle (if genuine) may be addressing those whom Apollonius saw as a counterfeit brand of Pythagorean, whose main interest (in addition to their fee)[14] was in Pythagorizing Platonic scholarship rather than in the Pythagorean life. A reference to 'Platonians' and 'Chrysippians' in Philostratus' *Life of Apollonius* (1.7) most certainly does not refer to sects as such, but rather to persons keen on the writings of Plato and Chrysippus respectively. Had there been a Platonic sect early in the first century A.D., then, as Glucker has observed, there is a strange lack of evidence in sources where one might have expected some.[15]

In these circumstances it is reasonable to suppose that Platonic scholars devoted to the Socratic element in Plato, even though they may have seen much probability in the Pythagorizing elements, would naturally have tended to describe themselves as 'Academics', while those who were opposed to the New Academicism in any form (particularly if they had seen Pythagorean influence on Socrates as well as Plato)[16] would have regarded themselves as 'Pythagoreans'. Thus they could stake a claim to a still more ancient and venerable heritage, speaking with greater authority and revealing directly what Plato had preferred to signal obliquely.[17]

Much also depends upon the type of 'Academic' which was to be found from one generation to the next. While persons as moderate and well respected as Eudorus of Alexandria adopted the title, it did not have to suggest destructive sophistry; but it clearly began to do so at some stage of Philo of Alexandria's creative career.[18] Nor was this entirely new, for the Academic-sophist Philostratus, who had consorted with Cleopatra, was regarded by Plutarch (or his sources) as unworthy of the Academic title.[19] Theomnestus of Naucratis may also have been an *Academic*-sophist,[20] and was certainly some kind of cross between a sophist and a philosopher. Philostratus (author of the *Lives of the Sophists*) thought that such people were deemed to be sophists, *like Carneades*, because of their rhetorical powers, but it is extremely likely that rhetorical displays of argument *pro* and *contra* were the primary reason: that technique which Academic and sophist had long shared. Such hybrids as Philostratus (the Academic-sophist) were probably to blame for Philo of Alexandria's low respect for Academics at *QG* 3.33 (where they are associated with Pyrrhonism and destructive sophistry), though one should remember that elsewhere Philo regards Academic values more highly,[21] as may be expected of one who is often thought to have been influenced by Eudorus. Thus I suspect that a change of attitude had been prompted by Philo's own experiences of Academics some time during his life.[22]

In Eudorus' day the description 'Academic' was no sign of a non-constructive approach to philosophy. Shortly before him Dio of Alexandria, friend of Antiochus, seems to have retained the title 'Academic', unlike many of Antiochus' followers.[23] It is very unclear what the title implies in his case, though since he had once studied in the official Academy (not just Antiochus' school) he scarcely had to justify its use. Unlike Eudorus, he is seen as 'from the Academy' as often as 'the Academic'.[24] But it is still significant that he wished to continue to be associated with the Academy; and since it is unlikely that he had much time for 'scepticism' (as a follower of Antiochus), he may have adhered to the name of the Academy out of a love for its founder's writings, and it seems likely that his written works conveyed his message by means of relaxed discussions in Platonic style rather than by dogmatic treatise.[25]

Eudorus' loyalty to Plato was certainly part of his choice of the title 'Academic', and, since he is not referred to as 'from the Academy', there is real doubt as to whether he ever studied in the Academy; he may be too late to have done so. It is tempting to link him rather with the Posidonian school;[26] that he adopted the description 'Academic' may be due *either* to Dio's influence *or* to his attraction to the picture of

Academic thought expounded by Philo and preserved by Aenesidemus' account of the difference between Academics and Pyrrhonians.

As a follower of Plato, Eudorus saw Pythagoras as an ally too, regarding him as the source of some of the doctrinal elements in Plato's works;[27] but he detected different manners of expression in Plato, only one of which was Pythagorean.[28] A coherent message was thought to emanate from Plato's work in spite of this variety of expression,[29] and there is no doubt that Eudorus admired such teaching, which was designed to strike a chord in the consciousness of the reader, far more than he admired crude statements of doctrine. In all this he followed the outlook of the Fourth Academy, and as an Academic he did not feel obliged to follow Plato slavishly, or to be too dogmatic in his interpretation of Plato.[30] Eudorus continued to seek for what Cicero might have described as 'quid constantissime dicatur' (*Ac.* 2.9): the most consistent and most readily agreed position, no matter who had been first to expound it.

Any 'Academic' element in Eudorus' Platonism attracted others less than his Platonic scholarship and his rather doxographical approach to philosophy.[31] Hence we find Potamo of Alexandria, still in the Augustan age,[32] preferring the title 'Eclectic': even though the eclectic method of choosing one's doctrines on a given issue from the range available had been a feature of Academicism as Cicero knew it.[33] Potamo's criterion of knowledge seems to have been 'the most accurate impression', and it would indeed make sense to follow whichever philosopher had received the most accurate impressions on any given issue. Potamo's concern with accuracy is reminiscent of $K$ (cols. 2–3) and of the report that Academics refused to attribute accuracy to the senses.[34] But whereas $K$ seems to be concerned with the accuracy of the criterion 'by which' (i.e. the mind), rejecting extravagant claims for the accuracy of the senses,[35] Potamo does not mention accuracy in relation to the criterion 'by the agency of which' (= mind), but sees it as a possible property of the criterion 'through which' (= presentations, with probable emphasis on sense presentations). If one could assume that $K$ was written by Eudorus, one would see good reason for Potamo to be rejecting Eudoran Academicism: he attached a great deal more importance to the evidence of the senses, and believed that they were capable of an accuracy which no 'Academic' in the current sense could allow. His rejection of the title 'Academic' is certainly due to his quarrel with the overtones of mild scepticism, for he was content to acknowledge Plato's greatness by writing a *Commentary on the Republic.*

With Thrasyllus, whose love of the Platonic corpus was surely built upon the Pythagorizing elements,[36] a further blow is struck for the dogmatic view of Plato. The division of the dialogues into 'zetetic' and 'instructional' ones has the effect of overturning the view of Plato found in $K$, which I believe to have been the view of Eudorus. There (cols. 58–9) the chief character of the dialogues seems to have been their 'zetetic' element, while positive teaching emerges unobtrusively as a by-product. With Thrasyllus the majority of the dialogues are seen to place positive teaching ahead of mere questioning and mental stimulation, so that the chiefly Pythagorean doctrine (as they believed) came to be regarded as the highest achievement of Plato. For this reason a new brand of Pythagorean begins to emerge, people who use Plato as a source for their Pythagorism, but who, because their sect-name implies no outright allegiance to Plato, may pass over the 'zetetic' dialogues and the 'zetetic' elements within the allegedly dogmatic works. In this category Moderatus of Gades, Nicomachus of Gerasa, and Numenius may be included. Moreover the works of Plutarch are testimony to a great upsurge of interest in Pythagoro-mathematical elements in Plato shortly before his time.

Plutarch himself, however, retained the allegiance to both sides of Plato, and to the New Academy. Even though the *Moralia* never refer to Philo of Larissa, his outlook remains that of the Fourth Academy, clutching at a One-Academy thesis and adopting an ambivalent attitude towards apprehension (*Mor.* 1000cd). It is not difficult to see that Plutarch inherited a Fourth Academic outlook from his teacher

Ammonius. Ammonius' philosophical orientation is very like that of *K*, to judge from available evidence.[37] The semi-sceptic fragment B35 of Xenophanes is a favourite quotation of his (*Mor.* 746b), and the Delphic maxims which he praises invite and receive an Academic interpretation (387f, 431a). Both our cognitive faculties and the nature of the physical world obstruct our efforts to apprehend it (392a–e); thus Ammonius is willing to judge by the criteria of 'the likely' (435c) and 'the probable' (427f, cf. 428b), and he sanctions caution (391ef, 744b).

But Ammonius is not referred to as an Academic; he is not referred to as any type of philosopher. Nor for that matter does Plutarch refer to himself as either an 'Academic' or a 'Platonic'. Their allegiance to the Academy would seem beyond doubt, but there is no hurry to adopt the title 'Academic'. The reason, I believe, is not hard to find. That title had too often been adopted by destructive thinkers, by sophists who used the name to add respectability to their displays of argument or oratory. Their goals were very different from those of Philostratus the Academic-sophist, from those of the Academics known to Philo of Alexandria and mentioned at *QG* 3.33, and from those of Favorinus of Arelate: whose Academicism was close to Pyrrhonism, and whose interest in Plato is not known to have been extensive. Ammonius and Plutarch were the recipients of the Fourth Academic heritage, not of its name.

How Fourth Academic ideas were relayed to Ammonius is obscure; there is no need to assume that he had an Academic teacher, though it is probable that he had studied under somebody sympathetic to Philo of Larissa and Eudorus. Such sympathies are found even in the Stoic Arius,[38] and there would presumably have been pupils of Eudorus who could have passed his Academicism on to Ammonius. And equally there would have been books, both of Philo and of Eudorus. If Ammonius' sympathies had belonged to Plato and to his milder 'sceptic' successors, he could soon have sought out the books of those he admired and fully acquainted himself with their position. Oral tradition fails if the mind of the pupil is not apt to receive it; and if that mind is both apt and inquisitive then oral tradition is irrelevant, or at best a guide on a road upon which one is already embarked. In the case of Academicism tradition is still less important than in other philosophies: for part of its tradition was that there should be no firm teaching so that the mind of the pupil might develop naturally along its own road, guided only by reason (*Ac.* 2.60).

The influence of Philo of Larissa thus lived on for roughly two centuries, a philosophy of caution rather than of serious doubt. Whether it would have endured without Eudorus, however, is less clear. In Philo himself the link with Plato is tenuous, postulated by the theory but not supported by constant appeals to Plato. In Eudorus Plato becomes the dominant influence, thus opening the door to those who later preferred to be called Platonists. Just as Platonism had long ago grown into Academic-'scepticism', so now it was being reborn from Academic-'scepticism'. Ignorance was the beginning of philosophy.[39]

# NOTES

## Introduction

1. S.E. *PH* 1.220; cf. also Eus. *PE* 14.726d–7a.
2. I agree broadly with the thesis of John Glucker (*Ant., passim*) that the Academy died out *qua Athenian institution* after the death of either Philo of Larissa or Charmadas. Cicero seems to confirm this at *ND* 1.11 ('prope modum orbam in ipsa Graecia'), at *Fin.* 5.4 (the empty *exhedra*), and at *Ac.* 2.7. But I do not regard the survival of the institution as a precondition for the survival of a New Academic style of philosophy.
3. See epilogue; also my remarks in *CQ* 33 (1983), 182–3.
4. To Eudorus the standard Middle Platonist goal (assimilation to God) is now confidently attributed (e.g. Dillon, *MP* pp. 122–3) on the assumption that Stob. *Ecl.* 2.49.8–25 still follows Eudorus (see my remarks in *CQ* 33 (1983), 180 n. 136); Antiochus' goal is expounded at *Fin.* 5, and is phrased in terms of 'life in accordance with nature' and of virtue (e.g. *Fin.* 5.34); it is significant that the 'nature' concerned is *human* nature, part physical and part psychical. Thus Antiochus thought that man should live as man, not as God.
5. Relevant terms are εἰκός, κανών (see chapter 5 ii), πιθανόν, ἴδια δόγματα (see my remarks in *Dionysius* 5 (1981), 96), and ὁμολογούμενον (*ibid.*, 74ff). I discuss the passage more fully in *CQ* 33 (1983), 181–2.
6. See epilogue; also Tarrant, *CQ* 33 (1983), 182–3.
7. I consider it clear that Middle Platonism was inclined to work with a five-fold metaphysic of this kind, a metaphysic which emerges in various ways in extant evidence. In Moderatus the Neopythagorean we find a transcendent One, intelligible Ideas, Soul, sensible bodies, and their matter (Simpl. *In Phys.* 230.34ff Diels); the ontology is linked with a new interpretation of the five positive hypotheses of *Parm.* (cf. E. R. Dodds, *CQ* 22 (1928), 129–42), and is found in virtually the same form in unknown interpreters at Proclus, *In Parm.* pp. 638.14ff (Cousin), an unknown Rhodian (*In Parm.* 1057.5ff), and Plutarch of Athens (*In Parm.* 1059.3–7). Seneca (*Ep.* 65.7–10) attributes a five-cause system to Plato, which is very similar to another Platonic five-cause system in Galen *U. Part.* 6.12–13, pp. 339ff (Helmreich); I shall be arguing elsewhere that

Plutarch of Athens (*In Parm.* 1059.14—19) was also using the five-fold system of causes, no doubt from earlier material with which he was familiar (*In Parm.* 1061.18—20). Early interest in the *Parmenides*-related Pythagoro-Platonic tradition can be traced back to Eudorus on the basis of Simpl. *In Phys.* p. 181 (Diels). I deal with a five-fold element in the structure of Numenius' metaphysics in *Antichthon* 13 (1979), 19—29. Also relevant are several lists of five terms applying to a particular metaphysical entity, usually God (e.g. *Didasc.* 10 p. 164.28—30 Hermann, *ibid.*, 9 p. 163.12—16; Max. Tyr. *Or.* 29.7g; Aetius 1.7.31 (= *Dox.* p. 304a2, b23)). See also Plutarch's fascination with the role of five-fold elements in Plato's metaphysics (*Mor.* 388a ff and 427a ff). The five-fold metaphysic is observable in Plutarch's discussion of the Posidonian interpretation of the Platonic world-soul, soul being placed at the level of mathematicals, flanked by intelligibles and sensibles, with God and matter at the extremes. If it cannot be traced back to Posidonius, then it is perhaps possible to trace it back to Plutarch's immediate source, probably Eudorus. On this whole question see H. Tarrant, *Phronesis* 28 (1983), 75—103, particularly 82—5.

8. See for instance Dillon, *MP* p. 143 and W. Theiler, 'Philo von Alexandria und der Beginn des kaiserzeitlichen Platonismus', in *Parusia, Festschrift für J. Hirschberger* (Frankfurt, 1965) pp. 199ff.

9. Cic. *Ac.* 2.76—7 (cf. 1.44, 2.16), S.E. *Math.* 7.150—7, Numenius fr. 25.83—105 (des Places).

10. S.E. *Math.* 1.159: I take Sextus' source to be Antiochus of Ascalon; see chapter 5.

11. S.E. *Math.* 7.161—4, particularly where it is said 'this affection must be such as to indicate both itself and the phenomena which caused it' (161) and 'since there is no true [presentation] such that a similar false one could not arise' (164).

12. See chapter 3 iii and Tarrant, *Dionysius* 5 (1981), 66—97.

13. See section iii below; Cic. *Ac.* 2.34, S.E. *Math.* 7.143—4.

14. S.E. *PH* 1.235 and chapter 3 iv below.

15. See Tarrant, *Dionysius* 5 (1981), 84—8, and *LCM* 7.2 (1982), 21—2. The Philonians recognized the existence of presentations which were (a) true and (b) clearly impressed upon the mind: all that the 'Peripatetic' definition required.

16. One notes the comparative lack of Epicurean and Peripatetic material in extant parts of the *Academica*; this does not signal that disputes with these schools had ended, but the adoption of the notion of 'the evident' brought the Academics a shade nearer the Epicureans, while differences with the Peripatetics were now minor (*Fin.* 5.76).

17. Cic. *ND* 1.6, *Ac.* 2.105 (cf. 31), S.E. *Math.* 7.260.

18. Such as Antiochus firmly believed in, *Ac.* 2.21—2, 30; cf. S.E.

*Math.* 7.222–4. But I do not deny that Fourth Academics envisaged some concepts being formed this way.

19. For the link between the evident and general agreement see Tarrant, *Dionysius* 5 (1981), 74–8; also section iii below, and chapter 3 iii.

20. Such is the doctrine attributed to Plato at S.E. *Math.* 7.143–4, on which see chapter 5 iii.

21. The fact that Antiochus could rely on such an account at *Ac.* 2.21–2 suggests that it was not keenly disputed at the time.

22. Most clearly in S.E. *Math.* 7.218 (attributing the idea to Theophrastus) and Aenesidemus in Phot. *Bibl.* cod. 212 p. 170a37–8.

23. As at S.E. *Math.* 7.218ff.

24. By Epicureans, Stoics (Middle), Antiochus; for two possible early exceptions see Tarrant, *Dionysius* 5 (1981), 93: both concern God, whose existence was thought to be *apertum, perspicuum*, and *evidens* by Lucilius at Cic. *ND* 2.4. That Antiochus was used to seeing 'evident' as a description to be applied to *sensations* in particular is not obvious from any single passage, but rather from the cumulative effect of *Ac.* 2.17, 38, 45–6, and *Math.* 7.143–4, 160, and 216.

25. I hope to consider Eudorus' influence upon Middle Platonism more fully elsewhere, as my conclusions are bound to differ from those of Dillon (*MP* pp. 115ff), Theiler, 'Philo von Alexandria', pp. 199ff., H. Dörrie (*Hermes* 79 (1944), 25–35), inasmuch as I see Eudorus as an Academic in the tradition of the Fourth Academy rather than as a Pythagoro-Platonist under Antiochus' influence.

26. Here I speak of extant remains of the Middle Platonists, and I do not include Philo of Alexandria among these; even he, however, appears to have made no positive use of the Stoic criterion of knowledge (see Tarrant, *CQ* 33 (1983), 173–4 with n. 105), and he often displays a mildly 'sceptical' attitude.

27. It is worth noting that where Antiochus stresses the virtues of Stoic thought it is Zeno of whom he speaks (e.g. *Ac.* 1.35–42); but where Antiochus' Stoicizing is criticized the name of Chrysippus is liable to be mentioned (*Ac.* 2.143), no doubt because of the low standing of Chrysippus at the time (cf. 2.73: 'quintae classis').

28. Not before the *Sosus*-crisis (S.E. *Math.* 7.143–4) and still less so after (*Ac.* 1.30–2, and also 40: 'plurima autem in illa tertia philosophiae parte mutavit').

29. Any such assent would have been private; I base my claims on my reading of S.E. *Math.* 7.159–89, but A1 is vital to any New Academic philosophy, while B1 is the obvious lesson to be learnt from Carneades' discussion of rational conduct.

30. The fugitive approaching a ditch which might conceal dangers (*Math.* 7.186), and the snake-like coil of rope in a dark room (*ibid.*, 187–8).

31. ὁμολογία, on which see Tarrant, *Dionysius* 5 (1981), 74–8.
32. The Epicureans use their principle for determining the *truth or falsity* of beliefs: S.E. *Math.* 7.211–16, D.L. 10.34.
33. S.E. *Math.* 7.211 has καί, which I take to signify a weak disjunction (Latin *vel*), whereas D.L. 10.34 has ἤ.
34. See Glucker, *Ant.* pp. 77–8; also Tarrant, *Dionysius* 5 (1981), 73–4.
35. *Ac.* 2.78, Aug. *c. Acad.* 3.41.
36. Discussed throughout my article, *Dionysius* 5 (1981), 66–97.
37. E.g. 'Cotta' in Cic. *ND* 3.8–11, particularly 'quod esset perspicuum et inter omnis constaret' (8), 'evidens de quo inter omnis conveniat' (9), 'hoc perspicuum sit et inter omnis conveniat' (11).
38. The Academic might discover agreement that the number of stars was even, but he would still suspend judgment on such matters as these; they are *incerta* (ἄδηλα), and separated by most Academics from more persuasive presentations (*Ac.* 2.32).
39. I do not claim that such a definition was actually used but S.E. *Math.* 7.143–4 shows that it was a possible one.
40. S.E. *Math.* 7.175 (διὰ τὴν σπάνιον ταύτης παρέμπτωσιν, λέγω δὲ τῆς μιμουμένης τἀληθές); I cannot claim that this is the *correct* view of Carneades, but assume that it was Antiochus' view during his activity within the traditional Academy (see chapter 5).
41. See *Ac.* 2.47–53 (e.g. 53: 'quaerimus gravitatis constantiae firmitatis sapientiae iudicium, utimur exemplis somniantium furiosorum ebriosorum'); also 2.55 and much of 2.79–90.
42. Cf. n. 38 above; for accuracy see chapter 3 ii below.
43. Above p. 11; cf. chapter 6 ii below.
44. Cf. nn. 18 and 21 above.
45. The theory of S.E. *Math.* 7.218ff and, less explicitly, of *Ac.* 2.21–2, 30.
46. Cf. Tarrant *Dionysius* 5 (1981), 92–6.
47. For God see *SVF* 2.1009 (pp. 299.13, 300.5), cf. Antipater fr. 33 = Plut. *Mor.* 1051ef; for virtues *SVF* 3.218 (p. 51.41), cf. Cic. *Fin.* 5.59; other common notions are those of inference and sign (*SVF* 2.223, p. 74.7–9) and types of mixture (*SVF* 2.473). Interesting use of common notions to prove the existence (no more) of fate is found in Alexander of Aphrodisias *De Fato* 2 (p. 165.14–25 Bruns).
48. Hence the common notions could on occasion appear as a criterion of truth, as in *SVF* 2.473 (p. 154.29) and Galen *Plac.* 9.778.
49. On the usual application of the term 'evident' to sensations see n. 24 above.
50. A Stoic definition of knowledge, *SVF* 1.68, 1.411 (Herillus), 2.130, 3.112.
51. Hence Philo's willingness to entertain some notion of 'apprehension'

139

(see chapter 3 iv). It is interesting that Antiochus appears to have claimed that the existence of apprehensibles was evident (*Ac.* 2.60: 'quis enim ista tam aperte perspicueque et perversa et falsa secutus esset, . . . ?', referring to the Academic doctrine of non-apprehensibility).

### *1. Scepticism in the late Academy?*

1. *PH* 1.223, 226—7, 236, cf. 1—3, 213.
2. Anon. *In Tht.* col. 61; cf. *PH* 1.7, 13, 21—4.
3. *PH* 1.7; the precursors of Academicism had been an important topic in Cic. *Ac.* (e.g. 1.44—6, 2.72—4); the Pyrrhonist—Empiric Theodosius denied that Pyrrho could safely be regarded as the inventor of 'scepticism', D.L. 9.70.
4. I cannot doubt that Aenesidemus belonged to the first half of the first century B.C., for we must identify his opponents in the *Pyrrhonian Logoi* with the Fourth Academy of Philo of Larissa and Charmadas, and it is natural to identify the dedicatee of that work with Cicero's friend L. Aelius Tubero. There seems to have been no official semi-sceptical Academy beyond the first quarter of the first century, so that Aenesidemus cannot have been writing much later. There are two ways of explaining Aristocles' exaggeration in claiming that Aenesidemus revived Pyrrhonism ἐχθὲς καὶ πρώην (Eus. *PE* 14.763d): (i) the words are designed to imply a lack of any ancient Pyrrhonist pedigree, suggesting that Aenesidemus is an upstart, sprung neither from classical Hellas nor from the flowering of the Hellenistic Age; (ii) Aristocles may be following a source much closer to Aenesidemus, perhaps even Antiochus himself, or a pupil of Antiochus such as the Peripatetics Cratippus or Aristo. It is noteworthy that Aenesidemus himself made accusations of a lack of pedigree in referring to the 'Academy of today' (Phot. *Bibl.* 170a15) and that this was probably a jibe directed at Antiochus' so-called 'Old Academy', which did not even function in the region of the Academy (Cic. *Fin.* 5.1).
5. D.L. 9.115—16 produces a succession-list from Pyrrho to the writer's own times, thus reminding one that one should not take too seriously his method of linking Aenesidemus directly with Sextus and Saturninus. But the post-Aenesidemus part of the list includes many other figures known to us, and when we add the important figure of Agrippa (D.L. 9.88—9, cf. S.E. *PH* 1.165—77) we have a picture of much sceptic activity between Aenesidemus and Sextus.
6. Favorinus fr. 26 (Barigazzi).
7. Glucker, *Ant.* pp. 281—9, adequately establishes the philosophical affiliations of Favorinus.

8. On the Academic side the subject had certainly been tackled by Plutarch (Lamp. Cat. no. 64) as well as by Favorinus, and the Pyrrhonists surely dealt with it regularly, since it is the very first topic in Sextus' *Pyrrhonian Hypotyposes* (much as in Aenesidemus' *Pyrrhonian Logoi*): a standard Pyrrhonist *topos*.

9. D.L. 9.70; Theodosius, a medical man of the early second century A.D. (probably), called his book *Sceptical Summaries*; by failing to credit Pyrrho with the invention of 'scepticism' (*sceptike* = the art of balancing one presentation against another, see below) he implies that others had used it before Pyrrho.

10. ζητητικοὶ μὲν οὖν ἀπὸ τοῦ πάντοτε ζητεῖν τὴν ἀλήθειαν, σκεπτικοὶ δ' ἀπὸ τοῦ σκέπτεσθαι ἀεὶ καὶ μηδέποτε εὑρίσκειν (D.L. 9.70). Note that the ideas overlap, finding being the natural outcome of *scepsis* as well as *zetesis*.

11. Phld. *Rhet.* 1.191 (Sudhaus), Philo *LA* 3.238, *Ebr.* 98, 202, *Her.* 247, 279. Additional evidence that non-Pyrrhonist philosophers claimed to use *scepsis* at a time when revived Pyrrhonism was already established is found at D.L. 9.91 (end): the Pyrrhonists held that the dogmatists were naive, for demonstration from hypotheses was not *scepsis* but merely *thesis*. Had *scepsis* been already a loaded word and an established term for Pyrrhonist practices, then the dogmatists would not have been concerned that their own pursuits were not identical with it.

12. K. Janacek, tackling the term σκεπτικός in Philo (*Listy Filologicke* 102 (1979), 65–8) notes the connexion with Plato's treatment of sophists, but this cannot be taken to show that Philo did not have contemporary sophists in mind. Indeed *QG* 3.33 (not considered by Janacek) seems to prove that he did. Words used by Philo are: σοφίσματα, τριβόμενοι, γλισχρολογούμενοι, λογοπῶλαι, λογοθῆραι, γνωσιμαχοῦντες, συλλαβομαχοῦντες.

13. See Janacek, *Listy Filologicke* 102 (1979), 65–8, for a different view; but *QG* 3.33 is important evidence against him.

14. It is sometimes merely commendable (*LA* 3.238, *Ebr.* 202, *Her.* 247), sometimes idealized (*Her.* 279 in relation to Israel, *Ebr.* 98 in relation to Moses).

15. *Ebr.* 98 and 202.

16. *Ebr.* 166–205: the connexion was elaborated by H. von Arnim, *Quellenstudien zu Philon von Alexandria* (Berlin, 1888) pp. 79ff.

17. This possibility seems more likely to me. If Philo was as opposed to Pyrrhonism as *Cong.* 52 and *Fug.* 209 (let alone *QG* 3.33) suggest, then it is unlikely that he would have bothered to rework the material for himself.

18. Photius cod. 212, 169b21, 36, 170a12, 40, 43.

19. His definition of Pyrrhonian *logos* appears in the previous sentence. The term *scepsis* appears to be used too narrowly and 'naturally'

here for the phrase to be late, and the antithetic nature of Aenesidemus' *scepsis* is well known.

20. U. von Burkhard, *Heraklit-Nachfolge* pp. 42–4; D.L. 9.78: ἀντιθέσεις, 97 ἀπὸ τῶν ἐναντίων, 106 διὰ τὴν ἐναντιολογίαν; Photius 170b4ff and 10ff.

21. δύναμις ἀντιθετικὴ φαινομένων τε καὶ νοουμένων καθ᾽ οἱονδήποτε τρόπον.

22. Cic. *Ac.* 1.13, 46, 2.74, 129; *ND* 1.11; *TD* 1.8, 5.10–11.

23. *Meno* 81e1, *Rep.* 535d5; less so at *Rep.* 528c1.

24. *Meno* 81e1: the passage as a whole emphasizes the virtue of inquiry in the hope that we may find, and the context is well known to Cic. (*TD* 1.57) and to Plut. (fr. 215).

25. I regard the view that Plato was εἰλικρινῶς σκεπτικός (*PH* 1.222) rather than ἀπορητικός (1.221) as having been advanced by Menodotus; see below, chapter 4 iii.

26. D.L. 3.49; Albinus *Prol.* 3 (p. 148.24–9 Hermann); the division given at D.L. 3.49 is presupposed by Thrasyllus' classification of the dialogues at 56–61, and his name was still important as an *arranger* of Plato's work in Albinus' time (*Prol.* 4). He had also arranged the works of Democritus, D.L. 9.45–9.

27. *Prol.* 6 (p. 151.5–6 Hermann): 'the dialogues of the logical character, which is also zetetic'. Albinus feels the need to indicate how his classification would differ from that of Thrasyllus.

28. As also *Phdr.* and *Critias*; for possible reasons see O. Schissel (*Hermes* 62 (1931), 215–26) and myself in *CQ* 33 (1983), 162 n. 18.

29. See n. 26 above.

30. We know from anon. *Prol. in Plat. Phil.* 10 (p. 205.13–16 Hermann) that a group of aporetic works which argue for both sides of a case (*Lys.*, *Charm.*, *Euthphr.* etc.) was so used to support an extreme view of Plato as a sceptic, and from 206.11–14 that *Tht.* was so used. All four works are zetetic according to the Thrasyllan classification. When one comes to the view that Plato was part dogmatic, part aporetic, one observes that the early 'gymnastic' and 'aporetic' dialogues are held to be an indication of the non-dogmatic pursuits (*PH* 1.221). Anon. *In Tht.*, who probably adhered to this double view of Plato (see chapter 4 below), thinks that in his ζητήσεις at least Plato inquires and does not reveal his beliefs, affirming in no case that a proposition is true or is false, 59.13–17.

31. It is unlikely that the 'great quarrel' about whether Plato dogmatized or not had lasted until the age of Diogenes. I know of no thinker since Menodotus who would have paid much attention to alleged sceptic elements in Plato. Furthermore one expects that the term *dogma* was coming to be used in a narrower, more modern sense by this time, implying considerable conviction, but no such

conviction is implied by the term in Diogenes when he divides *dogma* into 'the opinion' and 'the thing opined'; though the verb δογματίζειν might seem to be developing such a sense, when it is compared with the passing of laws.

32. A weak sense of *dogma* occurs in anon. *In Tht.* (54.38–55.13), which I date shortly before Thrasyllus; in the same period it is used by Strabo to describe the teachings of the Brahmans and Sramans (15.1.59).

33. See below, chapter 4 iii.

34. See Philo of Larissa in Stob. *Ecl.* 2.39.20ff (Wachsmuth), Cic. *Ac.* 2.7: 'neque nostrae disputationes quicquam aliud agunt nisi ut in utramque partem dicendo eliciant et tamquam exprimant aliquid quod aut verum sit aut ad id quam proxime accedat'. The positive goal of their aporetic exercises is no doubt linked to their study of the νάρκη-phenomenon in the *Meno* (79e–80d, 84bc) and the labour-pains of philosophical discovery at *Tht.* 148e and 151a.

35. See below, chapter 4 iii.

36. 'Lucullus' espouses the Stoic view that the sage's *dogmata* cannot be betrayed *sine scelere* at *Ac.* 2.27; Cicero finds this view to his advantage, since Antiochus must choose between the sage of the Stoics and that of Polemo, 2.132ff. The Academic must suspend judgment in order to avoid a crime (133); a follower of Antiochus must defend perverse *dogmata* like the walls of a city (137). The Academic is free; his opponent is compelled to defend 'omnia quae praescripta et quasi imperata sint' (8).

37. Lucius Tubero, Phot. *Bibl.* 169b33.

38. Col. 54.43–55.7; see chapter 4 below, with nn. 3 and 45.

39. It is clear that the addition of some such adjective as 'obscure' (ἀδήλου) is required in the text, and this is what J. Barnes chooses (*PCPS* 28 (1982), 25 n. 69). It is surely correct, for the Logical sect is here associated with *dogma* in this specific sense, and the same sect is then said to claim knowledge 'concerning things obscure' (19.353). One wonders whether Clement's definition of *dogma* as 'a kind of *logical* apprehension' at *Strom.* 8.16.2 (misleadingly printed in *SVF* 2.121) is connected with the *dogmata* of the Logical sect.

40. As Barnes again perceives, there has been the common corruption of ἐναργείᾳ to ἐνεργείᾳ.

41. Note that D.L. 3.51 distinguishes between *dogma* as opinion and *dogma* as thing opined, which 3.51 also described as a ὑπόληψις. This should be enough to neutralize Clement's picture of it as a κατάληψις λογική at *Strom.* 8.16.2.

42. Barnes, *PCPS* (1982), 1–29, particularly 6ff.

43. See *ibid.*, 7–8 and 9 for the second class of *dogma* in Sextus.

44. More by giving official sanction to a specific policy than by

requiring unquestioning obedience (to judge from the comparison with opinion).

45. See Barnes, *PCPS* 28 (1982), 6ff for discussion of the 'colour' of the term.

46. See *LCM* 7.2 (1982), 21–2.

47. Gellius (*NA* 11.5.8) says that the Academics 'quasi decernunt' that things are not apprehensible, and Antiochus (*Ac.* 2.29) regards it as an Academic *dogma* too.

48. Aug. *c. Acad.* 3.41, quoted below, p. 54.

49. That Carneades resisted the claim to 'apprehend' that nothing is apprehensible (*Ac.* 2.28) does not entail his denial that Academics had a *dogma* of non-apprehensibility.

## 2. Charmadas

1. Besides examples from *PH* 1.220 we may point to the following cases where the periphrasis 'those around x + y' is used of a given school at a given time: *PH* 1.3, 1.230 (Carneades and Clitomachus); *PH* 3.200, *Math.* 11.30 (Zeno, Cleanthes, and Chrysippus). Comparable cases of 'those around x' occur frequently, e.g. Xenocrates at *Math.* 2.61 and 7.16, Arcesilaus at *Math.* 7.150, Carneades at *Math.* 7.173, 175, and 9.190.

2. See Glucker, *Ant.* pp. 109–11, with n. 41.

3. See Eusebius *PE* 14.4.16.

4. The mentions of Aenes. at *PH* 1.210–12 and 222 show that an Aenesideman account of positions related to scepticism was in the mind of *either* Sextus *or* his immediate source.

5. On his split with the Academy see below, chapter 3 v.

6. See below, chapter 3 i.

7. Interpretation of the passage: I offer my reading in *Dionysius* 5 (1981), 66–97 and in chapter 3 iv.

8. See *Ac.* 2.7; *De Or.* 1.84, 263, 3.80, 107, 145.

9. Among the pupils of Carneades there was a dangerous tendency to guess his opinions in this way (*Ac.* 2.78, 112); or perhaps to guess by his having defended some positions more keenly (2.139); Cicero says that he himself would not argue strongly against certain positions (2.112–13).

10. See particularly *De Or.* 1.85: 'excitabatur homo promptus'; also such verbs as *docebat* (1.85), *inludere/ostenderet* (1.87), and *negabat* (1.92).

11. *De Or.* 1.92: 'nisi quae cognitis penitusque perspectis et in unum exitum spectantibus et numquam fallentibus rebus contineretur'. This is related to the Stoic definition of an 'art', *SVF* 1.73, 2.93–7.

12. Apparently a disjunctive interpretation of the Stoic definition of

opinion as 'weak and/or (καὶ) false assent' (*SVF* 1.67 = S.E. *Math.* 7.151).

13. One may interpret the words 'quibus non scientia esset tradenda' in three ways: (a) as a repetition of the Platonic claim (*Gor.* 454e–5a) that rhetoric does not aim at imparting knowledge (knowledge 'does not have to be' handed down) because of the numbers involved and the shortness of time; (b) as a suggestion that it is inappropriate for knowledge to be squandered on the masses (knowledge 'ought not to be' handed down), and thus as another indication of the esotericism of the Academy, perhaps dependent on Plato's claim that one should only sow seeds in suitable mental soil (*Phdr.* 276b–e); or (c) as a combination of these two.

14. See n. 13 above; esotericism would naturally follow from the belief that important truths are 'penitus in media philosophia retrusa atque abdita' (1.87).

15. See Glucker, *Ant.* pp. 28–30 for Panaetius' love of Plato, which may, however, have been outwardly presented as a love of Socrates; see F85, F141–9, F290–1 (Edelstein–Kidd) for Posidonius' studies of Plato, which may, however, have been outwardly presented as studies of early Pythagorism (see F85, F151).

16. *Ac.* 2.16: 'in Charmada eloquentia'. This reinforces the picture received from the *De Oratore.*

17. With 1.87 ('ne hanc quidem ipsam dicendi rationem ac viam nosse') compare *Gor.* 464c6 (οὐ γνοῦσα λέγω ἀλλὰ στοχασαμένη). With 1.90 (*consuetudo, exercitatio*) cf. 463b4 (ἐμπειρία καὶ τριβή), also the main theme that oratory is a flattery, not an art (note *blandiri*). Note also that the knowledge–opinion dichotomy is applied to audiences at *Gor.* 454e–5a (cf. 1.92).

18. *Ac.* 1.13, *ND* 1.11, *TD* 5.11.

19. 508e–9a: almost as an afterthought 'Socrates' asserts that he does not *know* this, much as if Plato had suddenly remembered that he was still speaking through the mouth of 'Socrates'. Compare *Meno* 98b.

20. For the increasing confidence of 'Socrates' in this work see E. R. Dodds, intro. to his edition (Oxford, 1959), p. 16.

21. One might object that the 'persuasive and undistracted presentation' does not appear in the *Gorgias*, but we have a similar concept at 509a4–7, where 'Socrates' can disclaim knowledge but give additional grounds for belief by observing that nobody can consistently maintain the opposite theme.

22. Though Carneades would surely have objected to the results of διεξόδευσις being called 'knowledge', it is clear that some were not sure, e.g. Galen *Plac.* 9.778, where this criterion is credited with the same power as the Stoic criterion!

23. R. E. Witt, *Albinus and the History of Middle Platonism* (Cambridge, 1937) pp. 34ff.

24. See 1.41, 42, 2.19, 27, 36, 58 (*fides*); 1.42 (*fidelis*); 2.18, 36 (twice) (*confido*); 2.43 (*fidens*); 2.24 (*fidenter*); note also the profusion of πίστις-terminology in S.E. *Math.* 7.89–260 where Antiochus is a likely source (see chapter 5 below): e.g. 89, 90, 111, 124, 125, 126, 131, 134, 136, 138, etc.
25. *Strom.* 2.8.4; for the two kinds of belief see 2.48.2 and 8.5.3.
26. To judge from S.E., including passages of acknowledged Aenesideman material (*PH* 1.66, 77, 79, 88, 98, 115–17, 122, *Math.* 8.45); also D.L. 9.78.
27. See n. 13 above.
28. *Ac.* 2.36, cf. *Phdr.* 273d.
29. Or rather his rejection of what is apt to be believed even in the absence of contrary evidence, 273b8.
30. *Tim.* 29d, 30b, 48d, 53d, 55d, 56a, b, 68b, d, 90e. Note Cicero's interpretation of the *Timaeus*' 'likely story' as the Carneadean *probabile* (*Tim.* 8 (twice)) or *veri similitudo* (*Tim.* 8) or *coniectura* (*Tim.* 9).
31. E.g. *Orator* 8–12, *Brutus* 31, 120ff, 191.

### 3. Fourth Academic epistemological doctrine

1. One must assume that Clitomachus followed Carneades (and his immediate successors) with no radical change of direction, or at least that his attitudes were largely those which we have come to associate with Carneades — for most of our information about Carneades surely comes via the pen of Clitomachus. Carneades is not alleged to have had any esoteric *philosophical* doctrine, for Aug. *c. Acad.* 2.11 shows only that he was prepared to relax his scepticism on non-philosophical matters, and Numenius fr. 27.57–59 (des Places) gives the strong impression that any esoteric teaching of his was merely agreement with what anybody would regard as obvious: ἀπεφαίνετο ἃ κἂν ἄλλος τῶν ἐπιτυχόντων. I assume that details of epistemology were (i) matters debated by philosophers, and (ii) not obvious to the common man. It is thus safe to assume that Carneades propounded no detailed epistemology, and Clitomachus surely followed him in this regard. Certainly Clitomachus resists the notion that the sage will opine (*Ac.* 2.78), and ought thus to dissociate the Academy from doctrine on such obscure matters as theory of knowledge and the psychology that will naturally attach to an epistemology.
2. The changes in Philo's attitudes reported by Numenius (fr. 28 des Places = 8 Lang) do not imply that he had written anything in his early days of which he later came to repent. Such a reversal of previous written statements would have afforded the dogmatists

of the *Academica* great opportunities to score points similar to that scored by Cicero at 2.69 (on Antiochus' inconstancy). But in fact Antiochus had to ask Heraclitus of Tyre (as an expert) to compare the Roman Books with what he had *heard* from Philo and from other Academics beforehand, not with previous Academic literature which anybody could have read (*Ac.* 2.11). In part this may be explained by the probability that Philo was claiming aspects of his Roman-Book theory as earlier esoteric teaching, but his previous esoteric writings could still have been used against him if they conflicted with Roman-Book theory, and could have been held to support the accusations of lying (*Ac.* 2.12, 18). As for the more innovative epistemology attacked at *Ac.* 2.33–6, there is no hint that it was new or that it was exclusive to Philo, nor is it claimed there that it conflicts with Philo's earlier doctrine in spite of the harm which such a claim could have done.

3. See my article in *CQ* 33 (1983), 180ff; also introduction i and epilogue.
4. See particularly *Ac.* 2.78; also the reversion to Clitomachean orthodoxy at 2.98 in order to avoid accusations of invention such as Philo had met with. Note also that Cicero offers no refutation of the charge that Philo had lied.
5. There is a conscious attempt to recover the true Carneadean position at *Ac.* 2.148 and a commitment to it — as if rejecting any weaker brand of 'scepticism'.
6. See H. Tarrant, *LCM* 7.2 (1982), 21–2.
7. Metrodorus of Stratonicea had clearly been interpreting Carneades in a less forceful manner than Clitomachus, both with regard to the sage's right to opine (*Ac.* 2.78) and on the status of the non-apprehensibility gambit (Aug. *c. Acad.* 3.41). His interpretations were probably backed by claims to have known Carneades well, *Ac.* 2.16, *De Or.* 1.45, *Index Acad. Herc.* 26.4.
8. *Ac.* 2.112 has Cicero acknowledging that he would dispute less vigorously with a Peripatetic, who would not employ the Stoic definition of apprehension. At all times it is the Stoic definition that is debated in the *Academica*, and its extant portions make no attempt to show that all cognition is impossible. The existence of true presentations is not disputed, and Cicero appears to accept that some such impressions are *perspicua* (2.132: 'iam illud perspicuum est . . .'). He thus falls into the group of Academics who acknowledge the existence of true presentations impressed upon the mind with all due clarity (*Ac.* 2.34), and such presentations would be 'apprehended' in the Peripatetic sense of the term. The only quarrel is whether the sense concerned is an appropriate one, as the Stoic definition receives approval at *Ac.* 2.77.
9. Most obviously at *Leg.* 1.39.

10. *Brut.* 306, Plut. *Cic.* 3−4.

11. Glucker (*Ant.* p. 396) has an interesting discussion, emanating from Hirzel, *Untersuchungen* vol. 3, pp. 288−92, on the degrees to which characters in the *Academica* are prepared to tolerate Peripatetic epistemology: i.e. the beliefs that the sage will opine and that apprehension of a non-Stoic kind is possible. 'Catulus' accepts the former belief with reservations about the mental attitude which accompanied the sage's opinion, insisting that he must be aware that mistakes were possible. This reservation, and his unwillingness to tolerate the idea of apprehension in any sense, make 'Catulus' a more conservative Academic than Philo.

12. *Dox.* 403ab5−6 gives the same doctrine in almost the same words, tacking it on to the views of Leucippus, Democritus, and Epicurus; but Galen (*Dox.* 636.21) attributes the doctrine to 'others', i.e. persons other than the atomists. The *Florilegium* of J. Damascenus is also relevant: see Diels, *Dox.*, intro. p. 55.

13. Also involved in Plato's theory of vision are (a) the presence of light outside the eyes, into which the eye's fire may issue forth without fear of dispersion (45cd), and (b) particles proceeding from the object (67d), which meet with the visual ray at some intermediate point.

14. I assume that Diels' correction of καταληπτόν to καταληπτικόν is misguided (see 398b22 n.), and the sense which this gives to γνώριμον at 398b24 (see index s.v. Academici: 'sapientem λόγῳ percipere') is unnatural. The author cannot be discussing how the sage apprehends things, for his apprehensions do not differ in kind from those of the fool; moreover the passage follows discussion of how pleasure and pain *are apprehended* (by sensation or mind?, 397b34ff). The reason why the Stoic sage was thought to be recognized by sensation is clear in von Arnim, who places 398b21−3 immediately after *SVF* 3.567; for many of the attributes given to the sage there would be evident from the senses.

15. Cf. the Academic adoption of the Stoic concept of the sage for purely theoretical purposes in the *Academica* (e.g. 2.66).

16. It is unclear how far the Stoics conceived of the senses as 'assents', for they claimed that assent was up to us (*SVF* 1.61, 2.115, 974, 992), but the doctrine from Aetius does recur in the *Academica* (2.108 = *SVF* 2.73) as well as Porphyry (*SVF* 2.74), and is thus relevant to the Stoic−Academic debate in the period under review. The difficulties may be overcome by distinguishing between two degrees of assent and/or two senses of αἴσθησις ('bare sensation' and 'perception') of which the latter dominates. It is not only those Academics who regarded the opinion-free life as an ideal who must resist the necessary connexion between sensation and assent (and so with opinion, *SVF* 1.67, 2.90, 992, 3.380, 548); for even

Philo's school continued to advise considerable caution before assent was given, even (one assumes) in the case of true presentations which appeared evident, which would have been 'perceived' before they had been approved (if one uses the Peripatetic sense of 'perceive', at least). Note also that Arcesilaus, who was first to advocate a policy of suspending judgment, made a rigid separation of assent from sensation when defending that policy (Plut. *Mor.* 1122b ff): see G. Striker, 'Sceptical strategies', in M. Schofield, M. Burnyeat, and J. Barnes (eds.), *Doubt and Dogmatism* (Oxford, 1980) pp. 67−9.

17. See Witt, *Albinus, passim.* Other examples of the 'not without' phrase occur in this period in anon. *In Tht.* 73.10, in Potamo's moral goal (D.L. 1.21) and in an apparently deliberate emendation to the text of *Meno* 99e6 (Clement *Strom.* 5.83.4), which I believe to have been inspired by Antiochus (see *CQ* 33 (1983), 162 n. 21).

18. *Ac.* 2.19−21 appears to separate assent-stages (which have propositional content) from mere sensations, though one should note that the former 'non sensibus ipsis percipi dicuntur sed quodam modo sensibus'. The last phrase is not far from 'not without the senses' but would scarcely mean that the senses were 'not without assent'. At 2.37−8 we meet such phrases as 'non potest obiectam rem perspicuam non adprobare' or 'qui enim quid percipit adsentitur statim'. In such cases, one might suppose, assent is only theoretically separate from sensation; and where the object is not evident one may claim that there has been no αἴσθησις in the full sense of that term. The distinction between the two senses was perfectly familiar to the non-Stoic in the first century B.C., as is shown by anon. *In Tht.* 59.46−9.

19. See col. 35 of *Index Acad. Herc.* for the change of allegiance. What the change entailed we do not know, but we do not hear of changes of view or of studies with Peripatetics.

20. Reference to Peripatetics alone is made at 310b14−15, 394b21−5, 397b7−8, 398b1−4, and the present passage at 396b8−10; there is mention of Peripatetics also at 366ab29−367ab3 in an entry dealing mainly with Heraclides and at 273a25−274a2 in an entry dealing chiefly with Aristotle and Theophrastus.

21. Clearly they date from a period when the two versions of the Aetius doxography had diverged, so that none of the entries appears in the a-column (though difficulties remain over 403ab5−7, which could not then be a garbled version of the Academic entry which follows in the b-column: see n. 12). I cannot believe that the doctrines attributed to the 'Academics' apply to a period prior to that of Philo, and I think it likely that the Peripatetic entries (also concerned with epistemology only) owe much to the debate

between Philo and Antiochus. Note also a reference to Xenarchus the Peripatetic at 388b16−20, which may date from the same period as references to Peripatetics alone; Xenarchus is unlikely to have attracted attention before 45 B.C. at the earliest. Note too that the b-column has a number of additional entries for Posidonius, one at 403b12−13 following an Academic entry.

22. Porphyry, *Concerning the Faculties of the Soul* in Stob. *Ecl.* 1.364 (Wachsmuth). A Fourth Academic source seems likely.

23. See Glucker, *Ant.* pp. 38−9, and Tarrant, *CQ* 33 (1983), 161−87.

24. Empedocles, Xenophanes, Parmenides, Zeno, Melissus, Anaxagoras, and Democritus (also Metrodorus, Protagoras); the only striking omission is Heraclitus, who could not easily be credited with scepticism of sense-perception, though see S.E. *Math.* 7.126 (= A16 DK). Anaxagoras, Democritus, Metrodorus, Empedocles, Parmenides, and Xenophanes are all seen as important forerunners of Academicism at *Ac.* 2.72−4, where Heraclitus is also an important omission.

25. ψευδεῖς, 396b16: 'deceptive' might be a better translation, but even so the word is stronger than the Academics' 'inaccurate'.

26. 396b17−19: note that it is also gramatically dependent upon b12−16.

27. There is no explicit indication in Aenesidemus' extant attack on Academics (Photius, *Bibl.* 169b18ff) as to how Plato was regarded, though Photius assumes that he was included among those attacked by the work as a whole (170b37−9). It appears to be only the so-called New Academy which is accused of slipping into dogmatism in book 1 of the *Pyrrhonian Logoi*, with a possible allusion to Antiochus' school at 170a14−15. Like Sextus at *PH* 1.220−35, Aenes. probably saw a progression away from 'scepticism' since the Second Academy, but, unlike Sextus, he probably saw Plato as the origin of sceptic trends in the Academy (see chapter 4 iii).

28. Notably Anaxagoras and Democritus at 2.72−3.

29. At *Ac.* 1.46 we learn that Plato affirms nothing, saying nothing for certain. I assume that it is a lack of certainty in Platonic statements which Cicero wishes to highlight; there is of course no suggestion that Plato did not have opinions (cf. 2.113) or doctrines (cf. 2.118, 129, 142). From 2.74 it would seem that Plato's main claim to be a doubter is the fact that he followed Socrates in so many of his works. The One-Academy thesis demanded that Plato should have been seen as about as 'sceptical' as Philo himself wished to appear.

30. There is no reference to the Pythagoreans in the *Academica* apart from an account of their physical principles at 2.118; they were likely, however, to be credited with much of the doctrine found in Plato: see epilogue.

31. See F85 and F151 (Edelstein−Kidd).

32. Posidonius F85; Eudorus–Arius in Stob. *Ecl.* 2.49.20; Aetius 2.4.1–2, 2.6.5, 4.9.10; Numenius fr. 52 (des Places = T 30 Leemans).

33. It is natural to include *Phd.* because of the presence of the Pythagoreans Simmias and Cebes at the discussion of the soul's immortality. Evidence that *Phd.* was actually viewed in this way is thin, though Aetius links Plato's psychology with Pythagoras (4.7.1–2, 5, cf. 4.4.1) as does Cicero at *TD* 1.39.

34. Posidonius F151, Aetius 4.4.1 (the partition of the soul); Numenius fr. 35/36 (des Places) uses the myth of Er to reconstruct Pythagorean belief.

35. In Moderatus (Simpl. *In Phys.* p. 230.34ff Diels) and perhaps Eudorus (*ibid.*, p. 181.10ff); see Dodds (*CQ* 22 (1928), 129–42).

36. Stob. *Ecl.* 2.49.8–25 (via Arius) and Simplicius, *In Phys.* p.230.34ff Diels.

37. See 2.4.1–2, 2.6.5, 4.4.1, 4.7.1–2, 5, 4.9.10, 4.20.1, 5.4.2, 5.20.4.

38. See Glucker, *Ant.* pp. 121–35 and *passim*, and J. Dillon, *Dionysius* 3 (1979), 63–77; contrast perhaps J. H. Oliver, *AJPh* 98 (1977), 160–78.

39. Philo appears to have been dead by 84/3 B.C. (Glucker, *Ant.* p. 100 n. 11), and Charmadas must have been some years his senior. Heraclitus of Tyre is something of an unknown quantity, but cannot have been born much later than 135 B.C. and would have been an old man if he had survived until 55 B.C. If we are to take Strabo's reference to Eudorus as a contemporary seriously (17.1.5), then his philosophical career cannot have overlapped with Heraclitus' by very much. But the greatest obstacle to believing that Eudorus began philosophizing before about 70 B.C. is the fact that Cicero fails to mention him. I do not reject the notion of a link between Eudorus and the (Fifth) Academic Dio of Alexandria.

40. (i) He is the source of Posidonian and Diodoran material in Achilles *Intr. Arat.* 30.20 (Maass) and probably of other references to Diodorus and Posidonius there; (ii) he may be the source of the Posidonian interpretation of the Platonic world-soul at Plut. *Mor.* 1023bc (chapter 5 n. 17); (iii) his view of the Platonic goal (Stob. *Ecl.* 2.50.6–10 etc.) may derive from Posidonius' *Timaeus*-inspired (see 90a–d) view that one should follow the daemon within one, this being akin to a cosmic daemon (F187 Edelstein–Kidd); (iv) Posidonian emphasis on the control of one's passions ($\pi\acute{\alpha}\theta\eta$) may account for the prominence which Eudorus gives to the impulses ($\acute{o}\rho\mu\alpha\acute{\iota}$) in his division of moral philosophy (Stob. *Ecl.* 2.44.13–24, cf. 3–6).

41. See *Ac.* fr. 21 = Aug. *c. Acad.* 3.43: the Academic custom was not to reveal their honest opinion until the pupil had studied *until old age*; *Ac.* 2.60 seems to confirm this. Eudorus cannot have studied

with Philo or Charmadas until old age, and thus cannot have claimed special knowledge of Fourth Academic opinion, except for that which could be extracted from the Roman Books. In an age when many studied with more than one school it required more than attendance at a basic course before one qualified to make statements of doctrine on behalf of that school (or to use the school's name as a title).

42. On the term 'preference' (αἵρεσις), which replaced terms indicating one's organized philosophical school between the second century B.C. and the second A.D., see Glucker, *Ant.* pp. 174ff.

43. Cicero repeatedly gives indications of who taught whom, as do the Herculanean indices. But after this period such indications are scarce, suggesting less interest in oral tradition for the preservation of authentic school doctrine. Thus Aristo Alexandrinus and Cratippus came to call themselves Peripatetics when their primary studies had been with Antiochus' school, and Cicero saw himself as an Academic even though he may have spent more time studying with the Academy's opponents.

44. Antiochus may have had considerable influence at Rome, though even here Cicero, Cotta, Catulus, and Tubero retain a loyalty to the New Academy. His personal impact upon Cicero and others did not mean that he converted them to his Stoicizing Platonism, several intermediate responses being possible. In the East there is no indication at all that his philosophy swept all before him, and a lack of references to him among Greek writers suggests minimal influence.

45. For his characterization of the 'Academic' position see Photius cod. 212 169b31ff; it is at least possible that Aenes. had an Academic teacher, as the Academic L. Aelius Tubero (cf. Cic. *Lig.* 21) is presumably the man to whom the *Pyrrhonian Logoi* were dedicated, and he is described as (i) a sect-mate and (ii) an Academic in the Photian passage.

46. While it is probable that Cicero is not following Philo in the discussion of the senses at *Ac.* 2.79–90 (for the Roman Books are unlikely to have made a convincing reply to the *Sosus*, which had attacked them directly), it would seem that he did so when attacking the senses in the *Catulus* (see *Ac.* 2.79), for there Cicero seems to have taken the mild Philonian line while 'Catulus' put the Carneadean case. Some of the material which attacked the accuracy of the senses is preserved in the fragments of book 2 of the *Posterior Academics* (frs. 3, 6, 7, 8, 9, 10, 11). Glucker (*Ant.* p. 419) assumes with good reason that Philo is responsible for it, and that it came from the Roman Books, possibly via the *Sosus*. Attempts to reconcile Plato with the New Academy needed to dwell on the inaccuracy of the senses.

47. 'Lucem eripere', Cic. *ND* 1.6, *Ac.* 2.105, cf. S.E. *Math.* 7.260: τὸ ὥσπερ φῶς αὐτῶν ἀφαιρεῖσθαι.

48. Stob. *Ecl.* 2.40.18–20 (Wachsmuth).

49. It is the κριτήρια . . . τῆς ψυχῆς whose health must be guarded according to Philo (*ibid.*). According to the traditional types of criteria in Sextus (*Math.* 7.29–37, *PH* 2.14–17) the criterion 'through which' would be the only type which could be said to belong to the soul, and this is divided into intellect and senses (*Math.* 7.37, *PH* 2.16). If Philo is worried that false opinion may make the senses sick, then he is concerned with more than the outward physical well-being of the sense-organ. Note also that the Academic reply to Antiochus tackles the empty visions of dreamers and madmen under the heading of the sensations (*Ac.* 2.88–90), making it clear that the Academics recognized the existence of unhealthy sensations of a kind not dependent on the physical condition of the sense-organ so much as on the condition of the mind itself.

50. See above, n. 48: healthy opinions are, for Philo, the opposite of false ones.

51. The Middle Stoic polemic against the New Academy preserved at S.E. *Math.* 7.260 appears to be directed against persons who took a much stronger line against the senses than do the Academics of Aetius: perhaps against those who denied that there could be any real sense-perception at all.

52. S.E. *Math.* 7.161–2 (via Antiochus).

53. *Ac.* 2.99: 'itaque quae contra sensus contraque perspicuitatem dicantur, ea pertinere ad superiorem divisionem, contra posteriorem nihil dicere oportere'. One might say that Clitomachus accepted the term if it referred to what appeared evident rather than to what was self-evident.

54. See Tarrant, *Dionysius* 5 (1981), 66–97, especially section iv, and also chapter 5 below.

55. Eus. *PE* 14.739c = fr. 28 (des Places) = fr. 8 (Leemans).

56. See Tarrant, *Dionysius* 5 (1981), 66–97, especially section iii.

57. That Philo wished to propose a theory of practical certitude I do not doubt. *Ac.* 2.32 makes it clear that the Philonians (and compare even Carneades *apud* Numenius fr. 26 des Places) do not wish to make all things *incerta*; 2.35 shows that they wished to make confident statements, and 2.36 (*fides, confidere, confidant*) suggests strongly that they wished to feel confident of such statements. From Stob. *Ecl.* 2.39.20ff it seems clear that Philo required such confidence for the purpose of moral teaching and sound advice to others; Aenesidemus also gives the impression that Philo's Academy aimed at giving such advice (Phot. *Bibl.* 170a24–5).

58. Here the Academics believed that there were things which were

evident, but that such things did not require demonstration and could not become clearer by attempts to demonstrate (on account of a ready supply of counter-arguments). It is easy to see that such indemonstrables will not be able to be debated in a philosophical manner.

59. Clem. *Strom.* 8.7.3–8, 8.14.3; Galen *Inst. Log.* 1.1, *et saepe.*
60. See Tarrant, *Dionysius* 5 (1981), 66–97, especially section vi.
61. E.g. *Plac.* 2.256, 9.725, 778; *Opt. Doctr.* 4.50 (p. 90.8–10 Marquardt), *An. Pass.* ii. 94 (p. 74.3 Marquardt).
62. The purpose of *Math.* 7.219–25 in some earlier source had surely been to relate the activities of memory, thought, concept-building, and knowledge to initial evident sensations, upon which all were thought to rely. The conclusion at 7.226, in which more originality may be attributed to Antiochus himself (not, I think, to Sextus), still emphasized the necessity of reliable sense-data for the mind to work with. There is no suggestion that any other data are required.
63. In Photius *Bibl.* 169b25–6 (applying to all non-Pyrrhonists), 169b41–170a3 (of the Pyrrhonists *as opposed to* Academics), and 170a21–2, 28–38 (of the Academics).
64. The entry for 'those about Philo' is not *just* designed to refer to Philo, since Sextus offers this doctrine as part of a five-fold discussion of the five alleged Academies (cf. *PH* 1.220) – i.e. it is presented as the characteristic doctrine of the Fourth Academy. But the periphrasis demands that Philo himself did have this doctrine.
65. On the significance of *omnino* see Glucker, *Ant.* p. 80, n. 227.
66. 'Hoc cum infirmat tollitque Philo', *Ac.* 2.18.
67. *SVF* 1.59, cf. 2.60 (= D.L. 7.50). The Greek version (S.E. *Math.* 7.248) runs ὁποία οὐκ ἂν γένοιτο ἀπὸ μὴ ὑπάρχοντος.
68. Apparently looser expression, found at *Ac.* 2.112 (cf. 77), and perhaps closer to the Greek of S.E. *Math.* 7.151 (= *SVF* 2.90).
69. Here I preserve the MS text, without the alterations of Manutius–Baiter or of Lambinus.
70. See Tarrant, *Dionysius* 5 (1981), 66–97, particularly section vii, for Academic use of common notions. The term appears at Cic. *TD* 1.57, and is important to both anon. *In Tht.* and Plutarch. Alexander *De Fato* 2 (p. 165.14ff), 6 (p. 170.7–8), and 7–8 (p. 172.4–19 Bruns) shows clearly how the existence of a common notion of an entity was in itself an argument for the existence of that entity, but not necessarily of any more than its existence (see 2 p. 165.23–4 and also Cic. *ND* 1.12–13). At 7 (p. 172.4) the existence of a common concept is taken to show that the thing's existence is evident.
71. In Plutarch's *De Communibus Notitiis* there is a close connexion between common notions, the evident, and everyday use of

language (συνήθεια), as I show in *Dionysius* 5 (1981), 66–97. Cicero has also learnt that terms should be used naturally if they are not to obscure progress towards the facts (*Ac. fr.* 19).

72. Probably = Gk. διόρθωσις, hence *correctio* here implied a 'correct emendation' (cf. *Fin.* 4.21) rather than the introduction of a new correct alternative.

73. I regard the acceptance by Philo of a weak sense of apprehension as the heresy of the Roman Books (*Dionysius* 5 (1981), 66–97 especially section v); if so previous Academics must have rejected the notion of apprehension of any kind, as the heresy is new (*Ac.* 2.11, 18). Thus there would have been no need for a distinction between the evident and any *special* sense of 'apprehensible'.

74. See Glucker, *Ant.* p. 77, who points out the significance of the plural, which can scarcely apply to the Roman-Book theory alone. This does not, however, mean that the people concerned did not include Philo (*pace* Glucker), only that their views are not specifically associated with the Roman Books. Glucker (p. 78) guesses that Metrodorus and followers are being criticized, but Metrodorus is only relevant to the *Academica qua* precedent for Philo (*Ac.* 2.78, Aug. *c. Acad.* 3.41); cf. D. Sedley, *Phronesis* 26 (1981), 71.

75. Aug. *CD* 19.1–3, reporting Varro, who in turn is said to have followed Antiochus.

76. For my discussion of the phrase ὅσον ἐπὶ . . . see *Dionysius* 5 (1981), 72–3.

77. Sedley, *Phronesis* 26 (1981), 72–3.

78. *Tim.* 27d–28a, *Rep.* 477a ff *et saepe*, *Phd.* 74b ff etc.

79. *Ac.* 2.87, 116–17; [Galen] *Isagoge* 14.684 (Kühn).

80. Sedley (*Phronesis* 26 (1981), 72–3) tries to show how Philo could have made use of *Tim.* 40d, 29cd, and 72d for his One-Academy thesis by ascribing to all concerned the belief that God apprehended things: a belief which Epiphanius attributed to the New Academy. While reluctant to believe that Philo's only concession to apprehensibility fell in the realm of theology, I concede that it is possible that Philo did attribute certain knowledge to God; for an important argument from the *Academica* falls back upon the idea that *God* might be able to provide a presentation which was both false and indistinguishable from an exactly similar true one (*Ac.* 2.47–50), and God himself could presumably not be deceived in any such way!

81. Brochard, *SG* p. 196, makes much use of the concept of truth in things, as if this could explain why Philo thought things were apprehensible (but not for us). But the Academics seem always to have debated about how we could distinguish true from false, and the problem had been one of recognition; and true presentations were not *ipso facto* apprehensible; it is only the existence of true

and *evident* presentations which makes a weak sense of 'apprehension' possible in Academic eyes.

82. See Photius 169b33: it is almost certain that Photius found reference to the 'sect' of Tubero in Aenesidemus' work, since his description of Tubero seems dependent upon the eulogy through which Aenes. made his dedication of the work to Tubero.

83. On the term as a whole see Glucker, *Ant.* pp. 166–92; for his use for internal sects see p. 166 and *Index Acad. Herc.* 18.7–12, 40–1, and 36.16–19.

84. See Glucker, *Ant.* pp. 191–2, particularly the following: 'Nowhere is the term used in such a context where it could refer unambiguously to a school of philosophy in its institutional sense. In some of the specimens . . . αἵρεσις comes near enough to a political, religious, or philosophical "faction" or "movement" regarded from the point of view which we would call its "ideology".'

85. Aenesidemus is trying to *persuade* Tubero that Philo's kind of philosophy is inadequate, and to *show* him that no position intermediate between scepticism and dogmatism was possible; it seems likely, then, that Tubero is not yet aware of inconsistency in Philo's position.

86. K. Janacek (*Eirene* 14 (1976), 93–100) argues that he does so, even preserving much of Aenesidemus' characteristic language.

87. See Tarrant, *Dionysius* 5 (1981), 89–92.

88. *Ant.* p. 117 n. 67.

89. See above, n. 70.

90. As stated in n. 73, I regard the position on apprehension to have been the heresy of the Roman Books, and this was regarded as *new* by Cicero (*Ac.* 2.11, 18). The reason why new doctrine on apprehension was proposed at this time is that (i) Philo wanted his theory to be seen to accord with Plato's, while (ii) Antiochus was now claiming (see chapter 5) that Plato used an equivalent term in the *Timaeus* (28a etc.) in such a way as to support the Stoic position. Philo is able to say that Plato would indeed have supported the non-technical use of the term, but not the Stoic use; see further my article in *LCM* 7.2 (1982), 21–2.

91. Such issues as anon. saw to be supreme, probably the criterion of knowledge and the moral goal, with Antiochus (*Ac.* 2.29). See also Tarrant, *Dionysius* 5 (1981), 65 n. 11 and chapter 4 below.

92. See particularly *Ant.* p. 305; but Glucker errs concerning the date of the work, and is forced to regard the author as very inferior in order to understand the passage as he wishes. Against G. Invernizzi's interpretation of the passage, see chapter 4 i.

93. Nor can one confine the author's claims to the thesis that contemporary Academics were at one with Plato, for any reply to (or version of) the Roman-Book thesis had to involve the whole history

of the Academy. It is also very difficult to find authors who would have adhered *dogmatically* to Platonic doctrine while calling themselves Academics.

94. See chapter 4 below.

95. *Ac.* 2.60; for Charmadas see also chapter 2 above, nn. 13–14. Also *Ac.* fr. 21 (Aug. *c. Acad.* 3.43), which was surely based on a Roman-Book claim as reported by Cicero. Naturally Philo's claims did not exclude Carneades from a list of those who disclosed their beliefs esoterically, and Numenius (fr. 27 des Places = 7 Lang = Eus. *PE* 14.738d/739a) does preserve the view that Carneades would admit the truth of such propositions as anybody would assent to, but I see no evidence for *Platonic* esoteric teaching by Carneades.

96. The fact that folly is used by Aenes. as the opposite of virtue in Academic thought agrees well with Stob. *Ecl.* 2.40.18–20, where Philo thinks of false opinions as the cause of ill-health of the mind, and with *Ac.* 2.129 where Plato is associated with Herillus on the question of the moral goal; this was knowledge for Herillus, and Plato was clearly being credited with a similar theory, though it was not in the interests of the Fourth Academics to say explicitly that Plato made knowledge the goal; however, the Fourth Academy themselves aimed at either the truth or the closest approximation to it (*Ac.* 2.7); it was the goal of their discipline, and hence perhaps life's goal also; and such a position could plausibly be attributed to Plato, who aimed at becoming like a God *to the greatest degree possible*, that being both true wisdom and true virtue (*Tht.* 176bc).

97. Note how Cicero's *Academica* shows both sides spending much time discussing the Stoic concept of the sage (e.g. *Ac.* 2.115: 'de sapiente loquamur, de quo ut saepe iam dixi omnis haec quaestio est'); next note how Arcesilaus' epistemology had been tied to Zeno's (*Ac.* 2.77, S.E. *Math.* 7.150–7); on Academic use of definition see *Ac.* 2.40, cf. 43; this no doubt included both Carneadean definitions and borrowed ones. Some Fourth Academics may, like Antiochus, have intended that definitions used should correctly mirror reality, in which case the complaints of Aenes. would have been justified.

98. In this sense it can take an indirect statement construction: 'affirm that $p$', e.g. 170a12; but in such cases it may still be better to translate 'distinguish that $p$'.

99. If, that is, 169b38–40 are not just Photius' brief précis of the Aenesideman material which appears in full at 170a14–38.

100. See *Jos.* 125–47, *Conf.* 104–6, *Ebr.* 170–4, 178–80.

101. According to my reconstruction of it (*Dionysius* 5 (1981), 89–92) the argument will not work unless the Academics (i) insist upon the virtues of hesitation, so as (ii) to deny that things are

known, and so (iii) to affirm that things are entirely non-apprehended, while still saying (iv) that things are in some sense apprehended.

## 4. Anonymous 'In Theaetetum'

1. He refers to his works on *Symp.* (70.11) and *Tim.* (35.11), and promises a commentary on the *Phaedo* (48.10).
2. G. Invernizzi, *Riv. Filos. Neoscol.* 68 (1976), 214–33. Compare also K. Praechter, (*Göttingische Gelehrte Anzeigen* 26 (1909), 530–47, especially 533ff).
3. 54.43–55.7; cf. also Praechter's plausible reconstruction of 47.35–7: [ἀλλ]ως μὲν γὰρ ἀπε[φαίν]ετο καὶ εἶχεν [δόγ]ματα (Praechter, *Göttingische Gelehrte Anzeigen* 26 (1909), 536). I prefer here [ἰδί]ως μὲν in order to maintain a contrast with ἐν δὲ τῷ διδάσκειν (37–8), but even if ἄλλως is correct it is clear that A did not consider the revelation of doctrine to be a part of the Socratic teaching-process. And this is where he would see a link between Socrates–Plato and the New Academy.
4. Chiefly in *CQ* 33 (1983), 161–87; cf. *Dionysius* 5 (1981), 68 n. 9 and *Phronesis* 29 (1984), 96–9.
5. On Platonics and Academics as distinct groups see Galen, *An. Morb.* 96 (cf. 60), *Pecc. Dignot. CMG V* 4.1.1 p. 62, *Opt. Doctr.*, *passim*; also Glucker, *Ant.* pp. 206–25, Ph. de Lacy, *AJPh* 93 (1972), 29. I know of no parallel for A's use of the adjective 'Academic' to describe Plato.
6. The correct text of *Meno* 98a seems to have been known to Albinus (*Prol.* 6, p. 150.27 Hermann), to Plutarch (*Mor.* 435b), to Atticus (apparent in fr. 4.80 des Places), and to Taurus. I discover through Jaap Mansfeld (Mansfeld, *Phronesis* 28 (1983), 59–74) that Ps.-Hero *Def.* 137.4 quotes a passage of Taurus dependent on 98a; furthermore Taurus appears to be following col. 15 of *K* (or a third text very closely related to col. 15). It is very difficult to believe that A has substituted a wrong reading for the correct one in some source of his own; moreover all three definitions of simple knowledge given by A are nicely tailored to suit his own epistemology, suggesting originality.
7. See for example Dillon's comment (*MP* p. 270: 'maintains a stupefying level of banality') which would be fair if and only if *K* belonged to a time when Platonism was in an advanced state of redevelopment.
8. We know of discussion among early Platonic interpreters as to whether the prologue requires (1) deep interpretation, (2) basic moral interpretation only, or (3) no interpretation at all (Proclus

*In Parm. I* p. 658.34ff Cousin). It appears from *In Tim.* 1.204.17 (Diehl) that Severus took position (3) on all that preceded *Tim.* 27b, whereas Porphyry took position (2) (possibly (1)) and Iamblichus definitely took position (1).

9. Praechter, *Göttingische Gelehrte Anzeigen* 26 (1909), 539 thinks that A took position (2), while Invernizzi, *Riv. Filos. Neoscol.* 68 (1976), 219 thinks that it would be more accurate to attribute to him position (3). In fact, regarding the brief prologue in which Euclides speaks to Terpsion, A thinks that it does have some content relevant to everyday ethics, but that this does not require interpretation (4.17–27). It should be noted, however, that refusing to interpret this brief introductory dialogue cannot be sensibly compared with refusing to interpret *Tim.* 17a–27b. A Severus would surely have refused to interpret *Tht.* 143d up to 145c, where Socrates begins to turn the conversation towards the subject of knowledge. A does interpret this section, which might be called a second prologue, at a greater length than one might expect.

10. In Polybius we find τεθαρρηκότως (2.10.7, 9.9.8) and τετολμηκότως (1.25.3, 9.4.2). In Lxx *II Ma.* we find λεληθότως (6.11, 8.1) and in Lxx *Za.* 14.11 we find πεποιθότως. The former of these occurs at *K* 59.19, the latter at 55.11. *K* also has the passive form σεσοβημένως, 10.34.

11. Aelian, Dio Cassius, Diodorus Siculus, Dionysius of Halicarnassus, Galen, Heliodorus, Josephus, Philo Alexandrinus, Philodemus, Plutarch, Pollux, Sextus Empiricus, Strabo. It should be noted that my methods were not infallible, and I may have missed occasional forms of this kind where the verb has been compounded within a prepositional prefix. There are, however, very few of these, and I should expect to have found most of them in authors which have been adequately indexed.

12. The forms δεδιότως (11.49) and ἠναγκασμένως (*Pomp.* 3) are not certain in Dionysius.

13. See my article in *CQ* 33 (1983), 179–87.

14. Stob. *Ecl.* 2.39.20ff (Wachsmuth), particularly 2.40.18–20.

15. With the passage from Albinus it would be usual to compare Theon *Expos.* p. 14.7–15.14: where, however, mathematics is the purgative factor. It is likely that Theon is directly dependent upon Thrasyllus (see my article in *Phronesis* 28 (1983), 98 n. 55).

16. D.L. 3.49.

17. See Tarrant, *CQ* 33 (1983), 167–8 and *K* 2.11–52 (cf. fr. 4).

18. S.E. *PH* 2.22, *Phdr.* 229ef.

19. Olymp. *In Phd.* 2.6 (14.7–20 Norvin), 6.14 (38.20–3), 8.17 (51.2–12), Damascius *In Phd.* 182.1.

20. The fourth argument to prove Plato's scepticism cited by anon. *Prol. in Plat. Phil.* 10 (p. 205.28–34 Hermann): Plato thinks that

cognition has two components, sensation and intellect, but the former's accuracy is repeatedly questioned, while the latter cannot be functioning properly when engulfed in bodily evils.

21. Anon. *Prol. in Plat. Phil.* 10 (p. 205.12–17 Hermann).

22. *Ibid.*, p. 205.18–21. Note that Proclus was aware of ephectic attacks on the reality of mathematics which centred on attempts to prove the non-existence of mathematical first-principles such as the unit (*In Eucl.* p. 199.3–9 Friedlein). This tactic is employed at S.E. *Math.* 4.20 against Plato: 'So much for the monad, on the destruction of which all number is destroyed.' Sextus here makes use of *Phd.* 96e ff (4.21–2) and a comparable set of puzzles occurs at *Tht.* 154cd.

23. Note that Aenesidemus is himself known to have been interested in the critical whole–part relationship, *Math.* 9.337, and that Sextus believes that the overthrow of the monad would secure the overthrow of all number, *Math.* 4.20. Other relevant passages may be 201d ff, where we meet a theory that there are no knowable units, and 195e–9c, where Plato fails to explain false opinion concerning the sum of 5 + 7.

24. Ps.-Ammonius' attack on 'ephectics' (*In Categ.* 2.8–3.8) is definitely aimed at Pyrrhonists, and it was Ammonius who first challenged the 'ephectic' view of Plato (Olymp. *In Phd.* 8.17 = p. 51.1–12 Norvin). Long before this Clement's attack on the ephectics had been headed 'against the Pyrrhonists' (*Strom.* 8.5). See also Philoponus *In Categ.* 2.3ff and Simpl. *In Categ.* 4.5.

25. Book 1 of the *Pyrrhonian Logoi*; see Photius *Bibl.* cod. 212, p. 169.36–170.41.

26. A particularly relevant passage is anon. *Prol. in Plat. Phil.* 5 (p. 202.22–7 Hermann); compare also Sextus' treatment of the Academic preference for certain presentations, *PH* 1.227–30.

27. Note the verb: ἀκαταληψίαν πρεσβεύει (205.14, 21, 31), designed perhaps to avoid strong terms for asserting a theory, while at the same time indicating a definite approach to things as being unknowable.

28. S.E. *PH* 1.1, Gellius *NA* 11.5.8.

29. Such anticipation seems to have been acknowledged even at S.E. *PH* 1.7, but is treated more elaborately at D.L. 9.71–3.

30. 'That perplexity is a road towards apprehension is clear to all'. Notice the verb διαπορεῖν (and compare 206.13), for the δια-compound was probably a favourite with Aenes. (Phot. *Bibl.* p. 170a27, 32). Note also that 205.6–7, ἐπιρρήματά τινα ἀμφίβολά τε καὶ διστακτικά (cf. also Elias *In Categ.* p. 110.13, Olymp. *In Phd.* 8.17.2, *In Alc. I* 24.19, Syrianus *In Meta.* 73.18 for similar terminology in 'ephectic' contexts) is reminiscent of Aenesidemus

in Phot. *Bibl.* 169b39–40: τὰ μὲν τίθενται ἀδιστάκτως, τὰ δὲ αἴρουσιν ἀναμφιβόλως (cf. 170a28–9).

31. See chapter 1.

32. For the phrase see *Math.* 7.264, and cf. μένεω ἐν τῇ ἐποχῇ at *Math.* 7.380, 8.118, 259.

33. Burkhard, *Heraklit-Nachfolge* pp. 21ff follows the emendation of P. Natorp (*Rh. Mus.* 38 (1883), 31–4) which would yield this view.

34. This is not characteristic of Sextus' view of Plato, and conflicts with *Math.* 7.281–2. The definition belongs to *Def.* 415a.

35. *PH* 1.92, 93, 124, 126, 127, 134, 140.

36. For his place in the Pyrrhonist succession-list see D.L. 9.116.

37. Note that the empiricism which Galen had known (and which Sextus rejects) had a positive belief in non-apprehensibility (*Sect. Intr.* 78, p. 11.20–12.1 Helmreich). I see no reason to suspect that Menodotus did not share in this positive belief, for his brand of empiricism permitted him to affirm that Asclepiades' views were *all false* (Galen *Subfig. Emp.* p. 84.18–32 Deichgräber); this would show (in Sextus' eyes) excessive confidence, so that he might be expected to hold the Pyrrhonist thesis with excessive confidence too.

38. Note that Sextus' sources only claimed that Heraclitism could be reached by way of *scepsis* (*PH* 1.210), that Democritism used the same material and had an affinity (1.213), and that Protagorism had an affinity (1.216). There is no evidence that claims of identity were made in these cases.

39. He is mentioned as a precursor of Pyrrhonism at D.L. 9.73 (for no obvious good reason), and Philoponus makes him a pupil (!) of Pyrrho at *In Categ.* 2.3ff, but he is not mentioned in Cicero's *Academica* where the epistemological views of several other early physicists are debated.

40. Significant is the omission of Xenophanes from the main discussion of *PH* 1.210ff, even though he is treated with respect by Sextus at *Math.* 7.49–52. Also relevant is the complete omission of Xeniades, Anacharsis, Gorgias, Metrodorus, Anaxarchus, and Monimus (cf. *Math.* 7.53–88).

41. Also *K* 61.23–30, D.L. 9.78 (πρὸς δὲ τὰς ἐν ταῖς σκέψεσιν ἀντιθέσεις) to 79 (ἀπὸ τῶν ἐναντίων . . . ἴσας πιθανότητας), Photius *Bibl.* p. 170b10–11; see also Burkhard, *Heraklit-Nachfolge* pp. 42–5. For Sextus see Janacek's index under ἰσοσθένεια.

42. Burkhard, *Heraklit-Nachfolge* p. 42: 'Laut P. 1, 210 galt es für Aenesidem als ein Spezifikum der Skepsis, das τὰ ἐναντία περὶ τὸ αὐτὸ φαίνεσθαι festzustellen.'

43. *PH* 1.209 ἐφεκτικήν (rare); 1.217 πρὸς τοὺς Πυρρωνείους (rare of

persons, cf. 1.13, 1.17 only), where relativism is the point of similarity, 1.221–2 ἀπορητικός in relation to Plato (elsewhere only at 1.7 in *PH*), 1.232 δοκεῖ τοῖς Πυρρωνείοις κοινωνεῖν λόγοις of Arcesilaus' complete unanimity with the Pyrrhonists.

44. See above p. 75 with nn. 34–5.

45. Invernizzi, *Riv. Filos. Neoscol.* 68 (1976), 220, denies this outright, but he is surely misled by the reference to *dogmata* which he thinks may only be held by somebody arguing the dogmatist cause. Philo's thesis, however, was not that Plato was a true sceptic who rejected *dogmata*, for Philo was nothing like a true sceptic himself. It was a theory of twin currents within the Academy from its foundation, aporetic and cautiously (perhaps esoterically) doctrinal.

46. According to 7.14–20 assimilation to God is the basis upon which Plato founds his theory of justice.

47. Stob. *Ecl.* 2.49.11: 'It is only possible through *phronesis*' (though this is glossed 'and this is that which is according to virtue'). I suspect that Eudorus wanted to confine the assimilation-process to the *rational faculty* (cf. 2.53.1–7), as would befit one who wrote in the Posidonian tradition, but not to confine it thereby to reasoning alone. It is interesting to compare *K* 58.42–9.

48. See Glucker, *Ant.* pp. 53–60.

49. Cicero refrains from saying that Herillus' position was identical with Plato's, and also suggests that the views of the Megarics (the good = what is one, alike, and the same) owed much to Plato (*Ac.* 2.129).

50. If, as I assume, R. Hoyer (*De Antiocho Ascalonita Diss.* (Bonn, 1883) pp. 26ff) was correct in seeing Antiochus behind the doxography of the goal of life at Clem. *Strom.* 2.127–33; for at 131 Plato is credited with a double goal, (i) the good itself and (ii) participation in it by assimilation.

51. Stob. *Ecl.* 2.49.18–2.50.10 credits Plato with at least four ways of expressing his assimilation-goal.

52. Note the words 'an intelligible [God] and harmonic principle of the cosmic well-ordered condition' (49.17–18) and the importance attached to *Tim.* 90a–d (49.19–21, 50.6–10, 53.1–7).

53. See Glucker, *Ant.* p. 54 n. 144 and pp. 58–63. 'Suspension of judgment' is the goal attributed to the New Academics by 'certain persons' according to Clem. *Strom.* 2.129 and Cic. *Fin.* 3.31, and it is also seen as Arcesilaus' goal by Sextus (*PH* 1.232).

54. We should probably see Democritus behind the remains of col. 62.

55. DK75 B1.

56. As seems to be the case in dialogues such as *Sph.* and *Phil.*

57. DK12 B10, 49a, 50, 51, 67, 82/83, 88, 103, and of course S.E. *PH* 1.210–12.

162

58. This can be seen in tropes 1–4, D.L. 9.79–82 and S.E. *PH* 1.40–117.
59. See my remarks in *Dionysius* 5 (1981), 78–84.
60. See *ND* 3.35 and cf. Aenes. at S.E. *Math.* 10.233.
61. Aenes. (S.E. *Math.* 8.8) and Antiochus (?) at *Math.* 7.126–34 both represent Heraclitus as saying that truth is what seems true to men generally, apparently a gross misinterpretation.
62. *Phoenix* 24 (1970), 309–19.
63. Sextus' attribution of strange interpretations of Heraclitus to Aenesidemus is not matched in Tertullian; the latter does sometimes attribute 'Heraclitean' doctrines directly to Aenes. (*De An.* 9.5, 14.5, 25.1), but the names of Aenes. and Heraclitus are kept separate at 14.5, where the mind-theory of Strato, Aenes., and Heraclitus is mentioned. At 9.5 the view that air is the soul's substance is attributed to Aenesidemus and Anaximenes, and 'according to certain people' . . . Heraclitus also. These words scarcely offer the impression that Tertullian has Aenes. in mind as the origin of this view of Heraclitus. One may compare 17.2 on the senses: 'horum fidem Academici durius damnant, secundum quosdam et Heraclitus et Diocles et Empedocles, certe Plato in Timaeo inrationalem pronuntians sensualitatem et opinioni coimplicatam'. Here it is the Academics and Plato who appear beside a sceptic view of Heraclitus; the name of Aenes. fails to appear. It may be objected that extant Heraclitean doctrines associated with Aenes. do not bring in the flux-doctrine at all, while it is this which A would have wished to trace in the Fourth Academy. But we could hardly expect Sextus to have cited Aenes. as an authority for attributing the flux-doctrine to Heraclitus — nobody needed any authority for that. And I doubt whether evidence is entirely lacking for an interest in flux in Aenes., since Aenesideman material in Philo (*Ebr.* 170, 172–4, 178–80) involves such a theory; moreover Olympiodorus (*In Categ.* 4.24–8) and Philoponus (*In Categ.* 2.8ff) connect Heraclitus *and the flux doctrine* with Pyrrhonism. Clearly Aenes. cannot have held any *dogma* about the flux-theory, but he must surely have made non-dogmatic use of it. And the third book of the *Pyrrhonian Logoi* would seem to have been a likely place for such a discussion (see Phot. *Bibl.* p. 170b9–12).
64. See Tarrant, *Dionysius* 5 (1981), 80 with n. 48. I should not, however, explain Aenesidemus' view of Heraclitism as a natural sequel of *scepsis* (S.E. *PH* 1.210–12) as something ascribed to Heraclitus in a dialogue. This view must have been expressed when discussing Pyrrhonism's sister-philosophies.
65. Cleanthes wrote four books of interpretation of Heraclitus (D.L. 7.114 = *SVF* 1.481) and Sphaerus wrote five books on Heraclitus

(D.L. 7.177 = *SVF* 1.620). It seems that the Middle Stoa did not retain this interest.

66. On this debate see David Sedley (*Phronesis* 27 (1982), 255–75).

67. *Strom.* 5.83.4, cf. 84.1–2; see Tarrant, *CQ* 33 (1983), 162 n. 21.

68. See chapter 3 ii, with n. 17.

69. Here I think of (a) *Ac.* 2.30 where the various assent-processes and concept-forming processes yield knowledge by the addition (note 'accessit') of *ratio* (= λόγος) and *argumenti conclusio* (= ἀπόδειξις) etc. And the combination of λόγος and ἀπόδειξις might easily be referred to as λογισμός; (b) S.E. *Math.* 7.143–4.

70. Examples of 'compound knowledge' are geometry and music, col. 15.

71. One exception is the 'wisdom' of *Tht.* 176c. I suspect that A is anxious to show that Plato is not discussing anything akin to the sage's wisdom of the Stoics, which must be regarded as basically 'systematic' if we heed two of the definitions of Stob. *Ecl.* 2.73.21ff (= *SVF* 3.112) which include the term 'system' (cf. also S.E. *Math.* 7.40 = *SVF* 2.132, where truth is found to be 'systematic' *qua* consisting in knowledge). Such a purpose would explain the lengths to which A will go to find details of Plato's text (*Tht.* 145c7–8, d8–9) which will support the contention that *Tht.* examines *simple* knowledge (14.42ff, 17.25–32).

72. See M. F. Burnyeat, *Aristotelian Society supp. vol.* 54 (1980), 173–91; J. Moline, *Plato's Theory of Understanding* (University of Wisconsin Press, 1981).

73. Comparison with S.E. *Math.* 7.226 (on Peripatetic epistemology), where sensation is the tool of reason, makes it probable that the criterion 'through which' is sensation. But comparison with *Didasc.* 4 (p. 154.13–18 Hermann), where reason is itself a tool, clouds the issue.

74. S.E. *PH* 2.16 and *Math.* 7.37 both make sensation and intellect possible criteria 'through which', but Potamo (D.L. 1.21) makes the mind his criterion 'by which' (agent), and *Didasc.* 4 makes only reason the criterion 'through which'.

75. See chapter 3 iii.

76. Stob. *Ecl.* 2.40.18–20.

77. E.g. *Ebr.* 169, *Conf.* 127, *Her.* 246; see M. Freudenthal, *Die Erkenntnislehre Philos von Alexandria* (Berlin, 1891) pp. 24–42.

78. Compare Potamo's 'criterion through which': the most accurate presentation, D.L. 1.21.

79. See chapter 6 below.

## 5. Interlude: Antiochus in the New Academy

1. Note how *Ac.* 2.21ff tries to refute the Academic position on the criterion by arguing that without it we cannot have reliable universal

concepts, memory, *ars*, or knowledge (as if the existence of such things could be taken for granted).

2. Why else is it possible for Cicero to ask at the end of *Ac.* 2.69 why Antiochus did not secede from the Academy and join the Stoa (sc. before he actually did secede!)? Since the explanation of his eventual succession is his acquisition of his own pupils, he must have had Stoicizing views before his acquisition of pupils. And since it seems that he had pupils for some time before the *Sosus*-crisis (Glucker, *Ant.* p. 18), his Stoicizing had probably been noticed at least as early as 95 B.C.

3. Aristus, Aristo Alexandrinus, and Dio (*Ac.* 2.12) were there with him and had apparently arrived from Athens, either with him or not long before him. See Glucker, *Ant.* p. 18.

4. David Sedley points out to me the parallel with *Ac.* 2.34: 'convicio veritatis coacti', applied to the Philonians.

5. The translation of *probabile* as 'probable' is highly misleading; the Latin means 'capable of being approved', and its Greek equivalent 'capable of being believed'. Carneadean philosophy has nothing to do with standard probabilism, cf. M. F. Burnyeat in M. Schofield, M. Burnyeat and J. Barnes (eds.), *Doubt and Dogmatism: Studies in Hellenistic Epistemology* (Oxford, 1980) p. 28.

6. Cf. *Ac.* 2.22−6.

7. *Ac.* 1.15−42, *Fin.* 5.9−14 (Peripatetic only) and 19−20. It is of course relevant that the Academic school since Carneades had approved of delineating various possible and actual positions during the course of an investigation, and that Antiochus was still working as an Academic.

8. *Math.* 7.89, 122, 126, 138−9, 141, 144.

9. Plato is held to have achieved the initial coupling between *logos* and the evident (i.e. evident sensation) at 141−4, while the Peripatetics (217−26) work towards a similar view from a position which begins by treating sensation slightly more favourably. Where Heraclitus rejected sensation, he is thought to have rejected irrational (*logos*-free) sensation (126). Carneades' arguments work against irrational sensation (165). Empedocles accepts the senses when reason controls them (124), on which see below. Note also that Sextus is particularly keen to do battle with those who link reason closely with the senses (as Antiochus, *Ac.* 2.30) in the pages which follow the doxography: 307−9, 356−8, and particularly 359−68.

10. Unless one excepts *Didasc.* 4 (p. 156.5 Hermann), where the term has a completely different significance, being opposed to discursive thought.

11. See chapter 1 above, my remarks in *CQ* 33 (1983), 183, and especially Glucker, *Ant.* pp. 213−15.

12. See Tarrant, *CQ* 33 (1983), 183 with n. 145.

13. 'And *certain persons* postulate a Fifth too, that of Antiochus and his followers.' Nobody could deny that Antiochus' school took a very new position, so that those who did not see it as an additional Academy had to see it as no Academy at all: cf. also 1.235, where the view is expressed that he taught Stoicism in the Academy (presumably before seceding, since he later taught at the Ptolemaeum).

14. It enables the omission of the adjective 'irrational' (*logos*-free), which is applied by Plato to sensation, while the source is committed to closing the gap between *logos* and sensation, and wants Plato to be seen to be doing likewise.

15. Compare S.E. *Math.* 7.364 (where Sextus may still have Antiochus in mind): ἐναργὲς γὰρ ἀξιοῦται ὑπὸ τῶν ἐναντίων τὸ ἐξ ἑαυτοῦ λαμβανόμενον ...

16. *Sph.* 226e8, 265a10, *Plt.* 282a3, 288c4, 294b1, 304e4, *Tht.* 148d6, *Phdr.* 273e2.

17. P. Thévenaz (*L'Ame du monde, le devenir, et la matière chez Plutarque* (Paris, 1938) p. 82), followed by H. Cherniss, notes that 1025a appears to assume what Plutarch had earlier rejected when criticizing Xenocrates (1013d), that Same and Other are in some sense responsible for rest and motion respectively. Moreover the use of the term ἰδέα at 1025c is reminiscent of the (Posidonian) use of the term at 1023b, which Plutarch misunderstands and criticizes at 1023c: just as Posidonius cannot have used the term *in its Platonic sense* to refer to the ever-moving soul (for Platonic Ideas are static), so one cannot suppose that the description of the Same as 'Idea of things in the same state' and of Other as 'Idea of things in a different state' was meant to refer to unmoved Platonic Ideas, for both of these two Ideas are then given an ἔργον: and of course the Other is source of motion at 1025a, but surely not an unmoved mover. Finally Cherniss (Loeb edn, p. 235 n. f) notes that at 1024d Plutarch derives Same and Other from One and Dyad (cf. 1025d: μοναδικῆς–δυαδικῆς), thus introducing number into the nature of soul almost as directly as Xenocrates and quite as directly as the Posidonians, both of whom he criticizes for their emphasis on number (1013cd, 1023cd). A further slight anomaly may be detected at 1025b (cf. 1025e–6a, 1024e), where Same and Other are apparently the dominant elements in the soul, while Divided and Undivided are intermediate elements (akin to air and water, *qua* intermediates helping to link fire and earth) while Plutarch's question at 1023f concerning the origin of the opining-and-sensing nature is answered (1024a) in a way which assumes that Divided and Undivided are the only proper elements of the soul. Note that at 1024ef the Other is responsible for sensation, and φαντασίαι need no special explanation, whereas Plutarch is

usually keen to identify the φανταστικὴ δύναμις with the Divided essence, and tends to link this with sensations too (1023d−4b). Thus some source, with views rather different from those found in Plutarch's criticism of earlier thinkers, must be sought for 1024d (ἦν δὲ τὸ θάτερον οὐ κίνησις) to 1026a (τὸ ἄπειρον ὁρίσας) inclusive. The source must be somebody generally respected by Plutarch for his views on the *Timaeus*, and Eudorus inevitably comes to mind. The basic interpretation underlying the passage owes something to Xenocrates (1012de) in that it attaches importance to the One and the Dyad and appears to derive (some) motion and rest from Other and Same, but differs in seeing One and Dyad as source of Other and Same rather than of Divided and Undivided; it owes something to Crantor (1012f) in attaching importance to the epistemic role of the soul and (almost certainly) in applying a principle of like-by-like cognition (the elements of reality being One, Many, Indivisible, and Divided, 1025e), but it differs in allowing Same and Other to dominate rather than the intelligible (undivided) and changeable (divisible) essences. The Posidonian interpretation *may* have been of this kind, and so may that of Eudorus, who sees merit but not perfection in the views of both Xenocrates and Crantor (1013b).

18. 1024f, κίνησις . . . περὶ τὸ μένον, . . . μονὴ . . . περὶ τὸ κινούμενον, 1025e, περὶ τε θάτερον ἐντυγχάνων τῷ θατέρῳ καὶ ταὐτῷ περὶ θάτερον, where I suspect earlier influence. Note too that the words περὶ τὰ σώματα (35a) must have been taken in a very literal spatial sense by Posidonius when he identified 'the essence around the bodies' with the limits of physical bodies.

19. *c. Acad.* 2.15: 'veterum physicorum . . . implorabat fidem'.

20. Hirzel, *Untersuchungen* vol. 3, pp. 78ff.

21. E.g. DK A2 (D.L. 9.21), A8, A29 (Pl. *Sph.* 242cd), A31.

22. But see my article in *Apeiron* 18 (1983), 73−84, where I argue that B1.31−2 may in any case be spurious.

23. *Didasc.* 4 (p. 154.18−30 Hermann), where we meet first with the division of *logos* into divine and human, then with the division of the latter into doxastic and epistemonic.

24. *Tim.* 30b7, 48d2, 53d5, 55d5, 56a1, b4, 68b7, 90e8.

25. *Dionysius* 5 (1981), 78ff treats the subject in more detail.

26. As one who saw a great gulf between the true nature of things (atoms and void), and man's conventional sense-based picture; cf. *Ac.* 1.44, 2.14, 32, 73.

27. Note that Meno's paradox on the impossibility of inquiry is solved at times with reference to the 'notion', e.g. Stoics in Plut. fr. 215f (and cf. Plutarch's own ἀνεννόητος at 215e) and *K* 47.13−24.

28. Cf. *Ac.* 1.44, *Ac.* 2.16. 76−7.

29. Note the words ἔδει . . . ζητεῖν.

30. See David Sedley, 'On signs', in *Science and Speculation*, ed. J. Barnes *et al.* (Cambridge, 1982) pp. 239–72, especially pp. 265–7, for more on the account of Epicurus' canonic.

31. See chapter 3 iii.

32. The term 'Aristotelian' should perhaps be qualified, since Aristotle's emphasis falls on the knowability of different objects *relative to us* and *by nature* (*An. Po.* 71b34–72a4, *Phys.* 184a16–26, *EN* 1095b2–4). While it does seem that what is most knowable to us is apprehended by sensation in Aristotle (sensation thus coming first in the cognitive process) the assertion that intellect is prior in potency perhaps gives a new loading to Aristotle's theory, designed to suggest an intellectual *power* present at the beginning of the cognition-process, though not achieving its own special activity until the end of it, like *mens* (= νοῦς) in the Ciceronian passage, where one should also notice *naturalem vim* (= φυσικὴν δύναμιν).

33. Compare the term *regula* at *Ac.* 2.29, 58; sensation is in fact said to be a tool analogous to the craftsman's ruler at *Math.* 7.226. The use of the terms τεχνίτης and ὄργανον strongly suggests that the writer has in mind the criteria ὑφ' οὖ and δι' οὖ.

34. See above, chapter 3 ii.

35. E.g. *Opt. Doctr.* p. 89.23–90.10 Marquardt, *Plac.* 2.256, 9.725, *et al.* Galen may, despite his rejection of Favorinus' Academicism, be quite relevant as a source for Fourth Academic attitudes. M. Frede, 'On Galen's epistemology', in *Galen: Problems and Prospects*, ed. V. Nutton (London, 1981) pp. 68–9 remarks that 'it is worth noting that if we did not have his explicit remarks to the contrary, . . . he might well be thought to be an Academic of the kind represented by Philo of Larissa, Cicero, or Plutarch. His sympathies are clearly on the side of Plato's school. He shares the eclecticism of these men . . . His writings are full of remarks against dogmatism which remind one of the anti-dogmatic tradition of the Academy . . .'

36. See *Ac.* 1.36–42 for Antiochus' attitude towards Zeno, who is also respected by his opponents. Chrysippus is mentioned only at 2.73, 75, 93–6, 138, 140, and 143; of these 73 and 143 look down upon him.

37. See *Ac.* 1.35.

38. Sedley, 'On signs' pp. 239–72, especially pp. 265–7.

### 6. God's thoughts as objects of knowledge

1. Aetius, *Plac.* 1.3.21 (*Dox.* p. 287.17ff), *Didasc.* 8ff, Atticus in Proclus, *In Tim.* 1.391.6ff (Diehl) = fr. 26 (cf. 27–8) des Places.

2. Aetius, *Plac.* 1.3.21 and 1.10.3, *Didasc.* 9, Atticus fr. 9.40 des

Places; also Syrianus *In Meta.* 1078b12 (p. 105.36ff Kroll), where
Plutarch is also mentioned as one of those who make the Ideas
*logoi* eternally existing in the world-soul.

3. D.L. 3.69, widely regarded as having Posidonian connexions, cf.
M. Untersteiner, *Posidonia nei placita di Platone secondo Diogene
Laerzio III* (Brescia, 1970).

4. I think of the chain of authors who wrote on the first-principles of
Pythagoras and Plato (Porph. *V. Plot.* 20, 21): Thrasyllus,
Moderatus, Numenius, and Cronius, all of whom may be expected
to have utilized some notion of a One and a Dyad as the foundation-
stone of their metaphysic (clear in the case of Moderatus in Simpl.
*In Phys.* pp. 230–1 and Numenius fr. 20 des Places); Moderatus
(Simpl. *In Phys.* pp. 230–1) and Numenius fr. 24.51–9 make it
obvious that the references in Porphyry are to a single set of first-
principles being attributed to *both* early Pythagoreans *and* Plato.
Nicomachus of Gerasa may possibly be included in this group of
Pythagorizers too.

5. Dillon, *MP* pp. 254–6.

6. We have a treatise by Plotinus on the subject (*Enn.* 5.5). The origin
of the doctrine is discussed by A. H. Armstrong *et al.* in *Entretiens
sur l'antiquité classique,* vol. 5 (Geneva, 1957) pp. 393–425.
Armstrong emphasizes an Aristotelian element in Plotinus' background.

7. Ph. *Opif.* 102, *Her.* 156, cf. Dillon, *MP* p. 159; Sen. *Ep.* 65.7: 'haec
exemplaria . . . deus intra se habet numerosque universorum quae
agenda sunt, et modos mente complexus est; plenus his figuris est,
quae Plato ideas appellat, . . .'; cf. Nicomachus of Gerasa *Intr.* 1.2.4
(p. 9.9ff Hoche).

8. For the Ideas as *logoi* within the world-soul (or immanent intellect)
see Plutarch, Atticus, and Democritus Platonicus in Syrianus *In
Meta.* 1078b12 (p. 105.36ff Kroll); also unnamed Platonists in
Alex. Aphr. *In Meta.* 991a23 (p. 103.1–2 Hayduck). The place of
the Platonic demiurge was at times a problem for Middle Platonists.
At *Didasc.* 12ff the demiurge is scarcely integrated into the metaphysical scheme of 10, having some resemblance to the first God
and other resemblances to the heavenly intellect (= the higher
function of the world-soul). And Numenius is said by Proclus to
have made the demiurge (Plato's demiurge, not Numenius') double,
a composite figure having features of Numenius' first and second
Gods (*In Tim.* 1.304.27ff = fr. 21 des Places).

9. See A. M. Rich, *Mnem.* 7 (1954), 123–33 (particularly 125–6),
J. Loenen (*Mnem.* 10 (1957), 45).

10. As particularly at *Didasc.* 9 (p. 163.29–31 Hermann), 10 (p.
164.24–7).

11. *Orator* 8: 'cogitatione tamen et mente complectimur'; 9: 'ipsius (Phidiae) in mente insidebat species'.
12. See Arist. *De An.* 3.4, 429a27–9.
13. Rich, *Mnem.* 7 (1954), 127ff, emphasizes the importance of the correspondence between Ideas as God's thoughts and as human thoughts.
14. Eudorus in Stob. *Ecl.* 2.49.16–18 (Wachsmuth).
15. See *Phd.* 64a, 81a etc.
16. See chapter 4 ii.
17. See Eudorus in Stob. *Ecl.* 2.49.8ff, *Didasc.* 28 (p. 181.36 Hermann), Pl. *Tim.* 90a–d.
18. See *K* 46.45–9: 'but before this they contribute to our actions by our having traces of them, but not clearly'.
19. Cic. *Fin.* 5.59: 'tamquam elementa virtutis'.
20. Albinus *Prol.* 6 (p. 150.21–2 Hermann): ἐπεγείρειν καὶ προκαλεῖσθαι and ἐκκαθαίρειν καὶ εὐκρινεῖς ἀποφαίνειν ὡς ἀρχάς suggests both processes. Plut. *Mor.* 1000e places more emphasis on the awakening, while frs. 215–17 perhaps place an emphasis on the analytical process of διάρθρωσις (cf. *K* 46.44 etc.). *K* 47.42–5 (ἀναπτύσσων . . . καὶ διαρθρῶν) has both processes in mind.
21. The *naturalis vis* which the mind possesses here ought perhaps to be credited with a knowledge of *how* to sort presentations correctly, and since this *vis* is prior to acts of sensation, any knowledge attributed to it would have to be innate.
22. See below, intro. ii and chapter iii.
23. Aug. *c. Acad.* 2.11, cf. Num. fr. 27.56–9 des Places.
24. τοῖς δ' αὖ μεγίστοις οὖσι καὶ τιμιωτάτοις οὐκ ἔστιν εἴδωλον οὐδὲν πρὸς ἀνθρώπους εἰργασμένον ἐναργῶς, . . .
25. Particularly that of Posidonius, F85, F140–8, F157–69, F187, F290 (Edelstein–Kidd).
26. See Plut. *Mor.* 1023b.
27. The ἀπόσπασμα. It is not important for our purposes whether this only became an ἀπόσπασμα of the divine (as opposed to the universe) with Posidonius, as J. M. Rist, *Stoic Philosophy* (Cambridge, 1969) pp. 266ff would have us believe.
28. *Fin.* 5.59: 'notitias parvas'.

## Epilogue: the Academic heritage

1. See D.L. 4.62.
2. One thinks of some of the Pythagorean writings falsely attributed to early Pythagoreans (Timaeus Locrus, Ps.-Archytas *On the Categories*, etc.), Ps.-Aristotle *De Mundo*, and the Chaldean Oracles. I think also of the philosophical digressions of *Epistles* 2 (312d–14c)

and 7 (340b–5c), which I regard as early Middle Platonic forgeries (*Phronesis* 28 (1983), 75–103).

3. Here I think not only of Eudorus' (and Euharmostus') famous emendation of Aristotle's *Metaphysics* (Alex. Aphr. *In Meta.* 988a7, p. 59.1–8 Hayduck), but also of the emendations to *Meno* 98a and 99e discussed above (chapter 4 iv with nn. 67–9). I shudder to think of the possibility that Thrasyllus, in editing the Platonic corpus, may himself have made slight alterations and additions (though this might explain a few little omissions in Cicero's translation of the *Timaeus*).

4. Dio, the follower of Antiochus, may merit the description for this reason alone (Strabo 17.1.11, cf. Stob. *Flor.* 19.17 p. 537).

5. Philo *QG* 3.33, Sen. *Ep.* 88.43–4, Tac. *Dial.* 31.6.

6. If one may judge from Plutarch, Ammonius, and the author of *K,* all of whom appear to show some allegiance to the Academy, not just to Plato.

7. *K* 54.43ff, Plut. Lamprias Catalogue no. 63. There could, of course, be differences in emphasis between the three defences of the unity thesis.

8. See *ND* 1.11, *Ac.* 2.74, *TD* 5.11.

9. *Fin.* 5.87, Numenius fr. 24 (des Places, = 2 Lang), cf. D.L. 3.8.

10. Posidonius T91, T95 (with regard to Platonic psychology), cf. Cic. *TD* 4.10. Eudorus with regard to assimilation to God, in Stob. *Ecl.* 2.49.8–9, 16–21; *K* 70.8; Numenius fr. 7.7 des Places and fr. 52 (on matter).

11. Aetius 1.7.18 (cf. 30, 31), 4.2.3 (cf. 4, 5), 4.4.1, 4.5.10, 4.7.5, 4.9.10, 5.4.2, 5.20.4, Ps.-Archytas *On Intellect and Sensation*, Ps.-Aresas *On the Nature of Man*, Ps.-Aristaeus *On Harmony*, Ps.-Brontinus *On Intelligence and Discursive Thought*, Ps.-Timaeus *On the Soul of the World and on Nature*; for full references see H. Thesleff, *An Introduction to the Pythagorean Writings of the Hellenistic Period* (Åbo, 1961) pp. 8ff. I leave open the question of the date of these works: they either contributed to the confusion between Pythagoras and Plato, or perpetuated it.

12. *K* 2.11 and fr. 4, Apollonius of Tyana *Ep.* 42 (the address).

13. E.g. Proclus *In Tim.* 1.162.12–13, where even Panaetius becomes a *Platonicus*; cf. Glucker, *Ant.* pp. 216–19.

14. *Ep.* 42: 'He will not receive a fee for philosophy, even if he needs it.' (Refers to Apollonius himself.)

15. *Ant.* pp. 208–9.

16. Numenius appears to regard Socrates as a metaphysician in the same mould as himself, fr. 24.51–6, and also as a Pythagorean (*ibid.*, 57–9).

17. Numenius feels that one should state one's Pythagorean beliefs

more openly than Plato did, i.e. in a pure Pythagorean fashion, fr. 24.59–70 des Places.

18. See *QG* 3.33.
19. Plut. *Ant.* 80.
20. See Philostratus *VS* 1.6, Plut. *Brutus* 24 (perhaps referring to the same man); cf. my remarks in *CQ* 33 (1983), 182.
21. See *Ebr.* 166–205, *Fug.* 135–6, 188–93, 206, *Jos.* 125–47, *Her.* 246; cf. Tarrant, *CQ* 33 (1983), 173–8.
22. One notices that Philo is at times preoccupied with 'Egyptian sophists' (*Migr.* 76, *Somn.* 1.220), who probably had some parallel in the world that he knew, and that Philo sometimes associates sophistry directly with 'scepticism' (*QG* 3.33, *Congr.* 52, *Fug.* 209).
23. Dio at Strabo 17.1.11, Stob. *Flor.* 19.17, p. 537; contrast Aristo Alexandrinus and Cratippus (*Index Acad. Herc.* col. 35) and Cicero's Piso in *Fin.* 5.
24. Athenaeus 1.34b, Plut. *Mor.* 612e.
25. He may have made a speciality of writing *symposia* (Plut. *Mor.* 612e, Athen. 1.34b, Stob. *Flor.* 19.17).
26. See *CQ* 33 (1983), 180 n. 137.
27. Stob. *Ecl.* 2.49.8–12 Wachsmuth; Simpl. *In Phys.* p. 181.10ff.
28. Stob. *Ecl.* 2.49.18–23.
29. Stob. *Ecl.* 2.50.2–4.
30. See his tolerance of the conflicting views of Xenocrates and Crantor at Plut. *Mor.* 1013b.
31. This at least is what Arius Didymus (?) admired at Stob. *Ecl.* 2.42.7–10.
32. See the Suda, s.v.
33. *Ac.* 2.7–9.
34. Aetius *Plac.* p. 396b17–19.
35. See chapter 4 iv.
36. See Dillon, *MP* p. 185, Porph. *V. Plot.* 20, 21.
37. See Tarrant, *CQ* 33 (1983), 173, Plut. *Mor.* 385cd, 391e–2e, 427f, 435c, 746b.
38. Stob. *Ecl.* 2.39.20ff, 2.42.7ff.
39. Cic. *ND* 1.1 as emended by Manutius, cf. Arist. *Meta.* 982b12–21, in particular 17–18: ὁ δ' ἀπορῶν καὶ θαυμάζων οἴεται ἀγνοεῖν ... ὥστ' εἴπερ διὰ τὸ φεύγειν τὴν ἄγνοιαν, ἐφιλοσόφησαν ... and compare with Pl. *Tht.* 155d2: μάλα γὰρ φιλοσόφου τοῦτο τὸ πάθος, τὸ θαυμάζειν· οὐ γὰρ ἄλλη ἀρχὴ φιλοσοφίας ἢ αὐτή, ...

# BIBLIOGRAPHY

The following bibliography is designed primarily as an aid to reading the text. It contains only a few works not actually referred to there. Extensive bibliography on Middle Platonism is available in (1) below, and on Hellenistic philosophy in (2) below.

(1) Mazzarelli, C., 'Bibliografia Medioplatonica: parte prima', *Riv. Filos. Neoscol.* 72 (1980), 108–44. Also 'parte secunda' and 'parte terza' in the two following volumes: 73 (1981), 557–9, and 74 (1982), 126–59

(2) Schofield, M., Burnyeat, M., and Barnes, J. (eds.), *Doubt and Dogmatism: Studies in Hellenistic Epistemology* (Oxford, 1980)


*Books etc.*

(3) Arnim, H. von, *Quellenstudien zu Philon von Alexandria* (Berlin, 1888)

(4) Arrighetti, G., *Epicuro: Opere* (2nd edn, Turin, 1973), abbr. Arr.[2]

(5) Brochard, V., *Les Sceptiques Grecs* (Paris, 1887), abbr. *SG*

(6) Burkhard, U. von, *Die angebliche Heraklit-Nachfolge des Skeptikers Aenesidem* (Bonn, 1973), abbr. *Heraklit-Nachfolge*

(7) Diels, H., *Doxographi Graeci* (Berlin, 1879), abbr. *Dox.*

(8) Dillon, J., *The Middle Platonists* (London, 1977), abbr. *MP*

(9) Dodds, E. R. (ed.), Plato: *Gorgias* (Oxford, 1959)

(10) Donini, P., *Le scole, l'anima, l'impero* (Turin, 1982)

(11) Freudenthal, M., *Die Erkenntnislehre Philos von Alexandria* (Berlin, 1891)

(12) Glucker, J., *Antiochus and the late Academy, Hypomnemata* 56 (Göttingen, 1978), abbr. *Ant.*

(13) Hirzel, R., *Untersuchungen zu Ciceros philosophischen Schriften* (3 vols., Leipzig, 1877–83), abbr. *Untersuchungen*

(14) Hoyer, R., *De Antiocho Ascalonita, Diss.* (Bonn, 1883)

(15) Moline, J., *Plato's Theory of Understanding* (University of Wisconsin Press, 1981)

(16) Rist, J. M., *Stoic Philosophy* (Cambridge, 1969)

(17) Thesleff, H., *An Introduction to the Pythagorean Writings of the Hellenistic Period* (Åbo, 1961)

(18) Thévenaz, P., *L'Ame du monde, le devenir, et la matière chez Plutarque* (Paris, 1938)

(19) Untersteiner, M., *Posidonia nei placita di Platone secondo Diogene Laerzio III* (Brescia, 1970)

(20) Witt, R. E., *Albinus and the History of Middle Platonism* (Cambridge, 1937)

(21) Zintzen, C. (ed.), *Der Mittelplatonismus* (Darmstadt, 1981)

*Articles*

(22) Armstrong, A. H., 'The background of the doctrine "That the Intelligibles are not outside the Intellect"', in *Entretiens sur l'antiquité classique* vol. 5 (Geneva, 1957), 393–425

(23) Barnes, J., 'The beliefs of a Pyrrhonist', *PCPS* 28 (1982), 1–29

(24) Burkert, W., 'Cicero als Platoniker und Skeptiker', *Gymnasium* 72 (1965), 175–200

(25) Burnyeat, M. F., 'Can the Sceptic live his Scepticism?' in (2) above, pp. 20–53

(26) Burnyeat, M. F., 'Socrates and the jury', *Aristotelian Society supp. vol.* 54 (1980), 173–91

(27) De Lacy, Ph., 'Galen's Platonism', *AJPh* 93 (1972), 27–39

(28) Dodds, E. R., 'The *Parmenides* of Plato and the origin of the Neoplatonic One', *CQ* 22 (1928), 129–42

(29) Dörrie, H., 'Der Platoniker Eudorus von Alexandria', *Hermes* 79 (1944), 25–35

(30) Frede, M., 'On Galen's epistemology' in V. Nutton (ed.), *Galen: Problems and Prospects* (London, 1981) pp. 65–86

(31) Frede, M., 'Stoics and Skeptics on clear and distinct impressions', in M. Burnyeat (ed.), *The Skeptical Tradition* (Berkeley, 1983)

(32) Invernizzi, G., 'Un commentario medioplatonica al *Teeteto* e il suo significato filosofico', *Riv. Filos. Neoscol.* 68 (1976), 214–33

(33) Janacek, K., 'Zur Interpretation des Photius-Abschnittes über Aenesidemos', *Eirene* 14 (1976), 93–100

(34) Janacek, K., 'Das Wort "skeptikos" in Philons Schriften', *Listy Filologicke* 102 (1979), 65–8

(35) Loenen, J., 'Albinus' metaphysics: an attempt at rehabilitation, ii', *Mnemosyne* 10 (1957), 35–56

(36) Mansfeld, J., 'Intuitionism and formalism: Zeno's definition of geometry in a fragment of L. Calvenus Taurus', *Phronesis* 28 (1983), 59–74

(37) Natorp, P., 'Untersuchungen über die Skepsis im Altertum' *Rh. Mus.* 38 (1883), 28–91

(38) Oliver, J. H., 'The *Diadoche* at Athens under the humanistic emperors', *AJPh* 98 (1977), 160–78

(39) Praechter, K., review of H. Diels and W. Schubart (eds.), *Anonymer Kommentar zu Platons Theaetet* (Berlin, 1905), *Göttingische Gelehrte Anzeigen* 26 (1909), 530–47

(40) Rich, A. M., 'The Platonic Ideas as thoughts of God', *Mnemosyne* 7 (1954), 123–33

(41) Rist, J. M., 'The Heracliteanism of Aenesidemus', *Phoenix* 24 (1970), 309–19

(42) Schissel, O., 'Zum Prologos des Platonikers Albinos', *Hermes* 62 (1931), 215–26

(43) Sedley, D., 'The end of the Academy', *Phronesis* 26 (1981), 67–75

(44) Sedley, D., 'On signs', in J. Barnes *et al.* (eds.), *Science and Speculation* (Cambridge, 1982) pp. 239–72

(45) Sedley, D., 'The Stoic criterion of identity', *Phronesis* 27 (1982), 255–75

(46) Striker, G., 'Sceptical strategies' in (2) above, pp. 54–83

(47) Striker, G., 'Über den Unterschied zwischen den Pyrrhoneern und den Akademikern', *Phronesis* 26 (1981), 153–71

(48) Tarrant, H., 'Numenius fr. 13 and Plato's *Timaeus*', *Antichthon* 13 (1979), 19–29

(49) Tarrant, H., 'Agreement and the Self-Evident in Philo of Larissa', *Dionysius* 5 (1981), 66–97

(50) Tarrant, H., 'Two fragments of Cicero, *Academica* Book I', *LCM* 7.2 (1982), 21–2

(51) Tarrant, H., 'The conclusion of Parmenides' poem', *Apeiron* 18 (1983), 73–84

(52) Tarrant, H., 'The date of anon. *In Theaetetum*', *CQ* 33 (1983), 161–87

(53) Tarrant, H., 'Middle Platonism and the *Seventh Epistle*', *Phronesis* 28 (1983), 75–103

(54) Tarrant, H., 'Zeno on geometry or on knowledge: the evidence of anon. *In Theaetetum*', *Phronesis* 29 (1984), 96–9

Note: this book was substantially complete before the appearance of B. Wisniewski, *Philon von Larissa. Testimonia und Kommentar* (Wrocław, 1982), and it seemed unnecessary to include Wisniewski's fragment-numbers. The collection may, however, be of some help to my readers.

177

# INDEX OF NAMES

182